"President Bill Clinton is well known as a true friend of Israel. This fascinating and edifying book of correspondence between President Clinton and Rabbi Menachem Genack also reveals the former president to be a student of the universal message and spirituality of the Book of Books. It is a testament to the boundless thirst for knowledge of the unique mind of Bill Clinton, who fulfills the American dream and brings hope to the world."

—*Shimon Peres, President of the State of Israel.*

"This profound, thought-provoking, and inspiring collection of correspondence between Rabbi Genack and President Clinton is an exploration of some of the Torah's greatest lessons, and provides valuable insight into the central role faith plays in leadership. President Clinton's embrace of Rabbi Genack's letters is a testament to the wisdom we all—Jews and non-Jews—can draw from the Torah. Whether faced with the greatest challenges of the globe or the difficulties inherent in all of our personal journeys, this is a truly important and helpful book."

—*Cory Booker, Mayor of Newark, New Jersey.*

"This irresistible volume of correspondence between President Bill Clinton and Rabbi Menachem Genack is not only entertaining and enthralling, it opens an important new window onto the forty-second president and his constant quest for spiritual guidance and historical truth. Throughout their compelling dialogue, President Clinton reminds us anew of his deep faith and endless curiosity about what we know—and cannot know—about world history. And in preserving, publishing, and interpreting these letters and notes, Rabbi Genack has not only created a gripping historical archive, he has invited all of us to examine for ourselves the ideas and challenges that the President was brave and curious enough to confront himself."

—*Harold Holzer, Chairman of the Abraham Lincoln Bicentennial Foundation, winner of the National Humanities Medal, and author or editor of 46 books on Lincoln and the Civil War.*

"This compelling account of a fascinating, epistolary relationship between one of the world's most notable leaders and a religious scholar is enriched by the actual Talmudic and biblically based correspondence that fostered a complex, often profound, always human exchange."

—*Jonathan Kellerman is a best-selling novelist and Clinical Professor of Pediatrics and Psychology, Keck USC School of Medicine.*

"When I was working for President Clinton at the White House, I sometimes had the opportunity to pass on Rabbi Genack's letters. I know the president appreciated them, and when I read them myself I could understand why. Once, a letter must have been delayed, because President Clinton asked me, 'Where's my letter from Rabbi Genack? I've been expecting it.'

Whatever our daily lives, this is wisdom we can all enjoy—and learn from!"

—Ann F. Lewis was White House Communication Director
for President Bill Clinton.

"This is an illuminating, inspiring and unique book of short essays in the form of letters to President Bill Clinton, which are invaluable in addressing the challenges of leadership and public service. Written by Rabbi Menachem Genack and a wide group of his colleagues and acquaintances, the correspondence itself and President Clinton's obvious interest in it testify to the president's personal spirituality and to his intellectual curiosity. In sharing these letters to the president of the United States, Rabbi Genack demonstrates the boundless wisdom of the Torah and its enduring message."

—Joe Lieberman is the former U.S. Senator from Connecticut.

"This is a remarkable volume. It is unique, unprecedented: a scholarly Orthodox rabbi sending to a Christian president of the United States biweekly insights from the Bible. The exclamation 'only in America' is thoroughly relevant to this volume and the friendship that permitted, even encouraged it. Buy this book, read it and study it. You will enjoy not only the fact of this relationship, but also the wisdom of the Torah as taught by a distinguished American rabbi."

—Rabbi Dr. Norman Lamm is the
former Chancellor of Yeshiva University.

"Bill Clinton appreciated the Bible more than any American president since Abraham Lincoln. He especially appreciated the gems of wisdom from the Bible prepared for him by Rabbi Menachem Genack and by leading rabbis and scholars at his behest. These unforgettable messages and Clinton's fascinating responses make for a unique volume that is at once deeply inspiring and of great historical significance."

—Jonathan D. Sarna, Joseph H. & Belle R. Braun Professor
of American Jewish History, Brandeis University.

LETTERS

TO

PRESIDENT
CLINTON

LETTERS
TO
PRESIDENT CLINTON

...

*Biblical Lessons on Faith
and Leadership*

FOREWORD BY BILL CLINTON

EDITED BY RABBI MENACHEM GENACK

OUPRESS

STERLING ETHOS
New York

STERLING ETHOS
New York

An Imprint of Sterling Publishing
387 Park Avenue South
New York, NY 10016

ISBN 978-1-4549-0791-6

Distributed in Canada by Sterling Publishing
c/o Canadian Manda Group, 165 Dufferin Street
Toronto, Ontario, Canada M6K 3H6
Distributed in the United Kingdom by GMC Distribution Services
Castle Place, 166 High Street, Lewes, East Sussex, England BN7 1XU
Distributed in Australia by Capricorn Link (Australia) Pty. Ltd.
P.O. Box 704, Windsor, NSW 2756, Australia

In conjunction with OU Press,
an imprint of the Orthodox Union, www.ou.org

For information about custom editions, special sales, and premium and
corporate purchases, please contact Sterling Special Sales at 800-805-5489
or specialsales@sterlingpublishing.com.

Manufactured in the United States of America

2   4   6   8   10   9   7   5   3   1

www.sterlingpublishing.com

*Frontispiece: President Bill Clinton and Rabbi Menachem Genack
at the White House, July 16, 1999.*
[All photographs, except where noted, are official White House photographs. All
correspondence reproductions courtesy of the archives of Rabbi Menachem Genack.]

"What is man, that thou art mindful of him?
and the son of man, that thou visitest him?
For thou hast made him a little lower than the angels,
and hast crowned him with glory and honour."
—Psalm 8:4–5

"He crowns kings, yet kingship is His alone."
—Rosh Hashanah liturgy

For Sarah
A woman of deep understanding, compassion,
and wisdom

CONTENTS

FOREWORD

Rabbi Menachem Genack has become known to some as "Bill Clinton's rabbi." Indeed, though I am a Southern Baptist, he has been a trusted guide to me on matters of leadership, justice, and faith. Our friendship began while I was running for president in 1992 and has progressed through a written dialogue that continues to this day. As part of our correspondence, Rabbi Genack worked independently and in conference with other theologians and scholars to send me the series of meditations on Jewish scripture, or "missives," that compose this book.

Over the years, these individual missives were invaluable to me in addressing the challenges of leadership and public service. In my most difficult and trying times, the Bible has been a source of solace and encouragement; and, in times of joy and celebration, a medium for giving thanks. It has, at all times, been for me a wellspring of inspiration and guidance, and throughout my life, its sacred texts and solemn cadences have sustained my spirit and calmed my soul.

One of the biblical themes I find most profound is that which emphasizes the commonality of humankind. It is a theological perspective upon which Rabbi Genack's missives ruminate in great detail. His lessons were particularly timely near the end of my presidency when the Human Genome Project's findings revealed that people around the world are genetically 99.9 percent the same. Modern science confirms what we've always learned from ancient faiths—that the most important fact of life on this Earth is our common humanity.

When compiled, the letters Rabbi Genack and I exchanged both during and after my presidency paint a powerful portrait of an interconnected global society at the dawn of the twenty-first century. This was an era of incredible growth and innovation in the United States. It was a period that saw the rise of both the positive and negative forces of interdependence, including, after decades of conflict, the advent of ethnic and religious reconciliation in places like Northern Ireland and the Balkans. Though the promise of peace in the Middle East has not yet been fully realized, the dialogues that began during those years are still influencing the process now. For the role I played in these and other major events, the lessons embodied in *Letters to President Clinton* both inspired me to persevere and provided the moral clarity necessary to be effective. The missives' emphasis on stewardship, public service, and—above all—our common humanity, continues to drive my life today as a private citizen.

This book reflects Rabbi Genack's remarkable generosity—both of time and of spirit—as well as the depth of his convictions. I'm delighted to see this collection published. I can only hope that its wisdom may enrich others' lives just as it did mine.

—*Bill Clinton*

At the signing of the Middle East peace treaty on September 13, 1993, Prime Minister Yitzhak Rabin said the Jewish blessing "Shechiyanu," that God has kept us alive and sustained us to this time. Sara Ehrman had the renowned Hebrew calligrapher Yonah Weinrib write the blessing as a gift to President Clinton. It sat, as shown, on the credenza behind his desk in the oval office.

PREFACE

AT SOME TIME in the mid-'90s—I can't recall the exact date—I was contacted by one of my favourite American rabbis, Menachem Genack, with a strange request. Would I write a *Dvar Torah*, a short biblical reflection, for the president of the United States, Bill Clinton? As Rabbi Genack explains in his introduction, the two men had developed an unusual relationship. At the president's request, the rabbi had been supplying him regularly with Jewish reflections, partly for the president's own edification, and occasionally for use during speeches. I was happy to comply, as were other rabbis and Jewish thinkers around the world, and these short essays have now been collected into the book you hold in your hands. They are full of interest in their own right, but they are also part of a significant story about the relationship between politicians and religious inspiration in an age that was once deemed secular.

As it happens, I was no stranger to this story. I had already had the privilege of a friendship with the British prime minister at the time, John Major, as I was later to have with Tony Blair and Gordon Brown. In each case it had nothing to do with my official position as chief rabbi. Initially it came about because of an event that sent shockwaves through Britain: the murder of a two-year-old child, Jamie Bulger, by two ten-year-old boys in 1993. I had written an op-ed article in the *Times* about the social conditions that were leading to a rise in child crime in Britain. The next day, I received a call from 10 Downing Street, at the prime minister's request, saying that he would appreciate the opportunity to have a conversation about the issues raised by the article. So the relationship developed from then until the present with political leaders from all the major parties, including Tony Blair, a deeply religious man, and Gordon Brown, whose father was a minister in the Church of Scotland and whose own convictions were shaped by the religiously inspired traditions of "ethical socialism."

There is a profound and ironic difference between the political cultures of the United States and Britain. In the United States, Dwight Eisenhower said in a 1952 address, "Our form of government has no sense unless it is founded in a deeply felt religious faith, and I don't care what it is." Religious language of a generic kind is part of public discourse. In Britain, the opposite is the case. At least since Tony Blair, politicians tend not to speak about their religious beliefs. On one famous occasion, asked whether he prayed before making difficult decisions, Blair's press officer, Alastair Campbell, interjected, "We don't do God." British political leaders are wary of saying anything about their faith. This has less to do with individuals than with the culture: Europe simply is more secular than the United States, whether in terms of private beliefs, attendance at places of worship, or the place of religion within the media.

Yet even Europe is beginning to change. One of the signs of this was the recent publication of a book by the editor-in-chief and the management editor of the *Economist*, entitled *God Is Back*. Their thesis, which has been conventional wisdom in America for some time, is that Europe is out of step with the world, rather than the other way around. The world is de-secularising, and that includes China, where Christianity and Islam are growing apace. Within Europe itself, with its large immigrant populations, minority groups are increasingly defining themselves by religion rather than, as used to be the case a generation ago, by place of origin. Faith has entered the public domain in ways that would have been inconceivable a generation ago, and this book is part of that phenomenon.

This raises the following question: Are the essays in this book just *Divrei Torah*, occasional thoughts prompted by the Hebrew Bible, or do they intimate a larger possibility, a genuinely Judaic voice within the public domain?

I BELIEVE THAT JEWS IN AMERICA have a significant story to share with their fellow Americans, and it is not just about anti-Semitism, Israel, and the separation of church and state, subjects that have predominated until now.

Judging by my own experience of broadcasting and writing in the public domain, people want to hear about a whole series of values central to Jewish life. They want to hear about the sanctity of marriage, the family, and the home as the setting of some of our most important religious rituals. They want to learn about the Jewish passion for education, schools, and the life of the mind. They want to understand the idea of *tzedakah*, that unique Jewish fusion of the concepts of justice and charity.

They want to learn about the strength of community in Judaism. They are often astonished about the power of community in Jewish life and the way we mobilise energies through networks of support. A senior British politician once asked me for my definition of community. I replied, "Community is the place where they know your name, and where they miss you if you're not there." He had to struggle with this idea. He could not think of any community of which he was a part where such things were true.

The Catholic writer Paul Johnson wrote a magnificent book, *History of the Jews*. When I asked him what, after the years of study he put into the book, most impressed him about Judaism, he replied that it was the way Jews were able to balance individual responsibility with collective responsibility (Hillel's famous dictum, "If I am not for myself, who will be? But if I am only for myself, what am I?"). He said that there have been individualistic cultures—the contemporary West, for example—and there have been collectivist cultures—the Soviet Union and socialist states—but none he could think of other than Judaism that had managed to exemplify both at the same time.

Non-Jews want to hear about how Jews have walked the tightrope between contributing to the wider society and yet not losing their own identity—how they have achieved integration without assimilation. I have been consulted on just this question by Hindus, Sikhs, and Muslims. I was asked the same question by a leading figure within China. China's recent astonishing economic growth has led, it seems, to many young Chinese businesspeople becoming very rich, very young, and in the process losing their traditions in favour of a culture of conspicuous consumption. A leading Chinese businesswoman who heads one of the country's largest charities had read my books and wanted to know how Jews, with similar business success, managed to retain their traditions.

Non-Jews want to hear the Jewish voice on morality. They want to understand how to create a culture that emphasises responsibilities, not just rights. They are interested in Jewish medical ethics. They often find themselves confronted with two opposing positions, a scientific view that says that anything we can do, we may do, and a conventional religious attitude that frowns on many medical, especially genetic, interventions as "unnatural" and "playing God." They are fascinated by the Jewish approach, which welcomes medical technology while at the same time frowns on anything that threatens to rob life of its inherent sanctity. They are intrigued by the rabbinic idea that we are "God's partners" in the work of creation.

One of the first projects my office undertook when I became chief rabbi in 1991 was the creation of a Jewish Association of Business Ethics, the most creative of its kind in Britain. It does much of its work in schools. Leading financial journalists write ethically challenging scenarios. Actors then act them out. The schoolchildren discuss how they would act under those circumstances. A team of leading businesspeople and professionals then give their view of the students' reactions. Only at the end does a rabbi outline the *halakhic* view.

The business ethics programme is offered to all schools in Britain, not just those with Jewish students (the non-Jewish schools use the scenarios, study guides, and videos), and it has had huge success. This allowed us to be able to take a moral lead in the aftermath of the 2008 financial crash. I made a television programme for the BBC on the subject. We have now been asked by Jewish communities in the United States to share our experience with them.

These are just a few examples of the many possible. In Britain, the Jewish voice is listened to with attention and respect. It is moral without being judgmental (in Judaism we say "we have sinned," not "you have sinned"). It is religiously principled without being irrational or extreme. Above all it is modest and unthreatening. We do not seek to convert anyone. We do not try to impose Jewish values on a non-Jewish public by force of law. When a Jew speaks in the public domain, the tacit message is: "This is how we do things; this is how we see things; if it is interesting to you, please share it; if it is uninteresting to you, we will not feel bad." That is the best kind of voice in a diverse society, a plural public.

Where does this fit with Judaism itself? The answer lies in the words of Moses toward the end of his life: "Keep [these laws] therefore and do them; for this is your wisdom and your understanding in the sight of the nations, which shall hear all these statutes, and say, Surely this great nation is a wise and understanding people" (Deut. 4:6). Moses did not believe that the Jewish project was for Jews alone. He believed it would inspire others, not to become Jews, but to practise justice and compassion, honour the sanctity of life and the dignity of the human person, and see within all of us the image of God.

A similar idea is stated no less than five times in the book of Genesis, in slightly different words, but always the same principle: that through you "shall all the nations of the earth be blessed." And with this we come to a fundamental fact. *This is perhaps the first time in history that we can understand these words literally.* When, before now, were non-Jews interested in what Judaism had to say about the moral issues of their time? Not in ancient times when polytheism was the order of the day. Not in antiquity when Hellenism ruled. Not in the Middle Ages when Christian and Islamic empires bestrode the arena. Not during the Enlightenment, when rationalists saw Judaism as at best outmoded, at worst barbaric. You have to go back to the book of Jonah for the last time a Jewish prophetic voice was heeded by a non-Jewish society.

THERE IS ANOTHER REASON why a Jewish voice deserves to be heard in America today, and it is surprising how few Jews have fully internalized this fact. The American story is, to a degree unparalleled by any other national narrative, a Jewish story.

The scholar who best documented this was Perry Miller in his magisterial *The New England Mind*. But the man who placed it in a contemporary context was the sociologist Robert Bellah. In a classic essay in the 1960s, Bellah argued that underlying American political discourse was a "civil religion" with its own national narrative. Every American president in his inaugural address has invoked God. Almost every inaugural address articulates, or assumes, a story about how America came to be, and the values that frame its aspirations.

This is how Bellah describes the way American presidents have envisaged God: "He is actively interested and involved in history, with a special concern for America. Here the analogy has much less to do with natural law than with ancient Israel; the equation of America with Israel in the idea of the 'American Israel' is not infrequent." Successive generations of immigrants came to the new world as the Israelites left Israel, fleeing from persecution in search of a "new birth of freedom." The American story is a reworking of the exodus. As Bellah put it: "Europe is Egypt; America, the promised land. God has led his people to establish a new sort of social order that shall be a light unto all the nations." Here for example is Thomas Jefferson, speaking in his second inaugural in 1805:

> I shall need, too, the favor of that Being in whose hands we are,
> who led our forefathers, as Israel of old, from their native land
> and planted them in a country flowing with all the necessaries
> and comforts of life . . .

And this, Lyndon Baines Johnson in 1965:

> They came here—the exile and the stranger, brave but
> frightened—to find a place where a man could be his own man.
> They made a covenant with this land. Conceived in justice,
> written in liberty, bound in union, it was meant one day to
> inspire the hopes of all mankind; and it binds us still.

And this, Bill Clinton in 1997:

> The promise we sought in a new land we will find again in a land
> of new promise. . . . Yes, let us build our bridge. A bridge wide
> enough and strong enough for every American to cross over to a
> blessed land of new promise.

The American story is the Jewish story. The American covenant is modelled on the covenant our ancestors entered into at Mount Sinai. It would be a dramatic failure if Jews themselves, who have lived this story for more than three thousand years, did not contribute to the public conversation that is the ongoing commentary to this story in each generation.

THERE IS A MAJOR ISSUE AT STAKE for contemporary Jewish life. In America, the Jewish narrative since the 1960s has been dominated by the Holocaust. One of the greatest Jewish thinkers in the second half of the twentieth century, Emil Fackenheim, spoke of a new commandment by which Jews are bound: not to hand Hitler a posthumous victory. Against this, one of the pioneering Holocaust historians, Lucy Dawidowicz, toward the end of her life warned that the emphasis on, and the obsession with, the Final Solution risked creating generations of young people knowing "about the Greeks and how they lived, the Romans and how they lived, and the Jews and how they died." Judaism—other than on special days of remembrance—is not about the memory of death but about the sanctification and celebration of life.

It is precisely in America, the most religiously believing and practising society in the West, where Jews as a *religious community*—not Jews as an ethnicity, Jews as an interest group, or Jews as the victims of history—should live their values in the public domain. But they have not conspicuously done so until now.

To give a simple example from Britain: I have spoken to Christian groups, and been interviewed by Christian journalists, where the people involved requested that before the proceedings begin, we take time out to say a silent prayer. A group of young Muslims, high flyers in finance in the City of London, whom I had invited to our house, looked at their watches in the middle of our session and asked permission to take a five-minute break. They then went into the next room and said their afternoon prayers. This has never happened in a Jewish meeting except when there were other rabbis present. Jewish groups simply strike me as more secular than their Christian or Muslim—or even Sikh or Hindu—counterparts.

To be sure, this has begun to change. Several city law firms have lunchtime *shiurim*. A number of them construct a sukkah for use during Sukkot. We must continue and deepen the process. If Jews do not bring their personal commitments into the public domain, we will find ourselves caught in the either/or that has devastated Jewish life and still today threatens Jewish continuity: between a universalism that denies Jewish particularity, and a particularity that causes Jews to insulate themselves as far as possible from the wider society. The equation has been, either social integration accompanied by outmarriage on a massive scale, or segregation and withdrawal into a voluntary ghetto. Neither honours the full terms of Jewish engagement with the human project as a whole.

AND THERE IS AN ISSUE AT STAKE for the future of America and the West. Since 9/11, liberal democracy has been tested by the emergence of a radical religiosity that values neither liberalism nor democracy. Thus far, the response has been less than intellectually compelling.

At the end of his famous 1958 essay, "Two Concepts of Liberty," Isaiah Berlin quoted Joseph Schumpeter's statement: "To realize the relative validity of one's convictions and yet stand for them unflinchingly is what distinguishes a civilized man from a barbarian." To which the obvious question is: If one's convictions are only relatively valid, why stand for them unflinchingly? Liberal democracy cannot be defended against absolutist faiths on the basis of moral relativism.

I came to know Berlin in his later years. In 1997 I published a book, *The Politics of Hope*, in which I argued that the greatest danger to the free societies of the West was not totalitarian systems elsewhere but an inner loss of moral consensus and the institutions—marriage, family, and community—that sustained civil society. I was saying, in effect, that the challenge had changed in the intervening forty years. I was interested in Berlin's reaction. He asked me to send him the book, which I did. He promised to reply.

Months passed and I did not hear from him. So, toward the end of year, I phoned his home in Oxford. His wife, Lady Aline, answered the phone: "Chief Rabbi, we've just been talking about you." "How so?" I asked. "Isaiah wants you to officiate at his funeral." I told her to stop Isaiah from thinking such morbid thoughts, but evidently he knew. Four days later he died, and I officiated at his funeral. Isaiah may not have been a believing Jew but he was a loyal one.

I believe that in a de-secularising, re-religionizing age, we cannot defend liberal democracy on the basis of moral relativism and the thin concepts of autonomy and rights. Those of us who have religious commitments must defend them on the basis of absolute and nonnegotiable principles: the sanctity of life, the dignity of the human individual, and the principle that America and Judaism share, namely covenant and its associated idea of moral reciprocity. I may not buy my freedom at the cost of yours. I cannot ask you to respect my faith if I am unprepared to respect yours. Freedom, the freedom of all-of-us-together, cannot be adequately defended without the religious premises (often nowadays called the "Judeo-Christian tradition") that brought it into being in the first place.

This is not to say that all members of a liberal democracy should be religious. It is, however, to say that there is a religious defence to be made of liberal democracy because it has achieved what no religion on its own has ever achieved: an environment in which people of deeply clashing faiths can live peaceably together. This is known in Judaism as the principle of *darchei shalom*, and it flows from Jeremiah's letter to the Babylonian exiles in the sixth century BCE. He told them to "seek the peace of the city whither I have caused you to be carried away captives, and pray unto the Lord for it: for in the peace thereof shall ye have peace" (Jer. 29:7).

That is the principle by which Jews in the Diaspora lived. They did not seek to impose their faith on others. Instead they sought the freedom to be true to their faith while being a blessing to others regardless of their faith. They became contributors to the human covenant while staying loyal to their own.

Liberal democracy asks us to do what the Bible itself implies by the way it structures the Genesis narrative. It speaks of our shared humanity prior to and as a precondition of our particular commitments of faith (in Jewish terms, the Noahide and Abrahamic covenants respectively).

The real religious divide today is not between Jews, Christians, and Muslims, but between those in each of the faiths who see religion as a form of the will to power, and those who see it as the will to life, all life. Fundamentalism is the attempt to impose a single truth on a plural world, and it owes more to imperialism than to humility in the face of our God-created diversity.

So there is much at stake for both Jews and Americans as a whole in how Jews think about their relationship with the wider society and how they speak in the public arena. In my 2010 book, *Future Tense*, I set out my own account of Judaism as the voice of hope in the conversation of humankind. *Letters to President Clinton* is an important and valuable part of that conversation, which I hope will continue and deepen in the years to come.

— *Chief Rabbi Lord Jonathan Sacks*

Rabbi Genack and his wife, Sarah, with Bill and Hillary Clinton
at the White House, June 19, 1995.

INTRODUCTION

THE WORLD KNOWS President William Jefferson Clinton as a world leader and international statesman. I have had the privilege and opportunity to know him also as a student of the Bible.

My relationship with President Clinton dates to his first presidential campaign. In addition to my professional work at the Union of Orthodox Jewish Congregations of America, I serve as a congregational rabbi in Englewood, New Jersey. In June 1992, I was asked to introduce then-governor Clinton as a presidential candidate at a local fund-raising function. In my presentation, I alluded to President George H. W. Bush's difficulty with the "vision thing." (In 1987, journalist Robert Ajemian had written an article about President Bush for *Time* magazine, where he recounted an anonymous anecdote. A friend of Bush's had apparently suggested that he spend some quiet time at Camp David to formulate his plans for the 1988 presidential campaign, to which Bush is said to have responded in exasperation, "Oh, the vision thing.") I quoted a verse from the book of Proverbs (29:18): "Where there is no vision, the people perish." Governor Clinton enjoyed the remarks, and told me that he would refer to the verse in his speech accepting the nomination—which he did. In the next few years the president graciously included me in joint prayer meetings, delegations to the Middle East, state dinners, and other events. I would prepare, in advance, a brief essay containing insights from the Bible that I felt would help him navigate whatever national issues he was facing and pass it along to him. At a certain point, the Secret Service objected to my handing documents to him personally, and the president arranged that I send him the documents initially through Nancy Heinrich, in charge of Oval Office operations, and then through his director of communications, Ann Lewis. Currently, the missives are sent to the president through Hannah Richert, Advisor at the Clinton Foundation.

During the president's second term, he suggested I take a more formal and regular approach to sending him the essays. I asked friends and acquaintances of mine, including Bible scholars, political leaders, authors and scientists, members of the clergy, and laypersons, to contribute. Many of the authors are well-known, and all are in their own right distinguished and thoughtful writers. In each case, I requested that the author express in his or her own way contemporary messages found in the Bible's ancient wisdom.

I was spurred by the president's responses, many of which are included in the coming chapters, indicating not only that he had received the essays but also that they had captured his attention. On one occasion, I sent him an essay about the biblical story of Judah and Tamar in which I mistakenly cited a passage as being from Genesis 28. The president responded with a note that tactfully corrected the citation to Genesis 38. His Bible is clearly on his bookshelf.

The president's firm grasp of biblical literature was on full display when he delivered remarks at the Commerce Department following the untimely death of Commerce Secretary Ron Brown in an airplane crash in 1996. His speechwriters had half an hour to quickly compose some comments and wanted to include a favorite Bible verse of Brown's. After consultation, they came up with a paraphrase of the verse; no one knew the exact wording. The president scanned the text and told an aide, "Oh, this is Isaiah 40:31. It sounds like the New English translation. I prefer the Kings James Version myself. That's the one I'll use." And he did, quoting from memory in the middle of the speech: "But they that wait upon the Lord shall renew their strength; they shall mount up with wings as eagles; they shall run, and not be weary; and they shall walk, and not faint."

In 1997, Christopher Edley Jr., a former advisor to President Clinton who is now dean of the University of California Berkeley School of Law, spoke at an Orthodox Union forum where he related an anecdote about the president: at an informal gathering of advisors in the Oval Office, President Clinton had reached into his desk and pulled out a weathered copy of the Bible and quoted from it to bolster a point he had been trying to make about public policy. Edley found himself amazed at the indisputable relevance of the biblical quotation to current affairs.

For this book, Dr. Martin Marty, a distinguished professor of religion at the University of Chicago, shared with me a story about a meeting of several Christian theologians and religious leaders that President Clinton convened at the White House in 1994. Several people at the table said that they were praying for the president. He asked what they prayed for. A prominent evangelist said he was praying from the following verse in 1 Chronicles:

> If my people, which are called by my name, shall humble
> themselves, and pray, and seek my face, and turn from their
> wicked ways; then will I hear from heaven, and will forgive
> their sin, and will heal their land.

The president correctly said, "I believe that is in Second Chronicles." (2 Chron. 7:14)

A little later at the same meeting, Pentecostal superstar pastor Max Lucado said that he was also praying for the president. Clinton asked what he prayed for. "That you be given a Mordecai." (Mordecai, who rose to leadership in the Persian kingdom, was a cousin of Queen Esther's. Together they initiated the Jewish people's redemption from Persian rule.) As Dr. Marty remembers it, Mr. Clinton then said, "Oh, now I am Queen Esther," thus evidencing for the rest of the group the deep biblical knowledge of informed Baptists—at least of this one! Bill Clinton was not alone, certainly, among the occupants of the White House, in his fascination with Scripture. Abraham Lincoln, though not formally religious in the sense of church attendance or denominational affiliation and probably an agnostic at one stage in his life, was deeply religious, if unconventional. He often spoke and wrote in a biblical cadence, particularly in his second inaugural address. He drew strength of spirit and courage of conviction from wellsprings of Scripture and spirituality in the face of travails that would surely have broken a lesser man.

Fifteen years after Lincoln's death, Joshua Speed, a personal friend of Lincoln's, shared a moving recollection of the president's esteem for biblical wisdom:

> As I entered the room, near night, [Lincoln] was sitting near a window intently reading his Bible. Approaching him, I said, "I am glad to see you so profitably engaged." "Yes," said he, "I am profitably engaged." "Well," said I, "if you have recovered from your skepticism I am sorry to say that I have not!" Looking me earnestly in the face, and placing his hand on my shoulder, he said: "You are wrong, Speed; take all of this book upon reason that you can and the balance on faith and you will live and die a happier and better man."

SOME YEARS AGO, it occurred to me that publication of the essays would serve as an interesting and important historical footnote, shedding light on a little-known aspect of President Clinton's persona and activities. He was receptive to the idea, and in September 2009, I delivered the draft manuscript of the book to him. After reviewing it, he told me he was pleased and agreed to my moving forward with the project. The day after I spoke with him, on September 15, 2009, I attended the *iftar* (the evening meal at which Muslims break their daily fast during the month of Ramadan) hosted by Secretary of State Hillary Clinton at the State Department in Washington. Secretary Clinton came over to me and said, "Bill called me last night and told me about the book. I think it's a great idea."

Letters to President Clinton: Biblical Lessons on Faith and Leadership is a compilation of almost one hundred of my communications with the president during his second term of office and after. Together, they constitute a wide-ranging discussion of how the Scriptures view faith and leadership, personal morality, and communal responsibility. The missives touch upon many important themes—with roots in the Bible—that are the foundation of American political theory. Perhaps the foremost of these is the dignity of man, a being created in God's image, and the primacy of the individual in contrast to society and the state—the essence of Jeffersonian democracy. Although written for a specific person facing unique challenges, the messages included here will be helpful to anyone who seeks to understand and benefit from the wisdom of biblical thought and its unique and profound insights into life. I am grateful to all of the contributors.

This book's existence is a tribute to President Clinton's enormously inquisitive mind and his appreciation for wisdom in its multifarious forms. It might seem improbable that an American president would encourage a correspondence based on a theological tradition that is not his own. This is not surprising, however, given Bill Clinton's philosophy that truth cannot be monopolized by a single group, but is diffused through different traditions. As he stated in his second inaugural address:

> Our rich texture of racial, religious and political diversity will be
> a Godsend in the twenty-first century. Great rewards will come to
> those who can live together, learn together, work together, forge
> new ties that bind together.

He echoes the declaration of Terence, the ancient Roman playwright, "I am a man; whatever concerns humanity is of interest to me." Among President Clinton's most attractive qualities is his compassion for other people and their communities' cultural experiences. I remember hearing him recount that as a college student, when he would be in New York, he would invariably find his way to 125th Street in Harlem and absorb the rhythm of its music, especially at the Apollo Theater.

In 2001 when President Clinton moved his new office to Harlem, just down the street from the Apollo Theater, there was a huge rally to welcome him. I took my daughter Ora, who was fifteen at the time, to the event. I wanted her to experience the joy of that day and what it connoted in terms of the diversity of America. President Clinton saw us in the crowd and asked us to join him at Sylvia's, the iconic Harlem restaurant.

Following that day, I wrote a letter reflecting on my visit, which was subsequently published in the *New York Times*:

> Mr. Clinton prides himself on the comment of Toni Morrison,
> the Nobel Prize–winning author, that he was our first black
> president. It was that extraordinary capacity to reach out . . . over
> the racial and ethnic divide and to bring people together that was
> on full display in Harlem. Ultimately, Mr. Clinton's legacy will
> be not only America's economic renewal, but also a more tolerant
> and connected society.

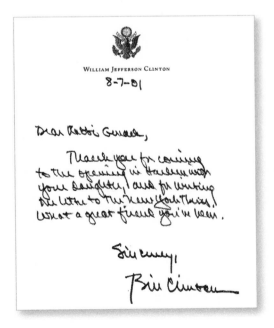

8-7-01

Dear Rabbi Genack,
    Thank you for coming to the opening in Harlem with your daughter, and for writing the letter to the *New York Times*. What a great friend you've been.
        Sincerely,
        Bill Clinton

Clinton would frequently comment that the three major American religions—Christianity, Judaism, and Islam—are all predicated on the notion of loving your neighbor. The president was fond of quoting the maxim of Hillel "That which is hateful to you, do not do to your fellow." I reminded the president that Hillel's maxim was offered in response to someone who had asked Hillel to recite the entire Torah on one foot. Hillel's statement of empathy and understanding embodies in many ways the essential values of religious life. In March 1997, President Clinton suffered a knee injury that required him to use crutches. Upon seeing him limping with his crutches, I jokingly remarked, "Now you are truly like Hillel!"

At one of the last prayer breakfasts of President Clinton's administration, just about the time Joe Lieberman received the nomination as the candidate for vice president, I spoke and told the following story. In the 1965 World Series between the Los Angeles Dodgers and the Minnesota Twins, the first game was played on October 6, which was Yom Kippur. Sandy Koufax was scheduled to pitch for the Dodgers, but Koufax, who was Jewish, declined to play because of Yom Kippur. Don Drysdale pitched instead of Koufax, and in the third inning had given up six runs. Walt Alston, the Dodgers manager, walked out to the mound to pull Drysdale from the game and apocryphally said, "Don, why couldn't you be Jewish too?" (Some accounts have Drysdale saying to Alston, "I bet right now you wish I was Jewish too.") While, at the time, I spoke in a humorous vein, I look back upon that prayer breakfast as marking a significant milestone in the history of our nation—it was the first time a Jew was on the national ticket. This was due to the extraordinary openness and tolerance with which the United States is blessed. Bill Clinton, always receptive to new and different experiences and traditions, played a role in fostering this openness and tolerance.

President Clinton's openness for traditions, cultures, and peoples other than his own is reflected in his affinity for the State of Israel and his unstinting efforts to forge a lasting peace in the Middle East. I recall a conspicuous example of this when I was with Mr. Clinton in Tel Aviv in January 2002, at the dedication of the Saban Institute for the Study of the American Political System at Tel Aviv University. After the formal dinner, the president asked me to come to his room, where he was meeting with several dignitaries. I reminded him that I needed to get back to Jerusalem that night and would miss the last bus from Tel Aviv if I went upstairs. Not to worry, Mr. Clinton said, assuring me that he would provide me with a taxi at the end of the evening, which he did. I vividly remember Mr. Clinton telling me that evening that he had discussed the Middle East situation with Jacques Chirac, the president of France, and that he had told President Chirac, "The reason the Israelis trust me is because they know that if Israel is in trouble, I would fight for Israel."

THE MISSIVES IN THIS BOOK are not arranged chronologically, but by category: Leadership; Creation; Faith; Dreams and Vision; and other topics. Although there is intrinsic value in the Torah the missives contain, they are also a footnote to a presidency. As such, we have appended a number of the president's responses.

We end where we began—with vision. To be a leader is to be a visionary, and for many, the profound inspiration of Scripture helps light the way. Today, with the challenges of his presidency behind him, Bill Clinton spends much of his time leading the Clinton Global Initiative, bringing together leaders of government, industry, and nonprofit organizations to confront the pressing challenges we face in the twenty-first century. I and my fellow contributors hope that the missives you are about to read here contributed in some small way to the president's spiritual awareness.

9/20/02

Dear Rabbi,
    Thanks for sharing your talk on the Declaration of Independence. It's <u>great</u>.

    Bill

Leadership

Thi section focuses on leadership, and the missives sent to the leader of the free world naturally draw on various biblical models of leadership.

For some contributors, Joseph is the model of a leader. When his father sent him on a potentially dangerous mission, Joseph quickly agreed. Ready willingness to assume the mantle of responsibility defines the leader. When the call comes that requires commitment, tenacity, and sacrifice—as it inevitably does to each of us—the true leader responds, "Here am I."

Another model is Moses. One contributor invokes Moses's smashing the tablets of the Ten Commandments and emphasizes that Moses did so on his own initiative, not God's instruction, as Moses deemed the people unworthy. For this contributor, the presidents who deserve celebration are those who have the vision and courage to transcend their limited assignment of power in order to preserve the life of the nation. Another sees leadership in Moses's confidence that God will be willing to forgive the people after their grievous sin of worshipping the golden calf. Leaders can meet great challenges and carry great burdens if they remain optimistic and, even in the midst of difficulty and confronted with defeat, can still glimpse the potential for success and triumph. Focusing on another dimension of Moses's character, one contributor reflects on the Divine gift to true leaders of a reserve of spirit and patience that is hidden deep within the crevices of character, but is available when all else seems somber and hopeless.

Joshua, Moses's successor, who led the Jewish people in the battle for the Promised Land, is yet another model. Here, the contributor notes that times of war produce great leaders, but freedom is more than the ability to win a war; freedom is the wisdom to create a society at peace with itself, with one another, and with God. Also discussed in this section is Queen Esther, whose internal regal character was inherited from matriarch Sarah, a spiritual dimension of leadership that serves as the wellspring of fortitude in times of difficulty and crisis.

Some of the missives, reflecting the author's profession, especially resonated with the president. Daniel Kurtzer, whom President Clinton appointed as the U.S. ambassador to Egypt, writes of emissaries and ambassadors in the Bible and their interaction with the leader. The president enjoyed this missive, and when the two met after Mr. Kurtzer's ambassadorial confirmation by the Senate, the president initiated a discussion of the missive's contents. Roald Hoffmann, a Nobel laureate in chemistry, ponders Moses's tragic fate, dying in the wilderness and being denied the triumphal experience of accompanying his people into the Land of Israel. He writes a poem about Moses that speaks of water and fire; aquifers and desalination; green mountains and ashen clouds. Though Moses struck the rock and lost faith in the people, he did well for them as a leader. As the Torah draws to a close, the land lies before them with a new beginning. President Clinton wrote that from Dr. Hoffman's letter and poem he took courage at the prospect of a new beginning.

Perhaps, though, the most poignant missive is from Yitzhak Rabin's granddaughter, Noa Rothman. She recalls that "when my grandfather was in America, he met a young, charismatic candidate for president of the United States and was thoroughly impressed by that first encounter. It was the foundation upon which an enduring friendship was based."

President Clinton had a special relationship with Yitzhak Rabin. The president admired Rabin's courage and willingness to take risks for peace, and he also came to admire Rabin's incisive and analytical approach to problems. Rabin's assassination was a source of profound sorrow for the president, and he ended his moving eulogy of Rabin with the touching personal farewell, "Shalom *chaver*, good-bye friend." At the mention of Rabin's name, tears would come to the president's eyes, something that I witnessed several times. The president said on more than one occasion that had Rabin lived, the negotiations with the Palestinians would have culminated in a peace treaty.

In reflecting on President Clinton's high regard for Rabin, I am reminded that how presidents and politicians are evaluated tends to fluctuate over time. I spoke to the president about Ulysses S. Grant, and he thought that Grant was underrated. He also felt that Alexander Hamilton was right about almost everything and that Thomas Jefferson was wrong about almost everything.

The essence of leadership is the ability to move the people and inspire their confidence during times of travail. What made Yitzhak Rabin great was his ability, in the most difficult of times, to be buoyed by a sense of hope and a clear vision of where he wanted to go. In fact, his Hebrew name, Yitzhak, which means "he will laugh," symbolizes the sense of optimism and confidence in a bright future during somber times that Rabin exemplified. Hope and a vision of the goal to be achieved and the direction to follow—these are qualities of leadership that President Clinton shared with Yitzhak Rabin. As President Clinton said at the conclusion of his acceptance speech at the 1992 Democratic Convention, "I end tonight where it all began for me: I still believe in a place called Hope."

Moving and inspiring the citizenry depends on the leader's ability to connect with people, an innate ability of Mr. Clinton's. An aphorism that floated around during Mr. Clinton's years in office effectively said, "When Bill Clinton speaks to a crowd of one thousand, each person thinks he is speaking to him, as opposed to other politicians, who when they speak to you, you get the feeling they are speaking to a crowd of one thousand."

Judah and Joseph

Menachem Genack, February 12, 1996

President Clinton was often criticized by his opponents for vacillating on certain issues. This letter highlights the fact that often the ability to change one's mind on important issues is the mark of a true leader.

LIKE A RED THREAD going through the Bible and the Talmudic tradition is the confrontation between Joseph and Judah over who will be the progenitor of the Royal House of David. We feel the tension below the surface as Judah approaches Joseph to plead for Benjamin (Gen. 44:18). It is remarkable that Jacob bequeaths royalty to Judah ("The sceptre shall not depart from Judah"—Gen. 49:10), rather than to his beloved son, Joseph. Joseph, after all, seems so suited to royalty, so perfect in every respect. He does not succumb to temptation. He is resolute and rules with brilliance and magnanimity over Egypt. Why then is the mantle of the kingship and leadership given to Judah, and ultimately to his scion, David?

Rabbi Joseph B. Soloveitchik, the preeminent Jewish theologian and Talmudist of the twentieth century, suggested that Judah is chosen for kingship because he is able to admit a mistake. According to the classical tradition recorded in the Talmud, Judah is chosen by God to be the forebear of the Davidic Dynasty, and the Messiah, when he admits his relationship with Tamar (Gen. 38:26). In fact, the name Judah is derived from the Hebrew "to admit." [Judah, a widower, admits that—unbeknownst to him—he had relations with his widowed daughter-in-law, Tamar, who'd been disguised as a harlot. She bore him two sons, one of whom, Perez, was the forebear of King David.]

Inherent to the human condition and our finitude is that we make mistakes and missteps. The critical element of leadership is the capacity to admit a mistake and not be wedded to a misguided and possibly disastrous course. What we seek in our leaders is not perfection or a misplaced, self-righteous stubbornness, but rather flexibility, and the ability to change direction in an ever-changing world drama. Humility requires that policies be susceptible to constant reevaluation and midcourse correction.

This was King David's great strength, and what set him apart from his predecessor, Saul. David was capable of admitting error, while Saul always explained it away, as he did when confronted by Samuel in the case of Agag (1 Sam. 15). [Saul had not followed God's commandments to destroy Agag, the king of the Amalekites, and his possessions.]

Lincoln, our greatest president, had a fundamental vision of where he wanted to lead America, but within that context he exhibited extraordinary flexibility. With his nuanced policy toward abolition, he was able to maintain the border states, while retaining the support of the Northern abolitionists. He changed commanding generals until he found Grant, the right one, to whom he gave his full support.

It is ironic that President Clinton is often assaulted by his Republican critics for waffling and changing policy when his ability to adjust to new circumstances and political reality, while remaining true to his basic vision, is the mark of real leadership.

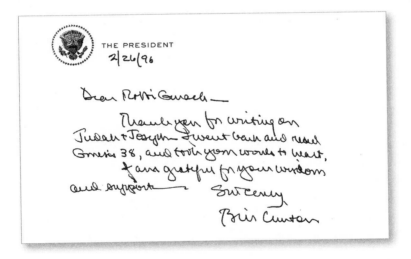

2/26/96

Dear Rabbi Genack:
    Thank you for writing on Judah & Joseph.
I went back and read Genesis 38, and took your
words to heart.
        I am grateful for your wisdom and support.
                            Sincerely,
                            Bill Clinton

Planning and Patience

Menachem Genack, December 26, 1996

At the end of a turbulent year for the Middle East peace process, including the difficulties following the Israeli archaeological excavation of the Western Wall near the Temple Mount, this letter emphasizes the value of patience in leadership —a value President Clinton gracefully exhibited as a mediator for peace in the Middle East.

DEAR MR. PRESIDENT,

I want to add my name—and a few words of Torah—to the list of those who have already expressed their deep gratitude for your continued leadership in advancing the Middle East peace process and supporting Israel.

Absent American involvement and influence, the world would be a much bleaker and more dangerous place. More specifically, without your leadership and engagement, the situation in the Middle East, which still bears such promise, would certainly atrophy, and a historic opportunity for peace in the region would be lost.

In this week's Torah portion (Gen. 42–45) we read about Joseph's dealings with his brothers in Egypt. He brilliantly orchestrates the bringing of Benjamin to Egypt, and only after he sees that his brothers have been transformed, and are now willing to protect a son of Rachel, does he reveal himself as Joseph—their estranged but forgiving brother—and thus effect a complete reconciliation. Leadership takes wisdom, patience, and determination, all attributes that you have exhibited in support of reconciliation in the Middle East.

It is most heartening to know that the Oval Office is occupied by a staunch friend of Israel, and someone who is firmly committed to the vision of peace, particularly in these critical times.

THE WHITE HOUSE

WASHINGTON

January 24, 1997

<u>PERSONAL</u>

Rabbi Menachem Genack
Orthodox Union
333 Seventh Avenue
New York, New York 10001

Dear Rabbi Genack:

    Thank you so much for the copy of your book, <u>Tradition</u>.
I appreciate your generosity, and I look forward to reading it.

    Thanks, too, for your recent letter regarding the Middle
East peace process. I share your commitment to continuing our
strong ties with Israel.

    I was pleased that Prime Minister Netanyahu and Chairman
Arafat reached agreement recently on the Israeli redeployment
in Hebron. This achievement brings us another step closer to
a lasting, secure Middle East peace.

    As always, I appreciate your friendship and wise counsel.

Sincerely,

Bill Clinton

The Trials of Leadership

Norman Lamm, June 13, 1997

Every president, most especially this one, must have the capacity to persevere even when confronted with negativity and pettiness. This missive reminds President Clinton to remain inspired even through such perpetual hostility.

THE BIBLICAL PARADIGM OF LEADERSHIP is that of Moses. He is the prophet supreme who was addressed by God "mouth to mouth" (Num. 12:8) and was regarded as the most "faithful in all mine house" (Num. 12:7). Moses is the one who defied the might of the entire Egyptian empire, the dominant world power at that time, and led his people to the shores of the Promised Land. Surely, his exercise of leadership was exemplary.

Yet Moses was only human, not Divine, and thus was subject to all the weaknesses of the flesh—and of the heart. Like all great leaders, before and after, there came times when he exploded in sheer exasperation. One can hear the frustration coming through the biblical text of his valedictory: "And I spake unto you at that time, saying, I am not able to bear you myself alone" and "How can I myself alone bear your cumbrance, and your burden, and your strife?" (Deut. 1:9; 1:12).

One of the things that most galled Moses was, undoubtedly, the ingratitude and pettiness of his people. He had inspired them with great dreams, with exalted visions of freedom and liberation, and all they could think of was: "We remember the fish, which we did eat in Egypt freely; the cucumbers, and the melons, and the leeks, and the onions, and the garlick" (Num. 11:5).

Moreover, according to the ancient Jewish Midrashic tradition [the body of classical rabbinic wisdom on the Bible], the people were spreading vicious rumors about Moses. They whispered about him dipping his hand into the till and helping himself to public funds, and they suspected him of seducing their wives! One can, therefore, hardly blame Moses for throwing up his hands in despair and crying out to God.

> Wherefore hast thou afflicted thy servant? and wherefore have
> I not found favour in thy sight, that thou layest the burden of
> all this people upon me? Have I conceived all this people? have

I begotten them, that thou shouldest say unto me, Carry them in
thy bosom, as a nursing father beareth the sucking child, unto
the land which thou swarest unto their fathers? Whence should
I have flesh to give unto all this people? for they weep unto me,
saying, Give us flesh, that we may eat. I am not able to bear all
this people alone, because it is too heavy for me. And if thou
deal thus with me, kill me, I pray thee, out of hand, if I have
found favour in thy sight; and let me not see my wretchedness.
(Num. 11:11–15)

The exasperation is dramatic and tangible. He has reached the end of his
patience, and his leadership is all but spent.

The Divine response is fascinating. Moses is told to gather seventy of the
elders of Israel to assist him in his duties,

And I will come down and talk with thee there: and I will take of
the spirit which is upon thee, and will put it upon them; and they
shall bear the burden of the people with thee, that thou bear it
not thyself alone. (Num. 11:17)

This response is puzzling. True, Moses will now have seventy helpers to
share the burdens of leadership. But why must the Lord "take of the spirit
which is upon" Moses in order to invest the seventy in leadership? Is God so
sparing in the "spirit" which is His that He must take it from Moses to put it
upon them? Why not take of His own spirit and directly grant it to them? The
answer proposed by one of the rabbinic sages is this: *God was telling Moses that
he has certainly not reached the end of his line. He has underestimated his capacity of leadership if he thinks he is ready to give up the post, abdicate, and vanish.
Indeed, he has enough "spirit" in him to provide for seventy others!*

Leaders, even of the caliber of a Moses, must be aware of the reserve
capacity of "spirit" that they possess and that they can summon for the exercise of their leadership. They must put up with pettiness and ingratitude,
with meanness and unfounded suspicions and rumors of the most vicious
sort—and not bend, not give up, and always rely upon the Divine gift to true
leaders: a reserve of spirit and patience that is hidden deep within the crevices
of character—but available when the circumstances require it, and when all
else seems so somber and hopeless.

Abandoned by His Flock

Joel B. Wolowelsky, June 27, 1997

Presidents, like all world leaders, face frustrations as they try to actualize their plans and hopes for their constituents. The most painful disappointment, however, is when efforts and labors extended on behalf of those citizens are not appreciated. Moses, leader par excellence of the Jewish people, faced such disillusionment, but history was grateful to him. Such a perspective should give sustenance to all leaders who must await a historical perspective to see their accomplishments fully appreciated.

SPEAKING AT THE CLOSE OF HIS CAREER as leader and liberator of the Jewish people, Moses mourns his inability to witness the fulfillment of his dreams. He had angered God years before, and now he must pay the price: exclusion from the Promised Land.

> And I besought the Lord at that time, saying, O Lord God, thou hast begun to shew thy servant thy greatness, and thy mighty hand: for what God is there in heaven or in earth, that can do according to thy works, and according to thy might. I pray thee, let me go over, and see the good land that is beyond Jordan, that goodly mountain, and Lebanon. But the Lord was wroth with me for your sakes, and would not hear me. (Deut. 3:23–26)

What right had Moses to blame his people for his plight? asked the late Rabbi Joseph B. Soloveitchik. It was he and not they who had sinned. It was God and not they who had passed a sentence that would not be commuted.

The answer, said Rabbi Soloveitchik, is to be found in the fact that Moses trusted in the power of prayer. When Israel had sinned, Moses pleaded their case: "Yet now, if thou wilt forgive their sin—; and if not, blot me, I pray thee, out of thy book which thou hast written" (Exod. 32:32). He knew that prayers are answered, and he understood that the prayers of the community are even more precious to God than those of an individual.

Moses expected no less from his flock than he had offered them as their shepherd. He was sure that when the cruel sentence was passed, his people would pray on his behalf. "If Moses our leader cannot enter the land," he expected them to declare, "then we too shall remain outside." He knew that God himself could not have refused such a demonstration of communal identity and concern.

But Moses was disillusioned. Israel was too intoxicated with the prospects of the fulfillment of its own dreams to take note of his crisis. "*I* pleaded with the Lord," we can imagine him crying. "I, alone, deserted, bereft of your support, pleaded with the Lord. Had *we* pleaded together, we would have been answered. But He would not answer me when He saw me standing alone."

Such is often a leader's fate. He makes his people's concerns his own, knowing full well that his loyalty may not be reciprocated. He creates and shapes dreams, aware that it may be only others who will see their realization.

Future generations, however, have a better perspective. The descendants of those who left Moses behind in the desert have continuously longed for his guidance, taking solace in the fact that his teachings did enter the Land with them, sustaining them as they study the work of their master.

Moses

Menachem Genack, August 29, 1997

Sometimes a leader must risk all, as Moses did, to be true to his principles.

MOSES'S NAME WAS GIVEN TO HIM by the daughter of Pharaoh when she "drew him out of the water" (Exod. 2:10), but his parents had surely named him already at birth. According to the collection of classical rabbinic wisdom known as the Midrash, Moses's Hebrew name was Tuvia. Yet strangely, even after he is repatriated with his family and people, he is always called in the Bible by his Egyptian name, Moses.

This retention of his Egyptian identity offers us an important lesson about why Moses is chosen for leadership. Moses was brought up in the palace by the daughter of Pharaoh. He is in every respect an Egyptian. He appears to the daughters of Jethro as "an Egyptian" man (Exod. 2:19). As a prince of Egypt with extraordinary leadership ability, he is a contender for the throne.

Yet when Moses sees an Egyptian smiting a Hebrew slave, his sense of justice and his outrage compel him to act. He kills the Egyptian oppressor, risking all and becoming a fugitive. He is transformed by his principled act from a prince of Egypt into a wanted man.

Moses could have made a very different calculation. "I will bide my time," he could have said. "One day Egypt will be my realm and I will then ameliorate the suffering of the slaves. I will be silent now. When authority is securely in my hands I will begin a period of 'perestroika' and reform the harsh Egyptian society."

But Moses's sense of justice would not tolerate such a "reasonable" calculation. He could not be part of the brutality that was Egypt. He instinctively acts, sacrificing all.

It is as an Egyptian, as a privileged royal, that Moses rejects his class, his society, and its values. At great personal peril, he asserts the then-unknown principle of the freedom and dignity of man. It is, therefore, Moses the Egyptian, and not Tuvia the Hebrew, who is destined to be the giver of the Law and the "father of Prophets" who will mouth the Divine imperative, "That which is altogether just shalt thou follow" (Deut. 16:20).

The Journey in the Desert

Julius Berman, September 15, 1997

This missive is a particularly relevant essay for the Clinton administration. President Clinton came to office with an ambitious agenda of reform but was forced to trim his goals in order to make it possible for them to be enacted into law. Even with the groundbreaking legislation that he signed into law, there might be reason for some to think that he failed because his entire agenda did not come to fruition. Julius Berman's missive responds to that mistaken criticism.

> These are the journeys of the children of Israel, which went forth
> out of the land of Egypt with their armies under the hand of
> Moses and Aaron. And Moses wrote their goings out according
> to their journeys by the commandment of the Lord: and these are
> their journeys according to their goings out. (Num. 33:1–2)

FORTY YEARS OF WANDERING IN THE DESERT after the Exodus from Egypt are about to end. One would expect that the narrative would turn to the preparations for the conquest of what will eventually be called the Land of Israel. Not so! Instead, the Bible veers off into an extensive travelogue, recounting the road map of the Children of Israel's four-decade journey from Egypt to Israel. "They journeyed from . . . and encamped in . . . . They journeyed from . . . and encamped in . . . ." Forty-two times in all.

This type of repetitive recitation is contrary to the basic elements of biblical style. The commentators extensively analyze every word in the Bible, building on the principle that not one word—indeed, not a single letter—is superfluous. Yet here there is passage after passage that does nothing more than list the myriad of resting spots on the way from Egypt to the Promised Land. What is the significance?

To appreciate the relevance of this extensive narrative, we must focus for a moment upon the people involved in the journey. Tradition informs us that with only two notable exceptions (Joshua and Caleb), none of the Jews who left Egypt arrived in Canaan. In other words, even though the yoke of Egyptian bondage had been removed, the ultimate redemption—arrival in the Promised Land—was not achieved.

Under the circumstances, one might suggest that these people had failed in their life's goal. After all, the ultimate objective of the Exodus was not simply physical redemption, but the spiritual experience of the Revelation on Mount Sinai, and its culmination in the entry into the Land that had been promised to their ancestors.

But the Bible informs us—via repeated reference to the journey and the stops along the way—that this is not the case. By no means was life wasted because the ultimate objective was not fulfilled. Each step of the way—each "journey," each "encampment"—was an achievement in and of itself, and remained so even if the ultimate goal could not be attained.

Indeed, that is the true appreciation of life. As Robert Browning put it:

> Ah, but a man's reach should exceed his grasp.
> Or what's a heaven for?

What was true with respect to the Dor HaMidbar, the Generation of the Desert, is equally applicable to every individual. When one is young and has a full lifetime ahead of him or her, one's dream of the future has no bounds; these are worlds to be conquered, this is a universe to harness. And so should it be. But, as time goes on and the years pass at an ever-accelerating pace, reality inevitably sets in. Goals conceived in youth are no longer achievable; the obstacles are manifold. Does that mean that life has been wasted, that the inability to attain the ultimate goal reflects failure? No, says the Bible. Every step of the way as one travels toward the ultimate goal is an achievement in and of itself, even if the long-sought end has not been reached. "And they journeyed and they encamped"—on the journey of Life.

The lesson of the Bible is equally applicable to a political leader. Prior to taking office, a true leader formulates a vision for the future, then goes on to formulate plans and a course of action to actualize that vision. The days, weeks, and months go by, and it becomes clearer and clearer that many of those dreams will never see reality. Does that reflect failure? The Bible assures us that, to be sure, many of the lofty goals have not been attained, but much has been accomplished, and every step of the way is an achievement.

"And they journeyed and they encamped."

Preparation for Leadership

Marc D. Stern, October 15, 1997

A great leader has very human qualities that are often manifest in quieter, less obvious ways than expected.

THE BIBLICAL TEXT IS RETICENT. Its biographies are incomplete, almost anecdotal. The Bible rarely explicitly judges those it depicts. It is only by searching for patterns and considering what the text chooses to report—and what it omits—that one can discern its judgments.

Moses, destined to lead the Israelites out of slavery, grew up in the house of his future antagonist. The medieval Spanish Jewish commentator Abraham Ibn Ezra (d. circa 1164), saw more in this than an ironic comment on the arrogance of a genocidal king:

> And the thoughts of God are profound, and who can stand in
> His counsel. . . . Perhaps God arranged that Moses should grow
> up in the king's house so that his soul would be on a high plane
> and . . . not lowly and accustomed to slavery. (Ibn Ezra, extended
> commentary on Exod. 2:3)

Leadership needs a breadth of vision, boldness, and freedom of spirit that the slave is likely to lack.

Venturing out to the enslaved Israelites to experience firsthand the suffering of those whom he would lead, Moses chances upon the beating of a Jewish slave by a taskmaster (Exod. 2:11). He surely could have passed over this injustice in silence, rationalizing that he could do more for the Israelites where he was than he could by intervening to stop what was no more than one more injustice in a degrading system of slavery. Almost instinctively, however, Moses reacts to save the "oppressed from his oppressor" (Maimonides, Laws of Sanhedrin 2:7). The impulse to correct abuses of power is an indispensable quality in the leader of a people who are themselves about to exercise it.

Almost instinctively—but not quite. The text reports that Moses "looked this way and that way, and when he saw that there was no man, he slew the Egyptian, and hid him in the sand" (Exod. 2:12). Eschewing the simplest understanding—that Moses simply stopped to see if he was being observed—the Talmudic rabbis comment that he stopped to see, prophetically, if any of the potential descendants of the taskmaster would be righteous, such that their ancestor should be saved so they might live. Why should Moses care? He was, after all, about to right a great wrong and save one of his future followers. The "victim" of Moses's wrath was entitled to no sympathy. At the very least, he was a brutal cog in a vicious system.

By insisting that Moses nevertheless considered not only the immediate justifications for killing the taskmaster but also its likely consequences, the rabbis teach us that it is not enough to act in pursuit of a great and just end. One must consider intermediate results. The pursuit of justice can be a heady thing, obscuring competing moral considerations. Was Moses doing more harm than good by killing this Egyptian? Was the moral calculus what it appeared to be at first glance? Was there some other avenue available?

Moses flees to Midian to avoid Egyptian justice. Stopping at a well, he observes shepherds chasing away the daughters of Jethro, who had just drawn water for their sheep. Moses, the recently arrived refugee, intervenes on their behalf (Exod. 2:15–17). Unlike his first intervention on behalf of his own people, this was on behalf of strangers. It cannot be explained by tribal loyalty. It reflects a commitment to the universality of justice—not a reaction to those parochial loyalties—without which a leader has no legitimate claim to leadership.

God commissioned Moses only after he demonstrated his fitness for leadership. His majesty of spirit; his empathy with the people he would lead; his willingness to consider the consequences of his actions; and his revulsion at injustice, no matter who the victim, were prerequisites for that commission.

Influence or Power?

Jonathan Sacks, October 17, 1997

Chief Rabbi Lord Jonathan Sacks offers advice on how to best garner cooperation and to inspire people to share one's vision in the task of making a better world.

FACED ON TWO OCCASIONS with a challenge to his leadership, Moses's reactions could not have been more different.

One was the rebellion of the Levite Korah and his followers. Korah, Moses's first cousin, had called into question the whole basis of Moses and Aaron's leadership: "Ye take too much upon you, seeing all the congregation are holy, every one of them, and the Lord is among them: wherefore then lift ye up yourselves above the congregation of the Lord?" (Num. 16:3). Moses's eventual response was to call on God to suppress the rebellion. The ground opened up beneath Korah and his supporters and swallowed them alive.

The other challenge concerned Eldad and Medad. Moses had been commanded by God to take seventy elders who would bear the burden of leadership with him. Moses took six from each of the twelve tribes—making seventy-two in all—and two were then excluded by a lottery. These two, Eldad and Medad, remained within the camp while the seventy went with Moses to the Tent of Meeting. There the Divine spirit rested on them. But it also rested on Eldad and Medad, who began speaking in the tone of prophetic inspiration.

Moses's deputy, Joshua, saw this as a threat to the leadership structure. Here were two people not chosen as elders, but acting as if they were. Joshua ran to his master and said, "My lord Moses, forbid them." But Moses replied, with majestic generosity, "Enviest thou for my sake? Would God that all the Lord's people were prophets, and that the Lord would put his spirit upon them!" (Num. 11:26–29).

Why in the one case did Moses zealously guard his leadership, and in the other, wish it were shared by all?

There is a fundamental distinction between "power" and "influence." Both are modes of leadership, but their logic is different in the extreme.

Power is a zero-sum game. The more power I give away, the less I wield myself. Influence is *not* a zero-sum game. The more influence I give away, the more I exercise. Power works by division, influence by multiplication. If I share power with nine others, I have a tenth of the authority I would have had if I had ruled alone. But if I share my *influence* with nine others, it expands to much more than if I had been alone. That is why power generates conflict, whereas influence generates growth.

Judaism's rabbinic sages expressed this difference in the form of a beautiful commentary. When Moses came to hand on his leadership to Joshua, he was commanded to do two things: "Lay thine hand upon him" and "Put some of thine honour upon him" (Num. 27:18; 27:20). On this the rabbis said:

> "Lay thine hand upon him"—this was like one who takes a flame to light another flame.

> "Put some of thine honour upon him"—this was like one who pours liquid from one vessel to another. (Midrash Rabbah, Num. 21:15)

Moses was about to transfer to Joshua the two bases of his leadership: influence and power. Handing on influence is like taking a flame to light another flame. The first flame is not diminished. Instead, the total light is increased. Handing on power, however, is like pouring liquid from one vessel to another. The more that is given to the second, the less remains in the first.

This explains Moses's reactions to the two crises. Korah wanted to seize some, perhaps all, of Moses's *power*. Moses knew that this was a threat to his authority, to his capacity to lead, and therefore he had no choice but to counter it. The case of Eldad and Medad had nothing to do with power. Instead they had caught Moses's *influence*, his prophetic spirit. Moses knew that this was not a threat to, but rather an enhancement of, his authority. The more widely influence is spread, the more effective it becomes. "Would God that all the Lord's people were prophets!"

Leadership almost always has these two dimensions, but they are strikingly different. Power shared is power halved, but influence shared is influence doubled. Power is temporary and vulnerable. Influence is lasting and pervasive. The great leader is one who knows the strange but expansive truth that influence is stronger than power, and that it is not through our control over others, but through our ability to extend their imaginations, that we make our most lasting contributions to human history.

The Greater Challenge

Jonathan Sacks, October 17, 1997

Rabbi Sacks wrote this prescient letter for President Clinton, which in retrospect seems like a message directed at his successor, President George W. Bush. With all the planning that went into winning the Iraq War, this essay would have provided strong direction on what turned out to be the bigger challenge.

MOSES, THE GREAT PROPHET, WAS DEAD. The time had come for his successor, Joshua, to lead the people across the Jordan into the Promised Land. We can imagine Joshua's fears. Would he be equal to the challenge of leadership? How could he follow in the footsteps of Moses, the founding father of a nation? How, above all, could he take the children of slaves and teach them what it is to be a free people in a land of their own, wrestling with the dilemmas of power?

God spoke to Joshua's fears. First He said, "As I was with Moses, so I will be with thee: I will not fail thee, nor forsake thee" (Josh. 1:5). Moses was not Joshua, Joshua was not Moses. God does not ask us to be the same as our predecessors. Each generation presents its own problems. Every age has its own dilemmas. That is why each leader must be of his or her time. It took a Moses to lead the Israelites out of slavery. It took a Joshua to lead them into freedom. That is why there are no universal rules of leadership, and why there are many styles, not one. But God holds out this promise to all those who open their hearts to an inspiration beyond themselves: that with the challenge always comes the strength to meet the challenge. God is with the leaders of every generation as He was with the first. "As I was with Moses, so I will be with thee."

However, God then went on to say something so radical that it still has the power to make us think again:

> Be strong and of a good courage: for unto this people shalt thou
> divide for an inheritance the land, which I sware unto their
> fathers to give them. Only be thou strong and very courageous,
> that thou mayest observe to do according to all the law, which
> Moses my servant commanded thee. (Josh. 1:6–7)

Joshua was faced with the challenge of leading the people into battle "to inherit the land." That would require him to be "strong and courageous." But God indicated that there would be a yet greater challenge, one that would require him to be *"very* strong and courageous." This was to live—and get the people to live—by the moral and spiritual standards set out in the Books of Moses.

It takes courage to win a military victory. It takes even greater courage to win a moral victory. It is one thing to win a war. It is another and greater thing to win a peace, to create a just and compassionate society in which my freedom is not bought at the expense of yours.

Times of war produce great leaders, who become famous through history as the individuals who led their people in battle against the enemy. But times of peace are the greater test of leadership. It is easy to mobilize a people in defense of land. It is harder to mobilize a people in defense of principle, common humanity, and all that is best and most generous in human nature. The dilemmas are harder. The risks of losing are less clear-cut. But it is here that leadership is forged, here that it makes its greatest contribution to the life of a nation. Freedom is more than the ability to win a war. Freedom is the wisdom to create a society at peace with itself, with one another, and with God.

It is never easy, but the words of God to Joshua echo in the ears of all who take up the challenge in the same spirit, each in their own way: "Have not I commanded thee? Be strong and of a good courage; be not afraid, neither be thou dismayed: for the Lord thy God is with thee whithersoever thou goest" (Josh. 1:9).

The Hands of Moses

Jonathan Sacks, October 17, 1997

President Clinton came to office with an ambitious and broad vision for his administration—welfare reform, health-care reform, education change, etc. As he faced the daily challenges of leading and the nitty-gritty negotiating of the legislative process, it would have been easy for him to have gotten lost in the details. Rabbi Sacks offers an inspiring lesson about successful leadership in the midst of legislative battle.

IT SHOULD HAVE BEEN PLAIN SAILING from here on. Moses had led the people out of Egypt with signs and wonders. They had traveled toward freedom across the desert. They came up against an impenetrable barrier: the Red Sea. The Egyptian army was advancing with its chariots. The Israelites could not go forward, they could not go back, and they could not stay where they were. Miraculously the sea divided. They crossed in safety. The Egyptians were stranded, their chariot wheels mired in the wet sand, and they were caught by the returning tide. At last, the Israelites were free and safe. . . .

But in human history, there is no "at last." Thinking they were alone in the desert, the Israelites found themselves the victims of a surprise attack by the Amalekites. Moses appointed Joshua his chief of staff and sent him into battle. He himself watched the progress of events from the top of a nearby hill. We then read the following:

> And it came to pass, when Moses held up his hand, that Israel prevailed: and when he let down his hand, Amalek prevailed. But Moses' hands were heavy; and they took a stone, and put it under him, and he sat thereon; and Aaron and Hur stayed up his hands, the one on the one side, and the other on the other side; and his hands were steady until the going down of the sun. (Exod. 17:11–12)

It is a moving and marvelous image: Moses willing his people to victory in the first war they faced, and he himself needing support as the burden weighed heavily upon him.

Yet there is an obvious question, and it was asked almost two thousand years ago by Judaism's rabbinic sages:

> Did the hands of Moses make or break the war? No—the text teaches us that so long as Israel looked upwards and subjected their hearts to their Father in Heaven, they prevailed, but otherwise they fell. (Mishnah, Rosh Hashanah 3:8)

There was nothing magical about the effect of Moses's hands. They merely communicated a message about where to look. So long as the Israelites looked down, they saw the enemy, the forces arrayed against them. Their morale suffered. They began to lose. But when they looked up, they remembered that Heaven had been with them in the past. They had come through difficulties and survived. They rediscovered hope and its begetter, faith, and they prevailed.

The hands of Moses were symbols of the power of a leader to generate courage by teaching a nation where to look. *More than leadership is about strength, it is about vision.* No political, social, or moral achievement is without formidable obstacles. There are vested interests to be confronted, attitudes to be changed, resistances to be overcome. The problems are immediate, the ultimate goal often frustratingly far away. Every public undertaking is like leading a nation across the wilderness towards a promised land that is always more distant than it appears on the map.

Look down at the difficulties, and you can give way to despair. The only way to sustain public energies is to look up, without flinching, toward the far horizon of ideals and aspirations. A leader is one who shows the people where to look—down or up, short-term or long-term, at present dangers or at ultimate destinations. That is perhaps the leader's greatest power—to influence the mood of a nation.

The philosopher Ludwig Wittgenstein once said that his aim was "to show the fly the way out of the fly-bottle." The fly keeps banging its head against the glass in a vain attempt to find a way out. Yet the bottle has been open all the time. The one thing the fly forgets to do is to look up.

A leader is one who sustains a collective vision. Teach a people to look up, and you give them the strength to prevail.

Jethro

David Kazhdan

Here is an analysis of the curious presence of Jethro, Moses's father-in-law, in the biblical story of the revelation at Sinai.

THE REVELATION OF THE DECALOGUE, the Ten Commandments, is one of the central biblical dramas. The dramatic description of God's theophany at Mount Sinai is preceded by a somewhat prosaic recounting of the visit of Jethro, Moses's father-in-law. Yet we are somehow left with the impression that Jethro has accomplished an important task, that without his visit the revelation could not have taken place. Indeed, Rabbi Elazar, one of the Talmudic sages, maintains that while in reality Jethro came a half year after the revelation, the Bible felt the need to relate it as a prelude to the Sinaic revelation. What could be so important about his visit?

On the morning after Jethro, a priest of Median, came to the camp, he saw Moses constantly surrounded by a throng of people from morning till evening. "What is going on?" he asks. "Why are all these people standing around you the whole day?" Moses tries to explain that people constantly come to him to inquire about God, to resolve their conflicts and to learn God's law. The only way to satisfy the needs of the people is to spend as much time as possible with them. "You are wrong," responds Jethro. "This is too much of a burden; both you and the people will wither away. Separate the tasks. Yes, you should remain an intermediary between the people and God, teaching them the statutes and laws. On the other hand, the resolution of conflicts should be run by a group of appointed judges. If you do this and God commands you to do so, you will be able to manage your tasks" (Exod. 18:13–24). Moses accepts the advice, and Jethro soon returns home.

What was so daring in Jethro's suggestion? Why was it not clear that God will approve his suggestion?

The concepts of truth and justice coincide in the biblical narrative from the beginning of Genesis. There, God is a friend, someone whom Abraham could even rebuke in his plea on behalf of Sodom and Gomorrah. This direct personal relationship existed till Jethro's arrival. Moses would treat every case as unique, something deserving to be brought to God Himself for final judgment. Jews were entering a new stage of their history. This was the time of their transformation from a group of individuals to a "kingdom of priests and an holy nation" (Exod. 19:6).The covenant on Mount Sinai was made with the nation. The individual Jew joined the covenant through his or her participation in this covenantal community. As a result, the relationship between the people and God had to become less direct than in earlier times. Indeed the Bible tells us that when God revealed Himself on Mount Sinai, the people were so frightened that they asked Moses to be an intermediary and to spare them from the awful, direct contact with God.

Jethro comes in the time of this transition from the immediacy of relations to mediation through community. He quickly realized that this change would lead to a removal of God from the day-to-day life of the individual people and suggested a way to combine the familiar structure of the direct relations between people and God with the new reality. While Moses will continue to bring the law to the people, it will be necessary to choose officers who will resolve day-to-day problems according to a firm law. There could be no other way for people to mature into a nation governed by a law and somewhat removed from its source. Realizing that there was no other possibility, Jethro confidently informed Moses—too close, perhaps, to realize it himself—and went on his way. The Jewish community went on to Sinai and its religious destiny.

Envoys Extraordinaire

Daniel C. Kurtzer, November 24, 1997

On November 5, 1997, the U.S. Senate unanimously approved President Clinton's appointment of Daniel C. Kurtzer as U.S. ambassador to Egypt, which led to his official appointment on November 10. Two weeks later, Dr. Kurtzer sent this missive to the president. In a fascinating essay, Dr. Kurtzer extracts from the Bible its principles of ambassadorship. During a brief meeting with the president shortly afterward to inaugurate Kurtzer's new role, President Clinton discussed this missive with Kurtzer and how it reflected on his new position as ambassador.

MANY AMERICANS HAVE AN IMPERFECT UNDERSTANDING of the role of ambassadors. Indeed, the most frequently asked question of an ambassador about to depart for his or her post is: "What is it that you do exactly?"

If contemporary experience is not enough of a teacher to answer this question, it may be possible to draw some lessons from biblical emissaries, mostly nameless and faceless people who appear at key junctures in unfolding dramas to deliver a message or carry out the bidding of the story's main personality. The Bible refers to these emissaries as *malach*, a curious choice of words, for it is part of the same root form of the Hebrew word meaning "work" and is translated often as "angel" or "emissary." Who were some of the human *malachim*, or emissaries, referred to in the Bible?

Jacob's functional envoy. In Genesis 32:4, Jacob sends emissaries to his brother Esau in an effort to appease him. Jacob is afraid that Esau will seek revenge for Rebecca's having conspired to steal Esau's birthright for her son Jacob. Jacob provides very specific instructions to his envoys, and the envoys report back that they had met Esau and that Esau was coming to meet Jacob with four hundred men. While this report does not calm Jacob's fears, it does provide Jacob with vital intelligence in preparation for his meeting with Esau.

Emissaries of Moses, the Commander in Chief. In Numbers 20:14–21, Moses employs emissaries to negotiate an arrangement that will allow the Israelites to pass through Edom without violence. Moses gives very precise instructions to the emissaries, appeals to the Edomites' good sense and common decency, and promises to disturb nothing along the intended route. The Bible reports Edom's threat to attack if the Israelites enter Edomite territory, forcing the Israelites to circumnavigate Edom.

Soon after, Moses sends envoys to Sihon, king of the Amorites, asking for permission to pass through Amorite territory. The text does not report Sihon's verbal answer but notes that Amorite troops were sent to fight the Israelites (Num. 21:21–23). Sihon's militant response is not puzzling in view of what had transpired between the failed diplomatic initiative to the Edomites and Moses's approach to him. During this interval, Aaron had died, the children of Israel had been forced to wander in the desert, and captives had been taken during a military engagement with the Canaanite king of Arad. "Diplomacy be damned," Sihon may have assessed, believing he could defeat the Israelites and capture booty. His calculated gamble failed, however, as the Israelites defeated his forces (Num. 21:24). In a strikingly parallel story in Judges 11:12, Jephthah tries Moses's diplomatic tactic with the king of Ammon and then defeats Ammon in war when the diplomatic opening is rebuffed (Judg. 11:32–33).

Alliance builders. The Bible also recounts (Num. 22) the effort of Balak, king of Moab, to induce Balaam, a noted soothsayer from Mesopotamia, to cast a curse on the Israelites. Balaam ultimately blesses the Israelites, after a humorous but fateful discussion with his very wise donkey. This effort to use an emissary to carry out a political-military mission fails ignominiously.

THE USE OF ENVOYS WAS AN ACCEPTED WAY of doing business throughout the ancient Near East. While the message brought back by emissaries was not always received well, their missions were usually of utmost importance. Do these biblical precedents offer lessons about the role of contemporary ambassadors?

- The identities of the emissaries appear to be singularly unimportant in the Bible. The leader who sends them is the central character in the story, not the people he dispatches. The Bible clearly intends to keep the ultimate responsibility for the direction of a diplomatic mission in the hands of the leader.

- One can but guess as to whether there was a "professional" cadre of emissaries chosen for successive diplomatic missions, or whether such envoys were picked serendipitously for each mission. The episode of the twelve "spies"—actually a senior fact-finding mission [one senior representative from each tribe of Israel], according to contemporary Bible scholar Menachem Leibtag—suggests that this was the exception, i.e. that in other cases, Moses picked envoys from among veteran message-bearers. The use of professional envoys might have been designed for leaders to maintain tight control over their message.

- The purpose of diplomatic missions in the Bible is varied, though most activity appears directed at avoiding or preparing for war. The Bible sometimes spells out the content of the diplomatic dispatch and sometimes does not. This could be a function of the nature of the mission, the trust the leader had in his emissaries, or the economy of words throughout the Bible text.

- The Bible does allow envoys some leeway in carrying out their mission: for example, when Abraham dispatches his servant, identified in rabbinic tradition as Eliezer from Gen. 15:2, to choose a wife for Isaac (Gen. 24), Eliezer defines the criteria for selecting a bride and puts her through a test of his own making.

- Finally, biblical leaders are clearly interested in what their envoys have to say, and in receiving reports expeditiously. This brings to mind the possibly apocryphal story told about George Washington's comment about an emissary to France. When informed that no reports had been received from the emissary for a period of six months, Washington was reputed to have said: "If we don't hear from him within three months, let us address another letter to him!"

Here Am I

Menachem Genack, 1998

The year 1998 was a difficult one for President Clinton. Even in times of difficulty, a leader must retain a great sense of purpose and mission and not allow the turbulence of life to distract from the greater resolve for accomplishment.

"AND ISRAEL SAID UNTO JOSEPH, Do not thy brethren feed the flock in Shechem? Come, and I will send thee unto them. And he said to him, Here am I" [*Hineni*, Hebrew for "Here am I"] (Gen. 37:13).

Rashi, the great medieval commentator (d. 1105), notes that the language of Joseph's response suggests both humility and eagerness. "He was eager to fulfill the request of his father," Rashi observes, "despite the fact that his brothers despised him."

How could Joseph express such a readiness to journey alone to his brothers, knowing they resented him so strongly? It was because Joseph was so imbued by his Divine mission that he assumed this journey, even to the point of self-sacrifice.

The biblical text itself hints to us to look earlier at another great man of faith, Abraham. Much of the same language used to describe Abraham's journey to sacrifice Isaac is used to describe Joseph's journey to his brothers in Shechem. There too Abraham responds to God's charge with extraordinary readiness: "And it came to pass after these things, that God did tempt Abraham, and said unto him, Abraham: and he said, Behold, here I am [*Hineni*]" (Gen. 22:1). The Bible relates that Joseph's brothers "saw him afar off" (Gen. 37:18); when Abraham journeys toward the mount, he "lifted up his eyes, and saw the place afar off" (Gen. 22:4). Joseph's brothers declare that after Joseph's destruction, "we shall see what will become of his dreams" (Gen. 37:20). After Abraham is relieved from sacrificing Isaac, he names the mount *Adonai yireh*, which means "in the mount of the Lord it shall be seen" (Gen. 22:14).

Joseph knew that even if he could not necessarily read it in the events themselves, there was nonetheless a Divine logic to his life. He sensed that each of the experiences would play a role in fulfilling the dreams of the sheaves and the stars. Thus, when Jacob sent Joseph on this potentially dangerous mission, Joseph responded unequivocally. This is the force of his response: "*Hineni*."

When Joseph and his brothers were finally reunited in Egypt, Joseph reassured his brothers that his earlier travails were not the result of their hostility, but were, rather, a part of God's plan. His speech is filled with this awareness: "So now it was not you that sent me hither, but God" (Gen. 45:8). "For God did send me before you," he tells them (Gen. 45:5). "And God sent me before you" (Gen. 45:7).

To each of us comes a call that requires of us commitment, tenacity, and sacrifice. It is at such moments that we are judged. Did we respond, "Here am I"?

> I heard the voice of the Lord, saying, Whom shall I send, And
> who will go for us? Then I said, Here am I; send me. (Isa. 6:8)

Isaac's Enigmatic and Heroic Legacy

Michael Rosensweig, January 14, 1998

Isaac, one of the three biblical forefathers of the Jewish people, introduced self-sacrifice and discipline as essential ingredients of leadership.

"THE ACTIONS OF THE PATRIARCHS are signposts to their descendants." This rabbinic perspective, which underscores the relevance of intense biblical study, projects that a profound understanding of biblical personalities, particularly the unique individual legacies of the three patriarchs, constitutes an exercise in self-discovery, a glimpse into our own spiritual potential and destiny.

Of the three patriarchs, Isaac is the least well-developed in the Torah. His story spans barely one weekly portion, in which he shares center stage with, and is often eclipsed by, the activities of others—Abraham during the Akedah (binding of Isaac); Jacob, Esau, and Rebekah in the struggle over the birthright and blessings. Moreover, when we do encounter Isaac in the narrative, he emerges as a most enigmatic figure. Occasionally, he exudes majesty and charisma. This is exemplified by his willing participation in the Akedah and by his dramatic first meeting with Rebekah, in which she literally falls off her camel in his presence (Gen. 24:64). In other contexts, however, Isaac appears to be at least partially manipulated by events that swirl around him, and his role is almost that of a transitional character: the bridge between a father who was the celebrated founder of monotheism and a nation, and a son, Jacob, whose evident achievements qualified him to bear the name and legacy of "Israel." Yet Isaac's status and stature in biblical literature and religious history is unquestioned, even as his contribution needs to be more fully assessed and understood. Who is Isaac really and what is his legacy?

The first verse in the weekly portion of Toledot [sixth Torah portion] provides a clue . . . "These are the generations of Isaac, Abraham's son: Abraham begat Isaac" (Gen. 25:19). This dual, apparently superfluous formulation establishes that Isaac's self-image as his father's son formed the foundation of his conduct and character. . . .

Yet Isaac's image of his father was a rather narrow one. After all, he experienced only the twilight of his father's career. Moreover, his primary interaction with his father took place in the absolutely unique and dramatic episode of the Akedah. The Torah, by repeating the phrase "they went both of them together" (Gen. 22:6, 8) emphasizes that this incomparable sacrifice cemented their relationship, inspiring the rabbinic insight that they approached the task with a singularity of purpose and commitment—"as one man with one heart." . . .

Isaac's fundamental religious personality was apparently profoundly reshaped by the event and implications of the Akedah. He could not simply put the experience behind him and rejoin society. He reappears in the biblical narrative only three years later to encounter Rebekah (Gen. 24:62–65). . . .

For Abraham, the Akedah was a test, a confirmation and culmination of an ambitiously balanced religious life. For the young, impressionable Isaac, it was apparently a defining experience, one that accented the role of charismatic gestures, extreme sacrifices, and the suppression of ego and personal need in the pursuit of spirituality. . . .

The spiritual model of Isaac contributes enormously to our spiritual heritage, even though the more complex and balanced religious agenda of Jacob, also named "Israel," is perceived to represent the ideal religious prototype.

Mankind is surely enriched by its legitimate diversity. The charismatic and wholly idealistic Isaac persona represents a critical element in the mosaic of religious society. He provides leadership, he occasionally even sets the tone in confronting various crisis situations, and he balances other elements in the daily challenges encountered by society. Moreover, the Isaac typology accentuates motifs that need to be integrated into every individual—idealism, heroism, the willingness to surrender and sacrifice for principle, and the capacity to eschew compromises that reflect a lack of will, devotion, and true commitment.

Yet, as noted, it is Jacob who emerges as the ideal patriarch. He most successfully integrated both his father's idealism-heroism and his grandfather Abraham's consuming commitment to compassion, enabling him to address the complexities of life armed with a broader and greater spiritual vision.

The contributions of all the patriarchs are particularly relevant as we struggle to resolve the knotty social and spiritual issues that confront us at the end of the twentieth century. . . . Never has the need to integrate idealism, pragmatism, and a broader spiritual vision been more imperative than in our own age. May the biblical models of the patriarchs, truly compelling and relevant, continue to inspire that leadership.

Human Anonymity and the Divine Plan

Judah Copperman, February 17, 1998

Leaders all begin their mission anonymously. It is their resolve to fulfill their mission that ultimately consigns their name to history.

THE BIRTH OF MOSES is recorded in the Bible (Exod. 2:1–2): "A man from the house of Levi . . . took to wife a daughter of Levi. And the woman conceived, and bare a son." This son is none other than Moses, the greatest lawgiver in history, How strange to find the birth of Moses, our Teacher, recorded in the annals of history in an anonymous context. Later the Bible records, "Amram took him Jochebed his father's sister to wife; and she bare him Aaron and Moses" (Exod. 6:20). Would it not have been simpler to write the names of the parents of the illustrious Moses when the Bible recorded his birth . . . ! Instead of this, we are held in the suspense of strict anonymity. The only hint given as to who the child really is, is the name given by an Egyptian lady (Exod. 2:10). It would appear that the theme underlining this method of recording history from the anonymous to the specific is as follows:

The Divine plan for the redemption of the people of Israel was devised, and ready for execution. The only question was, who would have the merit to be an active partner with the Almighty in bringing this plan into fruition? Amram and Jochebed, who were among the leaders of the Israelites in Egypt, brought a son into this world—a son who was gifted with those unique qualities essential for any partner with the Almighty in this historical upheaval. However, at the time of the birth of this savior, all the names are in strict anonymity, because it would depend upon the determination of these actors on the stage of history whether or not they would be privileged to fulfill their roles. (Destiny, in this view, is self-determined, not predetermined.)

Had these three actors failed to live up to expectations, it would have forced the Almighty, as it were, to seek His partner elsewhere. In that event, the names would have remained anonymous to this day. It was their determination and their ability to live up to the great expectations of them that took them out of the anonymity of Chapter 1 and recorded them for posterity in Chapter 6. Happy is the man who has the merit to utilize his great God-given abilities to participate as a vibrant actor in the God-given plan.

Sarah and Esther

Menachem Genack, February 23, 1998

Reminiscent of Ernest Hemingway's remark that "courage is grace under pressure," this letter was written to emphasize the importance of internal resilience and courage, not only political maneuvering, during times of crisis.

"AND SARAH WAS AN HUNDRED and seven and twenty years old" (Gen. 23:1). Jewish tradition, recorded in the Midrash, relates that Rabbi Akiva [d. circa 137 CE] queried how Queen Esther was able to rule from India to Ethiopia, 127 provinces (Est. 1:1). His answer was that Esther was the granddaughter of Sarah, who lived 127 years (Gen. 23:1).

Rabbi Akiva was puzzled—how did Esther, an innocent girl, ripped from the bosom of her family, and unschooled in the art of diplomacy outmaneuver her enemies and successfully rule over a vast empire of 127 provinces? Whence did she get the sophistication, poise, and strength to be queen, outwit Haman, the nefarious prime minister, and save herself and her people?

Rabbi Akiva believed that those qualities of leadership, and the ability to exercise them even in the face of great peril, were inherited by Esther from her ancestor Sarah . . . This association between Sarah and Esther can be found not only in the commonality of the number 127, but more fundamentally in the striking similarities in their lives. Like Esther, Sarah was abducted by a king—first by Pharaoh (Gen. 12:15) and again by Abimelech (Gen. 20:2)—and taken from her loving uncle and husband. Both Esther and Sarah were tragic figures; Esther was never reunited with her family, and Sarah died, according to rabbinic tradition, from the shock of learning that her beloved son was to be sacrificed by Abraham, and she never learned that God had in fact spared Isaac.

. . . "And Esther obtained favour in the sight of all them that looked upon her" (Est. 2:15). Her majestic nature was not learned, a function of external appointment, but rather radiated from the depth of her exalted personality. Her royal qualities were therefore not merely political, but more fundamentally spiritual. This internal regal dimension was inherited from Sarah. It is that spiritual dimension of leadership that serves as the wellspring of fortitude in times of difficulty and crisis.

Breaking the Tablets

Suzanne Last Stone, March 9, 1998

Focusing on the leadership skills of Judaism's greatest shepherd, Dr. Stone shows the importance of obligation prioritization. Moses was a lawgiver and spoke directly to God, yet his greatness truly comes to the fore as an advocate for his people.

"AND IT CAME TO PASS, as soon as he came nigh unto the camp, that he saw the calf, and the dancing: and Moses' anger waxed hot, and he cast the tables out of his hands, and brake them beneath the mount" (Exod. 32:19).

How can Moses be so consumed with fury, so ruled by his emotions, that he destroys the handiwork of God? After all, the golden calf is no surprise. God told Moses in grim detail what Israel had done before Moses descended from the mountain (Exod. 32:7–8). Indeed, Moses has just argued that God Himself has no right to be angry with Israel (Exod. 32:11).

According to the classical Jewish Midrashic tradition, the breaking of the tablets should be viewed not as an act of wrath or despair, but, rather, as an act of statesmanship—the continuation of Moses's effort to save the nation from Divine destruction. Moses reasoned as follows: If Israel has the Tablets of the Law, Israel will be formally bound to the Covenant, and legally liable for the death penalty for idolatry. Moses breaks the tablets in order to mitigate Israel's punishment. "To what can this be compared?" ask the rabbis. An earthly prince asks his faithful steward to betroth him to a maiden. The steward discovers that she has compromised herself in the meantime. The steward tears up the marriage contract, reasoning that it is better that the marriage never take place than that the maiden be judged as a married woman and subjected to the death penalty.

Moses not only subordinates the Covenant to the survival of Israel; he is willing to sacrifice his own destiny. Earlier, God said to Moses: "Now therefore let me alone, that my wrath may wax hot against them, and that I may consume them: and I will make of thee a great nation" (Exod. 32:10). But Moses rejected this course out of hand. Instead, he gave God an ultimatum: "Yet now, if thou wilt forgive their sin—; and if not, blot me, I pray thee, out of thy book which thou hast written" (Exod. 32:32). The Midrashic tradition links these verses with the breaking of the tablets, as follows:

> When Moses saw that there was no future hope for Israel, he
> united his life with theirs, and broke the tablets and said to God:
> "They have sinned, but so have I with the breaking of the tablets.
> If you will forgive them, forgive me, too. But if you will not
> forgive them, then blot me out of your book." (Midrash Rabbah,
> Exod. 46:1)

This understanding of Moses's action highlights the biblical conception of leadership. Although Moses's initial authority as leader stemmed from the fact of his conveying the words of God, his acceptance of this position implied a duty to *represent* the people *before* God—to secure the nation's survival, and to bear responsibility for the nation's actions. In doing so, a leader must have the courage to act on his own authority at critical moments in the life of the nation—and await the judgment of Heaven. God instructs the leader, as it were: "You have entered the [gladiatorial] arena. . . . You and I stand in the arena. Either you conquer, or I conquer you" (Midrash Rabbah, Exod. 28:1).

The tradition tells us elsewhere, "Three things did Moses do of his own understanding, and the Holy One Blessed Be He gave it His approval. [One is that] he broke the tablets" (Babylonian Talmud, Shabbat 87a). Later, God instructs Moses to place the remnants of the first tablets in the Ark of the Covenant, reminding him that they are "the first tables which thou brakest" (Deut. 10:2), as if to say: "Your courage is commended for having broken them" (Babylonian Talmud, Shabbat 87a).

America's greatest statesmen understood, too, that the founders gave us not only the Constitution—but also a model of action. History celebrates those presidents who have the vision and courage to transcend their limited assignment of power in order to preserve the life of the nation, and to announce its aspirations to the world. As Edmund Randolph, Virginia governor and, later, attorney general under President Washington, proclaimed: "There are great seasons when persons with limited powers are justified in exceeding them, and a person would be contemptible not to risk it" (Sanford Levinson, *Constitutional Faith*, 1988, p. 131).

Between a Grumbling People
and a Jealous God

Uriel Simon, June 8, 1998

A leader's job is to do what is right for his country and his people. Sometimes the public has different opinions on certain decisions a leader makes, and people can react with hostility. This insightful analysis of the Korah rebellion reveals Moses's important leadership practice of always doing what is best for his constituents despite personal risk. President Clinton found this message to be inspiring and sent handwritten letters of appreciation for the missive to both me and Dr. Simon.

MOSES AND AARON were chosen by God, not elected by the people. Naturally, then, Korah and his company, when they challenged Moses's leadership and Aaron's priesthood, concentrated their efforts on undermining this claim of Divine election. Korah's complaint against the two brothers was theological: "Ye take too much upon you, seeing all the congregation are holy, every one of them, and the Lord is among them: wherefore then lift ye up yourselves above the congregation of the Lord?" (Num. 16:3). In other words, the Lord, residing in His Sanctuary, is thereby ever present among His people; the injunction "Be holy unto your God" (Num. 15:40) was addressed to all the people. No one person, therefore, may maintain that he or she is holier than others and claim sole leadership on such grounds. Indeed, if sanctity is no longer seen as a matter of personal endeavor, but as an innate right—by dint of which every person is potentially a priest—there is no question of particularly worthy people being singled out by Divine choice. When the equality of all humankind as created in God's image becomes a pseudo-democratic slogan, bandied about by power-hungry demagogues, rather than a basis for human dignity and the rights and duties of the individual, the road is paved to anarchy.

Dathan and Abiram [co-conspirators of Korah], in contrast to Korah, put forward a purely political accusation: "Is it a small thing that thou hast brought us up out of a land that floweth with milk and honey, to kill us in the wilderness, except thou make thyself altogether a prince over us?"(Num. 16:13). That is to say: A leader who brought his people out of the fertile land of Egypt (a demagogic argument, ignoring the bitter reality: Egypt's slaves had no part in her plenty), promising to bring them to a land flowing with milk and honey, but who instead condemned the present generation (after the episode of the spies) to wander in the wilderness until they die out—such a leader had forfeited his people's trust; they no longer considered him a messenger from God, to be obeyed without question.

Faced with such total rejection, Moses realized that he could not resolve the crisis without requesting the punitive intervention of the invisible God. He therefore proposed two dangerous tests . . . The first test would show not only that God would punish Dathan's and Abiram's revolt by death, but that the punishment would be accomplished in an unprecedented way, demonstrating that rebellion against Moses was tantamount to rebellion against the Lord:

> If these men die the common death of all men, or if they be
> visited after the visitation of all men; then the Lord hath not sent
> me. But if the Lord make a new thing, and the earth open her
> mouth, and swallow them up, with all that appertain unto them,
> and they go down quick into the pit; then ye shall understand
> that these men have provoked the Lord. (Num. 16:29–30)

Korah's success in assembling "all the congregation" to witness his challenge to the leadership of Moses and Aaron aroused God's wrath, and He commanded Moses and Aaron, "Separate yourselves from among this congregation, that I may consume them in a moment" (Num. 16:21). But the two brothers could not agree to this harsh judgment; unwilling to abandon the people, they fell on their faces and implored the Lord to distinguish between the active rebels and the hangers-on: "Shall one man sin, and wilt thou be wroth with all the congregation?" (Num. 16:22). God responded, permitting them to save the rest of the congregation from the terrible fate of Dathan and Abiram by warning the people to distance themselves—demonstratively— from the camp of "these wicked men" (Num. 16:26). The people understood in time that a dreadful Divine punishment was imminent, and they heeded the warning and escaped death.

In the second test, 250 leaders of the congregation who had demanded to participate in the sacred service were summoned to offer incense in the Sanctuary together with Aaron, in order to determine who was permitted— and worthy—to do so: "Take you censers . . . put fire therein, and put incense in them before the Lord to morrow: and it shall be that the man whom the

Lord doth choose, he shall be holy" (Num. 16:6–7). As the death by burning of Aaron's two sons, a punishment for offering incense with unholy fire
(Lev. 10:1–2), was surely a vivid memory, it hardly seems reasonable that
the 250 leaders walked knowingly into a death trap, or that Moses would
have proposed such a measure. Rather, both sides to the dispute expected the
Divine will to make itself known not negatively, by branding those rejected,
but positively, by singling out the chosen one. Clearly, however, the Lord saw
the provocative challenge to Aaron's priesthood as a most severe offense, and
the punishment indeed recalled that of Aaron's sons: "And there came out a
fire from the Lord, and consumed the two hundred and fifty men that offered
incense" (Num. 16:35).

This should surely have been proof positive of the special sanctity of Moses
and Aaron. However, the people's rebellious spirit was kindled once again by
the very deadliness of the proof: "But on the morrow all the congregation of the
children of Israel murmured against Moses and against Aaron, saying, 'Ye have
killed the people of the Lord!'" (Num. 16:41). God's reaction was swift and terrible; once again, He commanded Moses and Aaron, "Get you up from among
this congregation, that I may consume them as in a moment" (Num. 16:45).

In God's view, obviously, the people, by accusing Moses and Aaron of killing the incense bearers, were not only identifying with the dead rebels but were
once again raising the banner of rebellion; Moses and Aaron, they reasoned,
had defended their own leadership at the cost of their rivals' lives, and so had
proven that they indeed exalted themselves above "the people of the Lord."

But Moses and Aaron once again disobeyed God's command, remaining
with their flock to obstruct the ultimate punishment, and again fell on their
faces. This time, however, they could not raise their voices in entreaty, for this
new challenge encompassed the whole congregation, and there was no distinction between leaders and hangers-on. Instead of abandoning the stubborn
people to an awful fate, Moses said to his brother Aaron:

> Take a censer, and put fire therein from off the altar, and put
> on incense, and go quickly unto the congregation, and make an
> atonement for them: for there is wrath gone out from the Lord;
> the plague is begun. (Num. 16:46)

And Aaron, though commanded by Moses to enter the very place that
the Lord had commanded them to leave, obeyed without question:

And Aaron took as Moses commanded, and ran into the midst of the congregation; and, behold, the plague was begun among the people: and he put on incense, and made an atonement for the people. And he stood between the dead and the living; and the plague was stayed. Now they that died in the plague were fourteen thousand and seven hundred, beside them that died about the matter of Korah. And Aaron returned unto Moses unto the door of the tabernacle of the congregation: and the plague was stayed. (Num. 16:47–50)

Moses and Aaron preferred to save the people, who had accused them of the most heinous crime, rather than save themselves. They risked their lives, acting on their own initiative, with the knowledge that God does not wish for sinners to die—only that they should repent their sins. And thanks to Aaron's efforts, standing fearlessly between the dead and the living, the terrible plague was halted; the Children of Israel were shown that their jealous God responded to the supreme devotion of their leaders. Blessed are the people that have leaders of whom they are not worthy.

THE WHITE HOUSE
WASHINGTON

June 23, 1998

Rabbi Menachem Genack
Orthodox Union
Kashruth Division
333 Seventh Avenue
New York, New York   10001

Dear Rabbi Genack:

Thank you so much for sending along Professor Simon's missive. I enjoyed reading it and have sent him a note of appreciation.

Sincerely,

Bill Clinton

Jacob and Israel

Menachem Genack, August 11, 1998

There is, Ecclesiastes tells us, a time for war and a time for peace. President Clinton faced many foes in his career. I encouraged him to stand firm on his principles and remain confident that there are issues on which compromise is impossible.

THE BIBLE GIVES US two apparently conflicting images of Jacob, who, after twenty years, is forced to confront [his brother] Esau. Twenty years earlier, Esau had set out to kill Jacob because of the blessings that Jacob had taken from their father. And now, returning from a long exile, Jacob prepares for his encounter with his brother. Immediately before this moment, Jacob, alone and away from his camp, is set upon by an angel. After a nightlong battle, Jacob heroically subdues him. When he then approaches Esau, however, Jacob is afraid (Gen. 32:7). Jacob is suddenly obsequious, bowing down seven times in Esau's presence (Gen. 33:3). What happened to the undaunted Jacob? How do we reconcile these two images?

The angel that Jacob struggled with, our tradition tells us, is in fact the angel of Esau, which means he represents the ideology of Esau. He reflects a this-worldly ideology of violence and self-centered power. Jacob does battle not so much with a specific figure but with an ideology, a principle. And his struggle to overcome the angel is a struggle for his own destiny. In such circumstances, there can be no compromise.

Jacob's loneliness, his solitude in battling with the angel, underlines this point. He is not only physically alone, but also existentially alone.

But his encounter with Esau is different. Here, Jacob is not doing battle with a pure ideology, but is confronting a practical challenge. Here, he must use realpolitik. Self-preservation requires deference and accommodating Esau's presence. But when it comes to principle, Jacob is uncompromising.

This dichotomy is reflected in the name that the angel, once subdued, gives to Jacob: Israel. "Thy name shall be called no more Jacob, but Israel: for as a prince hast thou power with God and with men, and hast prevailed" (Gen. 32:28). Jacob will, at times, be required to seek accommodation. But when confronted with matters of principle he emerges as Israel, who does battle even with angels.

The Royal Reach

Norman Lamm, November 6, 1998

Invoking the great psalmist King David, this letter reminds the president to transcend the disarray and disorder created by those who are intent on destruction. Even during times of crisis and personal calumny, the regality of a king must endure.

ONE OF THE MOST MOVING of all the psalms in the whole book of Psalms is Psalm 27. The most significant and characteristic verses in this deeply religious passage are the ones in which King David, the author, says, "One thing have I desired of the Lord, that will I seek after; that I may dwell in the house of the Lord all the days of my life, to behold the beauty of the Lord, and to enquire in his temple" (Ps. 27:4). Here is a deeply spiritual prayer of a sensitive, devout soul.

Yet when we turn to the Jewish exegetical tradition for its insight, we find one statement that, at first glance, is almost shocking. Rabbi Abba bar Kahana [third century CE] said that what David had in mind when he stated, "One thing have I desired of the Lord," was the kingdom of Israel. David clearly says that the one thing he asks is to dwell in the house of the Lord, and Rabbi Abba accuses him of political designs on the Israelite throne! David explains his prayer as the hope to behold God's graciousness—and a rabbi interprets his desire as one for power and influence! Isn't the rabbi being unfair to the memory of the "Sweet Singer of Israel"?

Of course he is being fair. On the contrary, if we understand his remark properly, he is not only being fair, but is paying David a handsome compliment. For this is what Rabbi Abba meant. David is throughout most of his life surrounded by enemies on all sides. Here are Philistines; there is Saul; and then there is his own son Absalom—all scheming to kill him, to do away with him once and for all. He is forced to flee for his life, to act insane lest he be trapped; he is hounded and hunted like a wild animal, hungry, cold, and tired.

What would one imagine should be the first prayer of such a man? "O Lord, destroy my enemies." "God, let me have my revenge against them." "Bread, O Lord, bread to sustain me." "One good victory, God, and I shall be happy."

Yet these are not the prayers of David. Caught in an almost hopeless situation, David has a vision that transcends the battlefield, that surpasses mere hunger, that stretches out beyond the din of war and reaches to Heaven itself: "One thing have I desired of the Lord, that I will seek after; that I may dwell in the house of the Lord all the days of my life. . . ." This, then, is what Rabbi Abba meant: David did not pray like a beggar. David did not grovel for crumbs. David did not limit himself to the petty needs of the hour. *David asked like a king*—he prayed like a sovereign; he never forgot that he was destined to become the great monarch of Israel. And a king, even if he is starving, remains proud, his vision large, his deportment grand, his goals lofty, his purposes elevated high above the crowd. By asking for the house of the Lord, by praying to behold God's goodness, by petitioning Him for the privilege of seeking Him in His temple, David acted like a prince, like a king. David had the "royal reach."

The question that confronts us in rare moments of truth and honesty is: How shall we define our own goals and ambitions? How shall we pray: like beggars, seeking only a bigger share of the pie; or like aristocrats of the spirit, striving for nothing less than the Kingdom of Heaven?

Our daily prayers reveal several such examples of the royal reach. We ask for wisdom—not merely that we might pass exams or appear well-read. We ask for forgiveness—not that we merely not be caught in some questionable act. We ask for redemption for our people—not merely for effective antidefamation and undisturbed leisure for ourselves. We ask for a full commitment to our faith—not just a pretty sectarian ceremony. And even when we plead for prosperity, it is not just for a better deal or portfolio, or a coup against a competitor, or more comforts and luxuries and status symbols, but: a blessing for plenty for all people in our times, for general prosperity and well-being; not that I make a killing, but that everyone makes a living. That is the royal reach.

A psychology of "asking for a kingdom" is unhappy with spiritual "tokenism" and "gradualism." It means that we must no longer be satisfied with mere water-skiing on the surface of life; we have got to do some deep-sea skin diving. As the poet Robert Browning put it: "A man's reach should exceed his grasp." We have got to reach for higher and higher goals.

How Things End

Roald Hoffmann, September 25, 2000

Toward the end of President Clinton's presidency, Roald Hoffmann, Nobel laureate in chemistry, sent him a letter with a brilliant poem regarding the final moments of Moses's life. As his term was coming to a close, the president, clearly moved by the letter's message, responded with appreciation for the letter's emphasis on "the prospect of making a new beginning."

OH, THERE MUST BE AN END—TO LIFE, to wandering in the desert, to a term of office. And with the ending, questions insinuate themselves: Why now? When I have so much to do? And . . . Could I have done better? Why?

In the synagogue every fall, Jews approach the end of the yearlong reading of the Torah, the last chapters of Deuteronomy. Forty years in the desert the people have wandered, led by Moses. Desperate for water, deluded by idols, the people wavered—even as they lived in the age of miracles, the power of God plain before their eyes!

Moses did not waver; he led the people with upraised hands and a clear mind. And yet here is how God spoke to Moses:

> And die in the mount whither thou goest up, and be gathered
> unto thy people; as Aaron thy brother died in mount Hor, and
> was gathered unto his people: Because ye trespassed against me
> among the children of Israel at the waters of Meribah-Kadesh, in
> the wilderness of Zin; because ye sanctified me not in the midst
> of the children of Israel. (Deut. 32:50–51)

And God took Moses to Mount Nebo, and from there Moses saw the land, bountiful, resplendent. And there, in sight of the Promised Land, Moses died.

Why? Well, at Meribah, the people complained:

> And wherefore have ye made us to come up out of Egypt, to bring
> us in unto this evil place? it is no place of seed, or of figs, or of
> vines, or of pomegranates; neither is there any water to drink. . . .

And the Lord spake unto Moses, saying, Take the rod, and gather thou the assembly together, thou, and Aaron thy brother, and speak ye unto the rock before their eyes; and it shall give forth his water. . . . And Moses and Aaron gathered the congregation together before the rock, and he said unto them, Hear now, ye rebels; must we fetch you water out of this rock? And Moses lifted up his hand, and with his rod he smote the rock twice: and the water came out abundantly. . . . And the Lord spake unto Moses and Aaron, Because ye believed me not, to sanctify me in the eyes of the children of Israel, therefore ye shall not bring this congregation into the land which I have given them. (Num. 20:5–12)

But what exactly was the great sin which the strength of the Israelites, their leader, committed at Meribah? What could merit that he should not reach where he, and only he, could clearly see? "'Tis a puzzlement," a question that has bothered many over the ages. Maimonides [Spain, d. 1204], the great Jewish rationalist thinker, saw the sin in Moses's clear anger at the people—for God had not been overtly angry in telling Moses how to respond to the complaints of His people. Nachmanides, the other pole of mystical Jewish learning in medieval Spain, saw Moses's fatal mistake in his saying "we," and not "God," as if the miracle were of his and Aaron's own magic.

Here is how a lesser American poet [Hoffman] reacted to it, faced with a striking painting of a burned mountainside:

In View of the Promised Land

The night before he died,
Moses our teacher dreamt
of the waters that once split
for him, now washing over
the burning bush on Horeb; Moses
woke, and smiled at his fate,
to lead a kvetching folk
from oasis to water hole; he,
drawn from water, giving
himself to fire, chosen

for expertise in the miracles
of aquifers and desalination!
Moses found it—again and
again—from the bitter waters
of Marah to the wilderness of Zin;
tired, there at Meribah,
he struck the rock twice, did not
speak to it, as was commanded,
as if to say, God, another miracle!
At Meribah Moses gave up
on his people; for this defiance
he would not enter the land
of milk and honey. They
say we do not know where
God buried Moses, having killed
him with a kiss. I know.
In every green mountain that
catches fire, in the yellow-red
night wounds of that fire,
on the day after, in black
that sucks light from the slopes
—there is Moses. The mistral
then comes, and blows the ashes
up in a cloud that exiles
day from the valley. In
the slopes is where Moses lies.
And drinks—rains, phase
of birth. The mountainside
grows green, as it must. And
Moshe Rabbenu smiles (as
the priests did not let him
in his book), now at peace
with his fire and his water.

As things end, we are always unsure of the value of what we have done.
We could have spoken more gently to our children, put in more time on that
introductory chemistry lecture; we could have somehow gotten a just health-
care plan through a recalcitrant Congress.

What was Moses's failure at Meribah? A small one, but oh so important. Faced with the disbelief of the people, Moses struck the rock twice, in anger. He had lost faith in the people of Israel, his own people.

What matters in this beautiful and terrible world is not that we reach the end. What matters is that one tried. And, yes, that one has faith in the people, those obstinate people. Moses faltered at Meribah, yet the people of Israel were hardly lost. For Moses, the same Moses who had been so angry at them, had done well for the people. The Torah draws to a close, but the land lies before them.

How do things end? With a beginning.

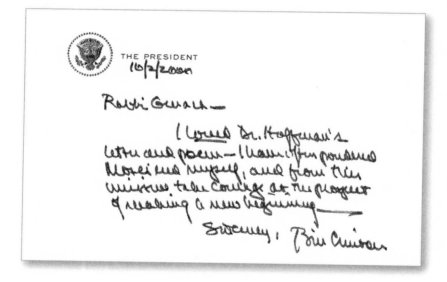

10/2/2000

Rabbi Genack:

I <u>loved</u> Dr. Hoffman's letter and poem—I have often pondered Moses' end myself, and from this missive take courage at the prospect of making a new beginning.

Sincerely,

Bill Clinton

Swearing on Lincoln's Bible

Menachem Genack, January 8, 2009

A few days preceding President Obama's inauguration, I sent this letter to President Clinton reflecting on the historic nature of the inauguration of the first African American president. Symbolically, President Obama chose to be sworn in upon Abraham Lincoln's Bible. Ironically, the Bible used for Lincoln's swearing in did not, in fact, belong to Lincoln; it was purchased by William Thomas Carroll, clerk of the Supreme Court, as Lincoln's own Bible was on route to the White House from Illinois with his luggage. Ironically, the presidential oath was administered to Lincoln by Chief Justice of the United States Roger B. Taney, the author of the nefarious Dred Scott decision and Lincoln's nemesis.

ON FEBRUARY 12, less than a month after Barack Obama takes the oath of office, we will celebrate the 200th anniversary of Abraham Lincoln's birth. How fitting that the two events will occur so close in time—the bicentennial of the birth of the man from Illinois who emancipated the slaves, and the inauguration of the man from Illinois who will become the first African American president. That is why Obama's decision to be sworn in using Lincoln's Bible is so rich in symbolism. Yet Lincoln's Bible is much more than a symbol. For Lincoln, the Bible was not only his most important literary wellspring; it was also a source of great comfort and inspiration.

Lincoln's religiosity has been a subject of endless debate. Lincoln was arguably both our least and our most religious president. He was not a churchgoer and rejected dogma and ritual; as a young man he was probably an agnostic. His wife, Mary Todd Lincoln, said that President Lincoln didn't believe in Christian tenets such as the Trinity. As Richard Carwardine notes in his book *Lincoln: A Life of Purpose and Power* (2006), Mrs. Lincoln maintained that her husband was not a "technical Christian."

Clearly, however, Lincoln lived his life with a deep religious sense. He may not have been a typical believer of the early- to mid-nineteenth century, when religious fervor was a major part of the American landscape, but he was still a man who in his own way communed with God.

Naturally, as a rabbi, I often view Lincoln's religiosity through a Jewish lens. I often tell my children that if they want to read a volume of *mussar*—a book about ethical and proper behavior—they should read a biography of Lincoln. His was an exalted personality serving a profound ethical purpose, with his great moral crusade wedded to a strategic and political genius that enabled him to successfully prosecute a war, win reelection, and preserve the Union, while never veering from deploring the evils of slavery.

As our prophets did, Lincoln recognized the power of words. He used words to challenge evil and to promote the good, to raise the spirits of a war-weary nation, and to ennoble Americans, even as he made clear that an ennobled America could never again include slavery within its borders. His speeches, with their biblical cadence, called upon the nation to live up to its highest ideals, to "the better angels of our nature."

Lincoln's magnificent second inaugural address—"With malice toward none, with charity for all, with firmness in the right as God gives us to see the right"—is a profoundly religious document. The [text of the] second inaugural saw the terrible carnage of the Civil War as Divine retribution for the evils of slavery. "Fondly do we hope—fervently do we pray—that this mighty scourge of war may speedily pass away," he said.

> Yet, if God wills that it continue, until all the wealth piled by
> the bond-man's two hundred and fifty years of unrequited toil
> shall be sunk, and until every drop of blood drawn with the lash
> shall be paid by another drawn with the sword, as was said three
> thousand years ago, so still it must be said: "The judgments of the
> Lord are true and righteous altogether" (Ps. 19:9).

The Gettysburg Address, in which Lincoln reaffirmed the Declaration of Independence's charge that "all men are created equal," reflects the Jewish concept that humanity is created *b'tzelem Elokim*, in the image of God. It was this notion, in Lincoln's thinking, that is "the father of all moral principle."

Lincoln was recognized in his time as a man devoid of prejudice, something remarkable in an era when even many of those who opposed slavery saw the Negro as subhuman and many of those who supported emancipation were horrified at the thought of social equality for blacks. His abhorrence of discrimination extended, of course, to Jews as well. After General Ulysses S. Grant issued his infamous General Order No. 11 banning Jewish merchants from the Tennessee military district, a delegation went to "Father Abraham," who immediately revoked the bigoted decree.

The idea of equality for Lincoln, though, was no abstraction; it was a deeply felt religious impulse. As Lincoln said to two women from Tennessee who had petitioned for the release in 1864 of their Confederate husbands from prison,

> You say that your husband is a religious man; tell him when you meet him, that I say that I am not much of a judge of religion, but that, in my opinion, the religion that sets men to rebel and fight against their Government, because, as they think, that Government does not sufficiently help *some* men to eat their bread on the sweat of *other* men's faces, is not the sort of religion upon which people can get to heaven. (*The Collected Works of Abraham Lincoln*, Roy P. Basler, Rutgers University Press, 1953–55)

Lincoln's political genius was rooted in his morality and empathy. His notion of God and what he saw as the Divine teleology in history were sources of courage and balance for him in the darkest days. His sense of God fostered in him a great degree of humility, a belief that he did not control events but rather that events controlled him; that he was not the captain of the ship, but rather a sailor, dealing with whatever storms and waves were sent his way.

Like Lincoln, Barack Obama takes office in a time of almost unprecedented challenges for America. As Obama places his hand upon Lincoln's Bible, let him be inspired by the spirit of Lincoln—his decency and his wisdom, his eloquence and his humility. May our next president, following Lincoln's example, always be true to the high standards that he has set for his administration and the nation. "I desire to so conduct the affairs of this administration," Lincoln said, "that if, in the end, when I come to lay down the reins of power, I have lost every other friend on earth, I shall have at least one friend left, and that friend shall be down inside of me" (*The Life of Abraham Lincoln*, Ida M. Tarbell, 1904).

In the Presence of Another Man
from Illinois

Menachem Genack, January 20, 2009

Doris Kearns Goodwin's landmark book *Team of Rivals* describes how Lincoln strategically used the talents of his political opponents. Perhaps the rival who served him best was William Seward, the U.S. senator from New York and a Republican presidential candidate, who became Lincoln's secretary of state. In a similar fashion, President Obama, who like Lincoln hailed from Illinois, also appointed to the post—to his great advantage—the senator from New York, Hillary Clinton.

WHEN BARACK OBAMA takes the oath of office today, the spirit of the sixteenth president, Abraham Lincoln, will hover over the ceremonies. Lincoln, in a sense, will be standing alongside Obama, reflecting that another man from Illinois has fulfilled the destiny that he himself set in motion with the Emancipation Proclamation.

Keenly aware of the monumental significance of his election, Obama has chosen to evoke Lincoln's accession to the office in a variety of ways.

- Obama boarded a train in Philadelphia that retraced part of Lincoln's route to his inaugural.

- During the ceremonies, Obama will take the oath of office on the same Bible Lincoln used.

- The theme of the inaugural is "A New Birth of Freedom," echoing the Gettysburg Address.

- Serendipitously, Obama will be inaugurated only weeks before the 200th anniversary of Lincoln's birth.

- Like Lincoln, Obama takes office at time of great peril for the United States.

Perhaps as he looks out at the enormous crowd gathered in his honor, Obama will sense the presence of Frederick Douglass, a black abolitionist and a noted orator, born in slavery, who witnessed Lincoln's second inaugural.

Douglass wrote in his autobiography [*Life and Times of Frederick Douglass*, 1881] that on Inauguration Day, March 4, 1865, "Reaching the Capitol, I took my place in the crowd where I could see the presidential procession as it came upon the east portico." Later, he attempted to enter the White House for the post-inaugural reception. When Douglass was stopped by the guards, Lincoln personally interceded to have him admitted, as Douglass wrote later in an essay:

> I could not have been more than ten feet from him when Mr.
> Lincoln saw me: his countenance lighted up, and he said in
> a voice which was heard all around: "Here comes my friend
> Douglass."
>
> As I approached him he reached out his hand, gave me a cordial
> shake, and said: "Douglass, I saw you in the crowd today listening
> to my inaugural address. There is no man's opinion that I value
> more than yours; what do you think of it?"

Douglass's response: "Mr. Lincoln, it was a sacred effort." He was correct; the second inaugural address was truly a religious document. . . . As many historians have noted, Lincoln was not formally a religious man. Yet he was fully aware of the presence of God in history and of the role of the United States as an instrument of God's will. The Gettysburg Address, like the second inaugural address, is a preeminent religious document. Lincoln's political philosophy was animated by a profound moral imperative, as he believed that the preeminent moral principle was that "all men are created equal."

And while Lincoln, according to his wife, was not a "technical Christian," in the Gettysburg Address he used Christian metaphors to indicate America's sacred mission. "Our fathers brought forth on this continent a new nation, conceived in liberty," is a metaphor for Jesus's conception. "We here highly resolve that these dead shall not have died in vain" refers to the Crucifixion. And "This nation under God shall have a new birth of freedom" denotes the Resurrection. The themes of the Gettysburg Address that "all men are created equal" and that "government of the people, by the people, for the people, shall not perish from the earth" set out a religious mission for the nation to fulfill.

As Obama takes the oath of office, we see the fulfillment of Lincoln's legacy. That legacy has now come full circle, from 1865, when a black man could barely enter the White House, to 2009, when an African American will be sworn in as president of the United States.

The rebirth of freedom implies a new beginning, a break from the past, a rethinking of old policies. As he takes office in these extraordinarily challenging times, it is well that Obama looks to Lincoln for inspiration.

"The dogmas of the quiet past are inadequate to the stormy present," declared Lincoln [in his annual message to Congress in December 1862]. "We must disenthrall ourselves and then we shall save our country."

2/12/09

Dear Rabbi Genack—
    Thanks for sending your fine essays on Lincoln—I enjoyed them, especially since I've been thinking about Lincoln, having just been a part of Henry Louis Gates' fine documentary, "Looking for Lincoln."
    I hope you're well.

                                    Best,
                                    Bill

A Father's Sacrifice

Israel Meir Lau, November 2009

In this moving letter, Chief Rabbi Lau recalls the president's eulogy for Prime Minister Rabin, which invoked the biblical story of the binding of Isaac. Rabbi Lau explains the heroic challenge of perpetual sacrifice.

DEAR PRESIDENT CLINTON,

Fourteen years ago the entire world mourned the murder of Israel's Prime Minister, Yitzhak Rabin. I spent that Saturday night at the Tel Aviv Medical Center, where Prime Minister Rabin was brought, along with Mr. Shimon Peres and the U.S. ambassador to Israel at that time, Martin Indyk. After I, as the Chief Rabbi of the State of Israel, authorized the burial to take place on the following Monday, Mr. Indyk informed me that he had spoken to you by phone a few minutes earlier, and that you had confirmed your plan to participate in the funeral on Mount Herzl.

Your eulogy, Mr. President, made a deep impression on all those present and those who heard it on the media, and your concluding words, which were said in Hebrew, "Shalom, *chaver* [Goodbye, friend]," will never be forgotten. They have become an international symbol and expression of true grief when one parts from a beloved and admired individual.

I, who like everyone else was moved by your words, was very close to you at the cemetery. I was aware of how deep your emotions were as you spoke. I was especially touched by the fact that you were the only speaker to mention the binding of Isaac, whose name in Hebrew was Yitzhak. This was a striking reference to the first name of the deceased prime minister, and was most appropriate given the fact that just that week, Jews in their synagogues throughout the world had read the story of the binding of Isaac in Genesis 22. The parallel was a perfect one, and I felt how terrible it was that the angel had not stopped the murderer with the words "Lay not thine hand upon the lad, neither do thou any thing unto him" (Gen. 22:12) that Saturday night in Tel Aviv.

Permit me, Mr. President, to share with you an idea which always comes to me when I read the story of the binding of Isaac. The story is generally seen as a demonstration of Abraham's devotion to God in being willing to sacrifice his son. But why should this not be considered a demonstration of Isaac's devotion as well? According to the rabbinic tradition, Isaac was thirty-seven years old at the time, and did not object in any way to fulfilling his father's plan as instructed by God. Why, then, is Isaac not credited equally?

The answer, evidently, is that a single test is not the same as an ongoing test over a period of time. Isaac's test was for a short time, and a person of his stature, who was willing to sacrifice himself out of respect for his father and in fulfillment of God's demand, had a relatively easy test (though I would not wish such a test upon anyone). Abraham's test, on the other hand, was very much greater, as he had to live with himself after the event and explain it to Sarah, and possibly even justify it to the rest of the world, where human sacrifices were regularly offered to the god Moloch. It was a terrible test—to live with the pain of the loss, and to be judged for having sacrificed his son.

Abraham nevertheless did not hesitate and was willing to fulfill the wishes of his Creator. That is why he was told: "Now I know that thou fearest God, seeing thou hast not withheld thy son, thine only son from me" (Gen. 22:12).

Mr. President, the Jewish people in the State of Israel have sacrificed close to 23,000 of our children on the altar of the revival of our nation in its land, as we are confronted by enemies who refuse to make their peace with our return to our ancestral home. At many memorial assemblies I look at the wrinkled faces of fathers and mothers who have lost their children, and I remember the binding of Isaac.

Permit me to show my appreciation for your sincere efforts to bring about peace, while you were president and to this day, in order to make further sacrifices unnecessary.

I would like to take this opportunity to offer my best wishes to you and to your wife, Secretary of State Hillary Clinton, and to your daughter, Chelsea. May you have many long years of joy and good health.

Optimistic Leadership

Menachem Genack, February 22, 2011

Lincoln apocryphally said, "People are as happy as they make up their minds to be."
I wrote this letter to President Clinton as a reminder of the integral role of optimism
in lasting leadership.

AFTER MOSES spends forty days and nights on Mount Sinai receiving the
revelation from God, he returns, tablets of the law in hand, to the catastrophic
sight of the Jewish people worshipping a golden calf. In response, Moses throws
the tablets down to the base of the mountain, destroying the tablets. This
is the classic interpretation of Moses's reaction, as captured in Rembrandt's
painting *Moses Smashing the Tablets of the Law*.

Another interpretation, contained in the Midrash, explains that the
tablets literally became heavier as Moses descended the mountain. The letters that were engraved in the tablets, the letters that spelled out the Ten
Commandments, objected to the idol worship and floated up to Heaven. The
tablets of stone resumed their original wholeness. Moses, enfeebled by the terrible sight of a nation gone astray, could simply no longer sustain the increased
weight of the tablets, which fell from his hands and were scattered at the bot-
tom of the mountain.

Rabbi Joseph B. Soloveitchik was puzzled by the second account. After
Moses, on behalf of the Jewish people, pleads for, and is granted, forgiveness,
God instructs Moses to carve out new tablets and bring them to the top of the
mountain to be once again inscribed with the Divine script. If Moses was not
able to bring the tablets *down* the mountain—working with the force of gravity—how would he be able to bring the tablets *up* the mountain? The second
tablets were no lighter than the first tablets that had fallen from Moses's hand.

Rabbi Soloveitchik answered that Moses was inspired and encouraged by
the forgiveness God had given him. Moses was optimistic, and that was the
key to his ability to lift the tablets back up the mountain.

Leaders carry great burdens and challenges. They can meet them and
succeed if they remain optimistic and, even in the midst of difficulty and confronted with defeat, can still glimpse the potential for success and triumph.

Attributes of a Leader

Noa Rothman, February 23, 2011

This letter was written by Noa Rothman, Yitzhak Rabin's granddaughter, whose eloquent eulogy of her grandfather at his funeral as the "column of fire before the camp" brought nations to tears.

IN MY LIFETIME, I have been influenced by people who were among some of modern history's greatest examples of leaders, people who governed by conscience, ethics, and morality. These attributes were ingrained in them by faith and they influenced who I am.

I make this contribution with regard for the person to whom I am writing, someone for whom I have great respect and a man whom my grandfather, Yitzhak Rabin, of blessed memory, called "*chaver*, friend."

In Exodus 18:21, Israel stands before Mount Sinai awaiting God's awesome revelation. From early morning until late at night, Moses sits and hears the people's problems and complaints, and teaches them the law. Moses's wise father-in-law, Jethro, sees this and notes that Moses cannot continue in this way, for his sake and for the sake of the people he leads. Rather, advises Jethro, Moses needs to delegate authority to others who will help him lead. Jethro then reveals to Moses four attributes such a leader needs: This person must be capable, God-fearing, honest, and just. As it turns out, these are not the only attributes of a leader. Four decades later, in Deuteronomy 1:13, as Moses begins his farewell speech to his people, he adds three more traits that a nation should seek in a leader: wisdom, compassion, and knowledge.

Because inevitably the Torah is not man's word, but God's, these seven attributes must be seen as a single unit. If so, asked the Mishnaic sage Rabbi Berechiah [thirteenth century], why were these seven attributes revealed in two parts—four at the start of Israel's momentous journey through the wilderness and three as that journey neared its end? The answer is, according to the Midrash:

> To teach us that if men with all the seven attributes are not
> found, then we select from those with four [attributes]; and if men
> with four are not found, then we select men with three attributes;

and if men with three are not found, then we select someone with but one attribute [the basic one required of every leader, and that is being capable of leading]. (Midrash Rabbah, Deut. 1:10)

There is more here than merely this answer. If we look deeper into the text, we are given the gift of truly seeing the wisdom of the Bible.

For one thing, besides the basic quality of leadership ability, Jethro's remaining three attributes emphasize moral character. Moses, on the other hand, emphasizes the intellectual side. A true leader knows the law, lives within it and administers it with compassion.

For another, Jethro was speaking to Moses based on his many years of experience as the leader of a group (Jethro, after all, was priest of Midian [an ancient region in Arabia]). Moses spoke to his people at the end of his career and articulated what he had learned through his experience.

The Midrash is correct; it is rare for one man to possess all seven attributes, but at the very least a leader must be God-fearing, i.e., humble and modest; and have an honest and just nature. In time, it is to be hoped, that leader will evolve through his experiences, and obtain wisdom and knowledge, and learn compassion on the deepest level.

My grandfather was among those lifelong public servants who evolved over time and who epitomized this explanation. Thus it was that in one of the most memorable speeches of his life, he could say, "We the soldiers who have returned from the battle stained with blood, we who have fought against you, the Palestinians, we say to you today in a loud and clear voice: Enough of blood and tears! Enough!"

My grandfather devoted his entire life to his country, his homeland. No matter which role he had at the time, be it war hero or peacemaker, his love and devotion to his nation was first and foremost. The proclamation above, given in 1993 at the White House signing of the Israeli-Palestinian Peace Accord, reflects the evolution of a leader who began his life fighting for a dream, spent much of his life defending that dream, and ultimately worked toward ensuring the long-term survival of that dream. He led a life imbued with tremendous faith and was wholly committed to the continuity of his people and his nation.

Of the seven attributes, one distinctly sets a person apart from his or her peers. To be a God-fearing person, to have faith, means to know that you are only mortal. Faith brings humility and modesty to those who have it.

Seemingly by default, it gives a person an air of honesty, integrity, compassion, and judiciousness. When Rabbi Berechiah spoke of capability as being the one absolute trait, he did not mean simply an ability to perform a task. Only by truly understanding and internalizing the lessons of our heritage that are taught to us from the time we are children can a person qualify as capable. Knowledge comes with age and experience; and willingness to learn from prior mistakes, personal and historical, brings about wisdom.

In 1992, when my grandfather was in America, he met a young, charismatic candidate for president of the United States and was thoroughly impressed by that first encounter. It was the foundation upon which an enduring friendship was based. My grandfather adored you as a person and had tremendous respect for you as the leader of arguably the most important nation in the free world. In everything you did, there were allusions to your faith. While mediating the Israeli-Palestinian and Jordanian-Israeli peace accords, you took direction from Proverbs 11:14, which states, "Where no counsel is, the people fall: but in the multitude of counsellors there is safety." You allowed the respective sides to negotiate by themselves for themselves, understanding that the issues needed to be discussed by the relevant parties and not directed by an interested outsider. You served as a mediator, possessing the unique ability to achieve compromise during times of impasse. You were fair to the process and committed to its resolution.

Compassion is the ability of a leader to identify with a person or group and demonstrate it. During the eulogy you delivered for my grandfather, the world saw an example of compassionate leadership. You addressed my family, but you spoke to an entire nation—identifying that this loss was both a family tragedy and a public one. By invoking the weekly Torah portion and connecting the binding of Isaac to that tragic day, you demonstrated not only your knowledge of Scripture, but of our culture, as well.

In closing your eulogy, you explained that the Jewish prayer for mourning does not speak of death, but that it does speak of peace. That is because the Kaddish originated as a prayer to be recited upon the completion of the study of a scriptural passage or a rabbinic text, and we have always believed that study of the Torah leads to peace. Other than several of the psalms, the Kaddish is one of the first documented prayers to include communal responses. It was written in the vernacular of the day, Aramaic, so that it could be more easily understood by all who heard it. The Kaddish evolved over time to have several functions, including (and most famously) as a prayer recited by mourners—not so much out of respect for the departed as out of concern for the living, to remind all who hear it that those who recite it need to be comforted by the community.

The Kaddish ends with words of peace, but it begins with words reflecting our hope for the coming of the messianic age. Our sages point out that in the Kaddish there are ten words of praise and consecration that correspond to what the Mishnah Avot ("Ethics of Our Fathers") refers to as the ten utterances of Creation. By communally responding and reciting these ten words, we all have a hand in Creation. Creation is about a world in harmony, not in conflict. It is about a world in which all people display the seven attributes of leadership as naturally as they breathe the air around them.

By referencing this prayer in your closing, you showed a commitment to the people to whom you were speaking, and you prayed alongside us for peace and renewal—both for Israel and for the world.

You and my grandfather, may his memory be a blessing, epitomized so many of the seven attributes of leadership. You both taught the world that good leadership can rest in hands that are capable, honest, just, wise, compassionate and knowledgeable. You continue to teach this lesson; I am sure my grandfather would have stood by your side in your many good works around the world that you have undertaken since leaving office.

And so I close this missive using the same words used by you, by millions of my ancestors, and by my people to this day. "May He make peace upon us, and upon all Israel, and let us say Amen."

Sin and
Repentance

onfession and repentance understandably became a theme of the missives toward the middle of President Clinton's second term when he faced impeachment charges. While the letters on the following pages do reference the "righteous indignation"—and implied political motivation—of those bringing charges, the missives' main focus is on the biblical models of failings and the need to confront oneself. Ecclesiastes (7:20) teaches us, "For there is not a just man upon earth, that doeth good, and sinneth not." Although this teaching can never be used to justify misdeeds, it exhorts us to widen our perspective and judge others based on a broad view of their talents, accomplishments, and overall spirit.

Applying a close analysis of the biblical language concerning sin offerings, one of the contributors asserts that the Bible views sin by a ruler as an inevitability, while sin by others is only a possibility. With power comes the responsibility of making decisions, and inevitably some of these decisions will be mistakes, misdeeds, or transgressions. Ultimate power carries the curse of hubris, itself a grave sin. Yet there remains the hope and reality of redemption. The Talmud makes the point that while error is inevitable for a ruler, the ruler who has the courage and humility to recognize his sin and ask forgiveness will receive atonement and even redemption.

Senator Joe Lieberman, in his missive, recalls the rabbinic tradition that Adam was expelled from the Garden of Eden at the close of the sixth day of Creation. With nightfall on that first evening of Adam's existence, he thought that his sin had brought the end of Creation, but when the sun rose the next morning, on the Sabbath, and with it the message of hope and redemption, Adam sang a song of praise to God.

"After the night comes the day, with its promise of salvation and the hope for a new and better tomorrow," writes Senator Lieberman. The president's reply captures his understanding of the moment: "Thank you for your reflections on night and day, sin and repentance. All of us need to reflect on these things, no one more than me."

Another missive perceives the shofar—the ram's horn sounded on Rosh Hashanah (the Jewish New Year), the holiday of repentance—as symbolic not only of the cry of the sinner, but also of God's reciprocal suffering. The penitent bemoans his failings and loss of innocence. So, too, the Almighty cries for His children who are alienated from Him, driven from His warm embrace. God, weeping for His afflicted children, assures them that they will be redeemed and returned to His presence.

In Jewish thought, repentance and the possibility for atonement are viewed as essential to human existence, so much so that in some metaphysical way, but also in a very real sense, repentance and atonement are inherent elements in the immutable structure of our universe. The Midrash interprets the "first day" referred to in the biblical account of Creation (Gen. 1:5) as a reference not only to the first day of the Creation process, but also to the day of Yom Kippur. The intent of this cryptic remark by the Midrash is that "first day" refers not only to that singular day, which was the first day of the Creation of the world, but also to another extraordinary and unique day— Yom Kippur, the day on which atonement for sin is granted by God. The possibility of atonement on Yom Kippur is so fundamental to existence that Yom Kippur was built into the very foundation of Creation.

The Thirteen Attributes of Mercy in Exodus define and describe God's compassion and readiness to forgive sin:

> And the Lord passed by before [Moses], and proclaimed, The Lord, The Lord God, merciful and gracious, longsuffering, and abundant in goodness and truth, Keeping mercy for thousands, forgiving iniquity and transgression and sin, and that will by no means clear the guilty; visiting the iniquity of the fathers upon the children, and upon the children's children, unto the third and to the fourth generation. (Exod. 34:6–7)

The first two attributes, which seem to be simply a repetition of the Divine name, "the Lord, the Lord God," are construed by our sages to refer to God's forgiving nature both before sin and after sin—that even before the occurrence of sin, God avails humanity of the possibility of repentance and atonement.

At the annual White House prayer breakfast held on September 11, 1998, in the midst of the impeachment turmoil, President Clinton delivered a speech in which he spoke of his own contrition and repentance and specifically referred to Yom Kippur:

> A couple of days ago when I was in Florida, a Jewish friend of mine gave me this liturgy book called *Gates of Repentance*. And there was this incredible passage from the Yom Kippur liturgy. I would like to read it to you:

> "Now is the time for turning. The leaves are beginning to turn from green to red to orange. The birds are beginning to turn and are heading once more toward the south. The animals are beginning to turn to storing their food for the winter. For leaves, birds, and animals, turning comes instinctively. But for us, turning does not come so easily. It takes an act of will for us to make a turn. It means breaking old habits. It means admitting that we have been wrong, and this is never easy. It means losing face. It means starting all over again. And this is always painful. It means saying I am sorry. It means recognizing that we have the ability to change. These things are terribly hard to do. But unless we turn, we will be trapped forever in yesterday's ways. Lord help us to turn, from callousness to sensitivity, from hostility to love, from pettiness to purpose, from envy to contentment, from carelessness to discipline, from fear to faith. Turn us around, O Lord, and bring us back toward You. Revive our lives as at the beginning, and turn us toward each other, Lord, for in isolation there is no life." (*New Prayers for the High Holy Days*, Rabbi Jack Riemer, 1971)

In a somewhat amusing misperception on my part, when Mr. Clinton quoted from *Gates of Repentance*, I thought he was referring to the monumental treatise on repentance written in the fourteenth century by the Spanish Jewish scholar Jonah Gerondi, who, wracked by guilt and remorse, wrote the book as penance for having attacked the philosophical works of Moses Maimonides, the great medieval Jewish thinker. It was only later that I discovered the president was not referring at all to Gerondi's *Gates of Repentance*, but rather to a different book that had no particular link to Maimonides—a twentieth-century prayer book of the same name used by the Reform branch of Judaism. Rabbi Joseph B. Soloveitchik makes the perceptive observation about the psychology of repentance that self-criticism is only part of the process; recognition of self-worth is also essential. As he wrote:

> A person is unable to repent if he lacks the courage to blame and
> to condemn himself. Regret is impossible without recognition of
> sin. On the other hand, one cannot imagine recognition of sin
> and commitment for the future unless man believes in his creative
> faculties and abilities. . . . The sinner must see himself from two
> antithetical viewpoints—the nullity of self and the greatness of
> self. Hence man's praise, like his shame, is part of confession.[1]

Rosh Hashanah, the Jewish New Year, is the day of judgment on which God scrutinizes our behavior and weighs our fate. Essential to an understanding of repentance in Jewish thought is the awareness that the Divine calculus of our sins and shortcomings is not a mechanical computation that satisfies the sterile rules of arithmetic but ignores the totality of the person. In judging each of us, the Almighty does not focus only on our deficiencies, He puts them in context, measuring them against our goodness and altruism. Only the omniscient God can know how to properly measure and weigh, on His Divine scale, the good against the evil for each person.

---

[1] Rabbi Joseph B. Soloveitchik, *The Rav Speaks: Five Addresses on Israel, History, and the Jewish People*, pp. 133–34. New York: Judaica Press, 2002.

When a Ruler Sins

Menachem Genack, September 1998

Humans are frail and subject to sin. However, the mistakes of a national leader are sui generis. With this letter, written a few days before Rosh Hashanah, I hoped to explain that the president has to recognize that a leader's error is in a category by itself and requires acknowledgment.

WHEN DESCRIBING THE REQUIREMENT of bringing a sin offering, the Bible usually uses the conditional case:

> If a soul shall sin through ignorance . . . (Lev. 4:2)
> And if the whole congregation of Israel sin through ignorance . . .
>   (Lev. 4:13)
> And if any one of the common people sin through ignorance . . .
>   (Lev. 4:27)

However, when speaking of the nation's leader, the statement is not made as a contingency, but rather as a declarative: "When [*asher*] a ruler hath sinned" (Lev. 4:22). There are several important lessons to be learned from this biblical text. The first is that the sin of the ruler is distinct and unique— sui generis. It is not simply a private matter that requires the same sin offering as the sins of the common people. Also, as opposed to all others, where sin is a possibility, the Bible states that the sin of a ruler is an inevitability. With power comes the requirement of making decisions, and inevitably among them will be mistakes, misdeeds, and transgressions. Ultimate power carries the curse of hubris, itself a grave sin. Yet there remains the hope and reality of redemption: "And the priest shall make an atonement for him as concerning his sin, and it shall be forgiven him" (Lev. 4:26).

In the original Hebrew text, *asher* has a dual semantic, meaning both "when" and "fortunate." Rabbinic tradition comments in the Talmud: "Fortunate is the nation whose ruler brings a sin offering" (Horayot 10b). The point the Talmud makes is that while error is inevitable as it relates to a ruler, the ruler who has the courage and humility to recognize his sin and ask forgiveness will receive atonement and even redemption.

The Weeping Shofar

Menachem Genack, 1998

The Hebrew month of Elul is a time of spiritual preparation for Rosh Hashanah. In the spirit of this time of repentance, I wrote this letter to President Clinton to express the Jewish belief that when someone truly repents and cries over his misdeeds, the Lord cries with him.

THE SOUND OF THE SHOFAR is, according to Jewish law, a weeping sound. The various sounds of the shofar represent different kinds of crying: the staccato cries of a child, the deep sighing of a distraught person.

But who is weeping? Undoubtedly, it is the one who sounds the shofar; as a penitent he bemoans his loss of innocence, his failings, his alienation from God.

But a careful analysis of the Rosh Hashanah liturgy underscores that the subject of the crying is not only the penitent, but that God Himself is crying. On Rosh Hashanah, we read from Jeremiah 31:15–16:

> Thus saith the Lord; A voice was heard in Ramah, lamentation,
> and bitter weeping; Rahel weeping for her children refused to be
> comforted for her children, because they were not. Thus saith the
> Lord; Refrain thy voice from weeping, and thine eyes from tears:
> for thy work shall be rewarded, saith the Lord; and they shall
> come again from the land of the enemy.

As Rachel cried for her children as they went to a cruel exile, God promised her that her children would return to their borders, to their homeland. So, too, God cries for His children who are alienated from Him, exiled from His presence, driven from His warm embrace. God, sobbing for His afflicted children, assures them that they will be redeemed and returned to His presence, and that the relationship of friendship and love will be restored.

"The Lord his God is with him, and the shout [trumpet blast] of a king is among them" (Num. 23:21). In the original Hebrew, trumpet blast, *teru'at*, also means "friendship," and the verse is interpreted by many commentators as "the friendship of the King is among them." The weeping sound of the shofar, God's sobbing for His wayward children, is the ultimate affirmation of God's love and friendship, and the eternal hope of return and salvation.

> And shalt return unto the Lord thy God, and shalt obey his voice according to all that I command thee this day, thou and thy children, with all thine heart, and with all thy soul; That then the Lord thy God will turn thy captivity, and have compassion upon thee, and will return and gather thee from all the nations, whither the Lord thy God hath scattered thee. (Deut. 30:2–3)

A Good Name

Menachem Genack, 1998

This letter reflects on the importance of one's own accomplishments and earned reputation, rather than mere status and position.

"A GOOD NAME IS BETTER than precious ointment; and the day of death than the day of one's birth" (Eccles. 7:1). Ecclesiastes was authored by King Solomon, son of King David, toward the end of his reign. The somber tone of Ecclesiastes contrasts starkly with the joyful and optimistic hue of Solomon's Song of Songs, which he wrote in his youth. Solomon, weary from the burden of leadership, was mindful of the fissures developing within his kingdom, and of the divisions within his land that would, upon his death, ultimately rupture and tear his realm asunder.

It might be from that perspective that Solomon, ruing the day he became king, observed that a good name, which one earns oneself, is better than precious oil—referring, I would suggest, to the specially designated oil with which kings of the Davidic dynasty were anointed. When a prince is born to his royal role, he is destined by pedigree to a station yet unearned. The day of death, when one garners all of one's life accomplishments, is more significant than the day of birth.

Forging Mettle

Menachem Genack, January 26, 1998

This letter was sent a few days after January 21, 1998, when the first mainstream media reports about the Lewinsky episode appeared.

DEAR MR. PRESIDENT,

We have often corresponded about models of leadership in the Bible. A great leader's mettle is often tested and forged in the cauldron of crisis. David's psalms, which have inspired all subsequent generations, were written during such periods of challenge in King David's own personal life.

Like millions of other Americans, I stand with you at this time. . . . You and your family are in my prayers:

> Wait on the Lord: be of good courage, and he shall strengthen
> thine heart: wait, I say, on the Lord. (Ps. 27:14)

THE WHITE HOUSE
WASHINGTON

February 11, 1998

Rabbi Menachem Genack
129 Meadowbrook Road
Englewood, New Jersey 07631

Dear Menachem:

Thank you for including me in your prayers. It meant a great deal to receive your thoughtful letter.

I appreciate your support and friendship.

Sincerely,

Bill Clinton

The Sins of Saul and David

Adin Steinsaltz, June 11, 1998

Here is a fascinating comparative analysis of the fates of King Saul and King David. While both sinned, Saul's sins abrogated his entire legacy. David's sins, however, did not prevent him from passing on the monarchy. This letter provides a compelling insight into this distinction.

SAUL AND DAVID were the first kings of the Jewish people. There are many points of similarity between them; both were young men from villages, both were anointed as kings by the prophet Samuel, both were war heroes who saved their people at times of distress.

Yet what a tremendous difference between their fates! King Saul was killed in battle and did not have descendants who continued his kingship, whereas King David died peacefully, his descendants formed a glorious dynasty of kings and rulers, and he received a Divine promise that the throne of kingship over the Jewish people would remain in the hands of his descendants forever.

The sages of Israel discussed the difficult question of the opposite fates of the two kings thousands of years ago, and some accounted for it by saying that King Saul was punished for his sins. However, King David also sinned! And the Bible, which shows partiality to no one, describes David's failures and sins, just as it describes his greatness.

In his public life, in his role as king, Saul succumbed to opposing emotions; indecisiveness on the one hand (1 Sam. 13), and uncompromising stubbornness on the other (1 Sam. 14:39–40); compassion and a gallant gesture toward an enemy (1 Sam. 15), on the one hand, and, on the other, cruelty and insensitivity toward the suffering of his own people (1 Sam. 16–19). Personal suspicion and paranoia occupied the army, the governing institutions, and the state, creating distortions in all the systems of government (1 Sam. 23–26), and were combined with personal feelings of regret and uncertainty.

David's sins, on the other hand, were private actions; they were his individual shortcomings. On the public plane, David did not allow for personal weaknesses to interfere with what was good for the people (2 Sam. 19:1–9). David's confession "Against thee, thee only, have I sinned, and done this evil in thy sight" (Ps. 51:4) was, to a great extent, true. As far as his actions as a leader are concerned, no blemish can be found.

It should be remembered that the Bible's test for public, political action is not the action's practical success. Saul's war against Amalek was a decisive event; from that point on, Amalek ceased to be a politically significant element. Still, the events of this war are counted among Saul's sins. On the other hand, many of David's wars did not bring about clear historical results, whereas one of his diplomatic activities resulted in a rough war (2 Sam. 10)— yet none of that is considered among his sins.

Individual sins are measured, and punished, on the individual plane, while public sins, or public fulfillment of commandments, receive their due reward on the historical plane, in the continuation of generations. "For David's sake did the Lord his God give him a lamp in Jerusalem, to set up his son after him, and to establish Jerusalem" (1 Kings 15:4). For kingship is based on the king's royalty, on his ability to transcend his flaws, on his adherence to what is proper and necessary for the kingship. And for this, he receives a reward for generations to come.

Respecting the Office

Menachem Genack, September 15, 1998

The president, like all political leaders around the world, is subject to intense personal attack from political opponents. But when legitimate rebuke moves into degradation of those who hold office, it is important to remember that respect due to an exalted office cannot be waived.

JEWISH TRADITION STATES in the Talmud that a king must be accorded honor and reverence, which he may not dispense with even if he wills it. This requirement to honor the king is derived by the rabbis from the very biblical requirement to appoint a ruler: "Thou shalt in any wise set him king over thee, whom the Lord thy God shall choose" (Deut. 17:15).

While the Bible requires us to honor our parents (Exod. 20:12), as well as an elderly person or scholar (Lev. 19:32), these may forgo the deference and dispense with the honor.

The difference between king and parent or scholar is that the honor due the king is not due to him personally, but to his exalted office. It represents not his personal prerogative, but the honor of the nation, which he has no right to waive. A nation is deeply invested in its ruler, who, in the words of Maimonides, is the "heart of the nation" (Mishnah Torah, Laws of Kings and Wars, 3:6). The honor due him is not merely due the person, but it is rather of a transcendent nature, involving the majesty of a nation and its history.

Noah

Menachem Genack, September 17, 1998

Ham's accursed trait, all too common in today's politics of personal destruction, was his attempt to discredit his father, Noah, for his failure despite the fact that Noah saved humanity.

> And [Noah] drank of the wine, and was drunken; and he was
> uncovered within his tent. And Ham, the father of Canaan, saw
> the nakedness of his father, and told his two brethren without. . . .
> And Noah awoke from his wine, and knew what his younger son
> had done unto him. And he said: Cursed be Canaan; a servant of
> servants shall he be unto his brethren. (Gen. 9:21–22; 24–25)

WHY WAS IT that Noah so chastised his son Ham? True, Ham saw Noah when he was naked and told his brothers, but why did Noah curse him so profoundly and reject him so totally?

The answer, Rabbi Joseph B. Soloveitchik suggested, is that Ham always wanted to find fault in his father, Noah, to diminish him, to expose his "nakedness" to the world. He hated his father. Ham wanted to show the world that his father was not the "righteous" and "wholehearted" man that the world thought he was, but rather a hypocrite. Ham bided his time, and one day he found his father drunk and naked in his tent, and he went and told his brothers.

The Bible does not want to justify Noah's behavior. His drunkenness and lusting were grievous sins. But what brought Noah to his inebriated state, if not the trauma of the Flood, the eradication of all living things? Did not Noah save the remnants of humanity, to courageously create a new world? Is not Noah, although fallen, none other than a heroic figure worthy of our consideration and compassion? He therefore deserved that his sin be kept hidden, and not publicized to all.

Ham's cynicism and mocking undermined leadership. His sin impeded the development of society, especially when a new world had to be created after the Flood. It is for that reason he is cursed; he is enslaved in his own mean-spiritedness.

The Naked Prophet

Menachem Genack, October 20, 1998

The Talmud tells us that certain great biblical figures sinned in order to teach people how to repent. This is not so much a lesson in biblical interpretation as it is a psychological insight. When a person is trying to achieve self-awareness, he needs guidance on how to break through confusion and regain his balance. Here I offered Saul as a biblical model for how to open oneself up to God and self-understanding.

> He came to Naioth in Ramah. And he stripped off his clothes
> also, and prophesied before Samuel in like manner, and lay down
> naked all that day and all that night. Wherefore they say, Is Saul
> also among the prophets? (1 Sam. 19:23–24)

WHAT DO THESE WORDS MEAN? Is it appropriate for a prophet to prophesy while naked? Rabbi Joseph B. Soloveitchik suggested that what the Bible refers to is not the external clothes we wear to cover ourselves, but the internal, subliminal coverings that shield us from confronting reality.

Saul knew that his grip on his realm was loosening. He knew that his dream of establishing a dynasty would be frustrated, never to be fulfilled. Yet Saul was unable to admit to himself that he was to blame. As Samuel had prophesied to him, "Because thou hast rejected the word of the Lord, he hath also rejected thee from being king" (1 Sam. 15:23).

Saul's many layers of psychological "clothing" protected him from the realization that he was at fault. As great as Saul was—and in many respects he was even greater than David—his own actions had brought about his doom. But he blamed David. If only David were not there to undermine his throne, things would be right again. If he could capture David, Saul would retain his kingdom. And so he constantly pursued David. But when Saul met Samuel and the group of prophets in Naioth, he felt the presence of God, and he confronted the bitter reality that it was not David who was at fault, but only himself. Saul stripped himself of the psychological armor, the substratum of psychological artifice that sheltered him from recognizing the bitter actuality. And that day Saul's pure soul, without pretense or artifice, was revealed before God, and Saul was "among the prophets."

Righteous Indignation

Menachem Genack, January 10, 2000

I write about the importance of consistency when criticizing others, and the risk of righteous indignation being used as a form of cynical manipulation.

> I am Joseph your brother, whom ye sold into Egypt. Now
> therefore be not grieved, nor angry with yourselves, that ye
> sold me hither: for God did send me before you to preserve life.
> (Gen. 45:4–5)

IN THE ORIGINAL HEBREW TEXT, the word "grieved" is *te-atzvu*, and the word "angry" is *yichar*. A similar linguistic construction is found in only one other place in the Bible—when Dinah [daughter of Jacob and sister of Joseph and the brothers] is raped by Shechem [prince of the city of Shechem]. The Bible records the indignation of Jacob's sons using a similar phrase:

> And the sons of Jacob came out of the field when they heard it:
> and the men were grieved [*va-yitatzvu*], and they were very wroth
> [*va-yichar*], because he had wrought folly in Israel in lying with
> Jacob's daughter: which thing ought not to be done. (Gen. 34:7)

The Bible intentionally uses the same construction to add its own implicit admonishment to the brothers, who had mercilessly sold Joseph into slavery.

When Dinah is raped, her brothers are indignant. In retribution, Simeon and Levi, with righteous indignation, wipe out the entire city of Shechem. Their action is motivated by their desire to protect a sibling, their sister Dinah, the daughter of Jacob. Yet, with regard to their brother Joseph, they judge him harshly, turn a deaf ear to his entreaties, and sell him into slavery, to an uncertain fate. Isn't Joseph, like Dinah, also a sibling, a child of Jacob? Doesn't he, as a brother, also warrant mercy and consideration?

The Bible means to criticize the zealotry of the brothers generally, and most specifically Simeon and Levi, who were the main antagonists of Joseph. For righteous indignation to be valid and genuine, it must be consistent, and in the case of the brothers, it was not.

Jacob takes note of this when on his deathbed he admonishes Simeon and Levi, cursing their wrath. "O my soul, come not thou into their secret; unto their assembly, mine honour, be not thou united: for in their anger they slew a man, and in their selfwill they maimed an ox" (Gen. 49:6). Jacob juxtaposes the massacre of the city of Shechem with Simeon and Levi's willingness to uproot Joseph, who is referred to metaphorically as an ox. Jacob is thus taking note of their terrible inconsistency in their respective actions related to Dinah and Joseph.

Righteous indignation is a dangerous emotion, though if pure and untainted by personal interest, it can be valid, indeed exalted. If applied, however, inconsistently, and alloyed with personal considerations, it is destructive, vengeful, and debased.

Night and Day

Joseph Lieberman, March 1, 2000

Senator Lieberman, who publically criticized the president on the Senate floor, was nonetheless an admirer of President Clinton. Clinton, as a student at Yale, had campaigned for Lieberman when he ran for State Senate in Connecticut; Lieberman was an early supporter of Clinton when he ran for president in 1992. After he sent this letter to the president, Senator Lieberman expressed that he regretted signing the letter "sincerely" rather than "affectionately."

And God called the light Day, and the darkness he called Night. And the evening and the morning were the first day. (Gen. 1:5)

THE BIBLICAL DAY BEGINS with night and is followed by the morning. The Jewish Sabbath is thus ushered in with the setting of the sun. The historian Benson Bobrick points out that in colonial times the Christian Sabbath began on Saturday night, and was likewise measured from sunset to sunset.

It has been puzzling to me that the day begins with night, the time of absence of light. Would it not have been more logical to calculate the day from the emergence of light, and then contrast the daylight period with its negation, night, the period of darkness? Why not coordinate the beginning of day with the morning-time, which initiates our daily activities, when we wake up?

One answer may be that the Bible thought that we could not properly appreciate the daylight if we did not first experience the night.

Night represents adversity, challenge, noncognition. Even the mighty King Solomon is seized by terror at night. "Behold his bed, which is Solomon's; threescore valiant men are about it . . . because of fear in the night" (Song of Sol. 3:7–8). Day, blessed by the warmth and light of the sun, is a period of security, productivity, growth, and hope. It is touched by all God's blessings. However, to appreciate and properly evaluate the gifts of the day requires the experience of the emptiness of the night, because the night teaches us the importance of faith and courage.

Psalm 92 is a song for the Sabbath day. In it the Psalmist chants, "To shew forth thy lovingkindness in the morning, and thy faithfulness every night" (Ps. 92:2). The morning, replete with God's bounty and benevolence, requires that we are grateful for His infinite kindness; but the night, enveloped in dark trepidation, requires faith.

There is a rabbinic tradition recorded in the Midrash that this psalm was written not by David, but by Adam. Adam came into being, sinned, and was expelled from Eden at the close of the sixth day. When the night of the first Sabbath descended, Adam thought that his sin had brought the end to Creation. The light was gone and he was surrounded by gloom. When the sun rose that Sabbath morning, and with it the message of hope and redemption, Adam sang this song of praise to God. After the night comes the day, with its promise of salvation and the hope for a new and better tomorrow.

THE PRESIDENT
3|15|00

Dear Joe —

Thank you for your reflections on night and day, sin and redemption. All you need to reflect on these things, no one more than me —— Sincerely,

Bill

3/15/00

Dear Joe:

    Thank you for your reflections on night
and day, sin and repentance. All of us need to
reflect on these things, no one more than me.
                    Sincerely,
                    Bill

The Ascent of Judah

Norman Lamm, December 30, 2000

The path to success as a leader is far from sequential. This letter, tracing the story of Judah's right to the legacy of Israel's monarchy, presents the Hassidic paradigm of "descent for the purpose of ascent," a road traveled by many biblical leaders.

I HAVE ALWAYS been fascinated by the figure of Judah as he winds his way through the last part of Genesis. He appears to me as a rather mysterious person, riven by inconsistencies: on the one hand, dark, introverted, somewhat reckless, impetuous; and on the other, a born leader, powerful, "a lion"; head of the Tribes of Israel, progenitor of King David and the Messiah.

He is both, of course, and that is what makes him so interesting as well as so important. But in order to understand him, we have to view him as one would a moving picture rather than a snapshot. Judah is a story in progress.

When we first meet Judah, he is in an untenable position. He was denied official leadership of the brothers because Reuben was the first-born and, by the rights of primogeniture, was the presumptive leader. Then there was Joseph, the *designated* leader as his father's favorite, and the son of his father's favorite wife, Rachel. Joseph wore the "coat of many colors"—not just a fancy sport jacket, but the uniform identifying the wearer as the heir apparent of the father. Yet *functionally* he, Judah, was the unofficial leader—with all the additional responsibilities that such an unanointed role carried.

In his conduct, he appears considerably less than admirable. Two events mark his life as a failure, as a moral debacle. He is the propelling force in the selling of Joseph, and he is disgraced in the matter of the Tamar affair [see "Judah and Joseph," page 4. In each case, he suffers a shattering shock at having his sins bared. . . .

But that is by no means the end of the story of Judah. In the end, surprisingly, he becomes the acknowledged leader of the Tribes of Israel, and progenitor of the House of David and the Messiah. Why? *Because Judah rises above his failures. He atones for his sins and goes on to greatness. He redeems himself.* The same Judah who counseled his brothers to sell Joseph into slavery now offers his own freedom and his very life to save Benjamin, Joseph's full brother. The same Judah who sought out a harlot and was dismayed to learn it was his daughter-in-law Tamar—whom he had wronged, and whom he had peremptorily ordered executed for suspected adultery—the same Judah openly and immediately confesses his terrible mistake. Realizing his dreadful error, he publicly concedes to Tamar, saying, "She hath been more righteous than I" (Gen. 38:26); justice (the Hebrew word for "righteous" is *tzedek*, which also means "justice") must now be done, and the price is my confession and restitution, and her exoneration. Only then can I go on to my destiny.

Judah has now overcome his deficiencies. He has learned from his mistakes. Judah is a study in growth, in development, a case study in how to overcome moral vulnerability and emerge all the stronger. And note well: the Torah *accepts* him in his new role; it does not thereafter condemn him to a life of endless and fruitless regret. So *tzedek* means that justice must be done, but also that the sin is not indelible: *teshuvah*, repentance, is possible. *Tzedek* means there must be no whitewash; but also that there must be no permanent blackening of one's reputation, no invitation to despair.

Martin Buber once said: "There are people who enjoy success after success, and they are failures. And there are those who experience failure after failure and they are successes." Judah exemplifies the latter.

Solomon said, "For a just man falleth seven times, and riseth up again" (Prov. 24:16). On which the great nineteenth-century Hasidic thinker Rabbi Zadok of Lublin comments, the "fall" of the righteous person is "a descent for the purpose of [a later] ascent." The fall is part of the getting up; it is, in the simile of an earlier Hasidic source, the backing up of the runner as he prepares to lunge forward and win the race. Which means that a failure overcome, a disaster studied and understood, a mistake pondered and corrected, leads to and eventually becomes part of the ultimate triumph itself. In the heavenly calculus of moral life, failure is often the stuff of success.

On his deathbed, Jacob looks back on the critical events of his life and sees Judah's development in a new perspective: "Judah is a lion's whelp: from the prey, my son, thou art gone up" (Gen. 49:9). What is Jacob driving at in this poetic metaphor? Rashi, the famed medieval biblical commentator, explains it best: the word "prey" is an allusion to Jacob's earlier words, which he later suspected were inspired by Judah, that Joseph was torn apart by a wild beast. . . . "Thou art gone up," is meant to imply, as Rashi puts it: you, Judah, emerged from your misdeeds with strength; you grew morally and you have "gone up" spiritually from your two dreadful failures. . . .

Imagine, now, if Judah had failed to offer his life for Benjamin, and if he had failed to confess to Tamar. Imagine if the Almighty had decreed that Judah must never emerge from his guilt and must wallow in the mud of his contrition forever—the people of Israel would never have benefited from the magnificent, centuries-long leadership of the House of Judah!

The rebuilding of one's life and reputation is never an easy matter. There is much grime to clean away, much regret at time lost and effort wasted, hard and lonely attempts to repeat what was once done and then undone and must now be redone. But precisely because of that, it is a nobler and more sacred task. As the Jewish tradition in the Midrash put it, "even the completely righteous cannot attain the place of those who sinned and repented."

Second Chances

Menachem Genack, April 11, 2013

During the 1992 New Hampshire primary, President Clinton promised voters, "I'll never forget who gave me a second chance, and I'll be there for you till the last dog dies." Indeed, President Clinton understands the value of second chances, a value this missive considers in light of a lesser-known biblical commandment.

WHEN IT COMES TO the important things in life, people don't often get a second chance. And yet that is exactly what we read about in the Torah concerning a festival that will occur in the Jewish calendar within the next two weeks—the Lord ordaining that if Jews are not able to observe the Passover holiday on its proper date, they may observe a "Second Passover" one month later (Num. 9:1–14). This ordinance contains a message of love, reconciliation, and family solidarity that resonates through the ages.

The very first Passover holiday was celebrated, of course, in Egypt as the Jews were being redeemed from slavery. But Passover was meant to be an annual ritual; the Torah recounts that one year later in the midst of their sojourn in the desert, the Jewish people are commanded by the Lord to observe Passover on the anniversary of the Exodus from Egypt in accordance with all of the rites and ceremonies—including the sacrifice of the paschal lamb— that attended that first Passover in Egypt (Num. 9:1–5). There was, however, a problem. A group of Jews had been rendered ritually impure because they had been in contact with a dead body. Now, under biblical law, one who is ritually impure due to contact with a dead body is prohibited from partaking of the paschal sacrifice. This group protested—why should they be excluded from the rest of the people and prevented from participating in the Passover holiday, surely the high point of celebration of Jewish national redemption?

> And there were certain men, who were defiled by the dead body of a man, that could not keep the passover on that day; and they came before Moses and before Aaron on that day: And those men said unto him, We are defiled by the dead body of a man; wherefore are we kept back, that we may not offer an offering of the Lord in his appointed season among the children of Israel? (Num. 9:6–7)

In one of the rare instances of Moses the lawgiver being at a loss for the right decision, Moses was baffled, and he presented the question to the Almighty: "And Moses said unto them, Stand still, and I will hear what the Lord will command concerning you" (Num. 9:8).

As rare as Moses's uncertainty was, the response given by the Lord is unique in biblical literature—a built-in, codified second chance to observe the holiday ritual a month later. Those who are unable to observe the holiday on the evening of the fourteenth day of the month of Nisan, the first month of the Jewish calendar, are to observe it on the evening of the fourteenth day of the month of Iyar, the second month of the Jewish calendar:

> And the Lord spake unto Moses saying, Speak to the children
> of Israel, saying, If any man of you or of your posterity shall be
> unclean by reason of a dead body, or be in a journey afar off, yet
> he shall keep the passover unto the Lord. The fourteenth day of
> the second month at even they shall keep it. . . . According to all
> the ordinances of the passover they shall keep it. (Num. 9:9–12)

And so the institution of the "Second Passover" was codified in the Jewish calendar for all time.

The following is based on an idea from my friend, Rabbi Ari Kahn.

The rabbis of the Talmud, as was their wont, were not willing to take this account at face value, and were convinced that some significant event must be at the root of the extraordinary institution of the Second Passover. From their exploration of the source of the Second Passover, we can distill a timeless message of forgiveness, reconciliation, and family inclusiveness that is as powerful today as it was thousands of years ago.

Just who, ask the rabbis of the Talmud, were these individuals referred to in the biblical account, who protested their exclusion from the paschal celebration, and what was the source of their ritual impurity? One of the answers, offered by Rabbi Yose [second century CE], is that these were the individuals who were entrusted with carrying Joseph's remains out of Egypt at the time of the Exodus, and their contact with Joseph's remains rendered them ritually impure. Rabbi Yose's answer harks back to the dramatic story in Genesis of Joseph and his brothers, generations before the Exodus. Recall that the brothers, driven by jealousy and meanness, throw Joseph in a pit in the wilderness and leave him for dead. Joseph, hauled out of the pit by slave merchants and taken to Egypt, ultimately becomes viceroy to the pharaoh, and through his wisdom saves Egypt and the entire Middle East, including his own family, from famine. After their father, Jacob, dies, the brothers fear the worst and plead with Joseph not to take revenge for their cruelty in years past. In one of the most touching expressions of kindness in the biblical narrative, Joseph, instead of exacting revenge, comforts his brothers and tells them he will care for them and their families:

> And Joseph wept when they spake unto him. . . . And Joseph said unto them, Fear not; for am I in the place of God? But as for you, ye thought evil against me; but God meant it unto good, to bring to pass, as it is this day, to save much people alive. Now therefore fear ye not: I will nourish you, and your little ones. And he comforted them, and spake kindly unto them. (Gen. 50:17–21)

The brothers had tried to cast Joseph out of the family, and Joseph, instead of exacting revenge, treats them like family. He craves to be part of the family of Jacob, and with prophetic vision he adjures them, in the penultimate verse of Genesis, that they should never again abandon him, and they should take his remains with them when the Jewish people ultimately leave Egypt (Gen. 50:25). And Joseph merited redemption with his people at the Exodus precisely because he afforded his brothers a second chance.

The essence of the holiday of Passover and the paschal sacrifice is the coming together of the family. Unique to the holiday of Passover is the Torah's requirement of the centrality of the family. The Torah prescribes that the paschal offering must be celebrated by each household (Exod. 12:3)—it is not an individual or communal observance, but is meant to be, first and foremost, a family celebration.

The same concept, the coming together of the family, is the underlying theme of the Second Passover. The Almighty would not countenance any Jew being deprived of the experience of bonding with his family on Passover and exulting in the freedom of the Jewish people. And if one could not participate in the Passover celebration at its proper time due to ritual impurity or being located in a distant land, he was given a second chance to celebrate with his family one month later.

This then is also why the drama of Joseph and his brothers echoes in the biblical narrative of the Second Passover. Joseph lovingly embraced his family.

Deprived for so long from being with his family, Joseph repaid his brothers' callousness not with revenge but with a second chance for love, reconciliation, and inclusiveness. They had attempted to drive Joseph out of the family; he bound them within the family ever more closely.

And it was those determined men who brought Joseph's remains back to their eternal bond with the family of Israel and who insisted on their right to celebrate Passover with their families, who assured that all Jews would have a second chance to share the family joy of the Passover holiday.

A second chance—for reconciliation, inclusiveness, and family bonding—the enduring message of the Second Passover.

Creation

The first chapters of Genesis contain fundamental lessons about the nature of the world and our role therein. The letters in this section draw from the Genesis narratives and explore some of the themes of Creation, including what it means that we were created "in the image of God"; the mandate to rectify a broken world; and the role of diversity in God's creative design. The missives ponder the message of human individuality as it emerges from the Creation story and how it impacts our understanding of each person's political and moral rights. Perhaps most significantly, the missives express the message of Genesis that the uniqueness with which every individual is endowed is a reflection of our being created in the image of God.

The great advances in science over the past century, especially in the area of medicine, have saved and improved countless lives but have also raised thorny ethical dilemmas. Rabbi Immanuel Jakobovits, former chief rabbi of the British Commonwealth, addresses the issue of humanity's mastery over nature—in effect "playing God"—as in the areas of nuclear power and cloning. Rabbi Jakobovits applauds these advances and affirms Judaism's view that man was meant to be a partner with the Creator. He cautions, however, that humanity must wield this power wisely and know how to control the forces it is able to unleash. The issue of human cloning came to the fore during the Clinton administration after the cloning of a sheep in Scotland was announced in 1997. Soon afterward, the president reacted at a press conference by saying, "Any discovery that touches upon human creation is not simply a matter of scientific inquiry; it is a matter of morality and spirituality as well. . . . Each human life is unique, born of a miracle that reaches beyond laboratory science."

In his missive, Rabbi Ahron Soloveichik, the brilliant thinker and teacher, finds in rabbinic commentary the message of the importance of human diversity and uniqueness as represented in the rainbow, the symbol of God's covenant with Noah and the entire human race in the aftermath of the great flood. This symbol has also been used by many outside the Jewish world to represent diversity—most famously by Jesse Jackson, whose vision of a "Rainbow Coalition" was articulated during his 1984 presidential campaign and evolved into the organization of that name that he founded.

Esther Wachsman reflects on the uniqueness of the individual and points out that, in Hebrew, the word for "alone" and "one" has the same root as the word for "together" or "united." Only by appreciating the great value of our own individuality can we see the reflection of that value in others and thus strive for brotherhood, togetherness, and unity. Esther Wachsman's missive is heart-wrenching to those who know her story. Mrs. Wachsman's son, Nachshon, was an Israeli soldier captured while off duty in 1994 by Hamas terrorists disguised as religious Jews. During a daring but ultimately unsuccessful rescue operation, he was killed by his captors. The whole episode was closely followed by the entire Israeli populace, and Nachshon's mother inspired the nation with her faith and courage in the face of such tragedy.

As part of a delegation to Israel in October 1994 for the Israeli-Jordanian peace treaty signing, I accompanied President Clinton to the Knesset, where he gave a memorable address that was a telling testament of his relationship with Israel and his compassion for the Israeli people. The president told of his first visit to Israel, in 1982. His pastor came with him, the president recalled, and they became very close. Later the pastor became desperately ill. On his deathbed he called for Governor Clinton and told him that one day, he might become president of the United States, and he must promise never to betray Israel, for God would never forgive him. President Clinton stated "and I never will."

The president's speech was succor to a people who had been traumatized by the murder of Nachshon Wachsman and a recent terrorist attack in Tel Aviv. In the audience that evening were Nachshon's parents, to whom the president addressed words of consolation. He concluded by stating that America would stand with Israel always.

In a later year, after Yitzhak Rabin was assassinated and President Clinton visited Rabin's grave in Israel, he paused first at the grave of Nachshon Wachsman to place a small stone on his gravestone as a sign of mourning.

The significance of each individual as part of the human community and the importance of diversity within the human community are significant themes in President Clinton's thought. Time and again, he called on citizens to stand up and contribute their unique skills to making this country even greater. In the speech marking the one-hundredth day of his first administration, President Clinton told about a letter he had received from a childhood friend. This friend told how she had been asked in conversation how we are going to save all of the kids who are in trouble in this country; she responded, "The same way we lost them, one at a time." Each person is distinctive, and we need to recognize everyone's place in this world.

In President Clinton's second inaugural address, he stated, "Our rich texture of racial, religious, and political diversity will be a Godsend in the twenty-first century. Great rewards will come to those who can live together, learn together, work together, forge new ties that bind together." Diversity, in President Clinton's eyes, is not a burden to be tolerated but a blessing to be celebrated.

President Clinton, when he addressed the nation after testifying before the Starr grand jury, decried the "the pursuit of personal destruction, and prying into private lives" in which no area of a person's life is exempt from public scrutiny. He defiantly asserted his right of privacy, declaring, "Even presidents have private lives." In one of my missives, I suggest that the Jewish view is that privacy is significantly more than a right. Rights can be waived under appropriate circumstances. Privacy is an existential need of the human being, built into the fabric of creation. The absence of privacy is a critical limitation on the ability of the human being to function, whether as a spouse, a parent, a president, or any other significant role. The president had asked me what he should speak about when he addressed the nation, and I told him that in addition to profound remorse, he should mention the right of privacy. In hindsight, this was poor political advice, as the president was criticized for not being sufficiently contrite. Nonetheless, the issue of privacy is fundamental, and the erosion of privacy in our media-driven society is a matter of deep concern.

These missives, which speak to that essential human dignity that defines every individual, and which emerges from the Almighty's plan of Creation, found a receptive ear in the forty-second president of the United States.

In His Own Image

Shlomo Sternberg, November 3, 1997

All humans, not only rulers, are created in God's image.

"SO GOD CREATED MAN in His own image, in the image of God created He him; male and female created He them" (Gen. 1:27). Philosophers and theologians have pondered this verse over the centuries, each with his own notion of the Divine aspect of man, and of the way in which there can be a human aspect to the Divine. But modern archaeology confirms the simplest and most direct intent of the verse, especially when placed in its original cultural climate.

In the ancient Near East, being created in the image of a god was a description used to distinguish the ruler from his subjects. Thus one cunei-form document reads, "The king, my lord, is the very image of [the god] Bel," and another says, "The king, lord of the lands, is the image of [the god] Shamash." Similarly, in Egypt, Pharaoh Thutmose IV is described as "the likeness of [the god] Re."[1]

But the Bible tells us that this phrase applies to the whole human race, which is conceived to be one family, in that we are all descended from a single pair of ancestors. The One God personally created man and woman as the supreme act of cosmogony, and created them—and hence, all of us—in His image. Human life is infinitely precious, and we each have free will and share in a unique personal relationship with God.

[1] See Nahum M. Sarna, "The Mists of Time: Genesis I–II," in Ada Feyerick, *Genesis: World of Myths and Patriarchs*, p. 51. New York: NYU Press, 1996.

Playing God:
The Limits of Man's Creative Genius

Immanuel Jakobovits, November 10, 1997

In March 1997, President Clinton issued a "Memorandum on the Prohibition on Federal Funding for Cloning of Human Beings." This letter reflects on the careful balance humankind must negotiate between scientific innovation and creative hubris.

THROUGH SPECTACULAR ADVANCES in medicine and technology, man has become able to manipulate the very building blocks of life, to generate human beings out of test tubes, and to change their genetic composition. Man is assuming increasing mastery over the conditions that determine his physical existence, and has even developed the capacity to generate life beyond the natural processes of its propagation. The charge is therefore increasingly made that by assuming functions that hitherto could be exercised only through natural processes, we are "playing God." Is such a charge justified?

In earlier times, a good deal of opposition existed to such artificial intervention in nature, on the grounds that this might challenge and usurp the Divine role in the propagation and preservation of life. Thus, there was religious opposition to, for instance, Edward Jenner's discovery of inoculation against smallpox, on the grounds that it interfered with the prerogative of the Creator. The objection extended even to the use of chloroform to ease the pangs of childbirth. It was argued that such analgesics conflicted with the biblical statement "In sorrow thou shalt bring forth children" (Gen. 3:16).

Judaism could never accept this reasoning. Man was meant to be a partner with the Creator, and not a passive victim of nature's capricious inroads into human health and security. Thus, man's task to apply the healing arts to the relief of pain and illness was mandated in Jewish tradition by the verse "And shall cause him to be thoroughly healed" (Exod. 21:19). As the great Jewish philosopher, codifier, and physician Maimonides observed, if we are to employ such reasoning and inhibit man from countering the curses of nature, we would consider it a violation of Divine prerogatives to utilize plowshares or other manmade instruments that ease the burdens of plowing. Man would be sentenced to perpetual serfdom. On the contrary, man is gifted with intelligence in order to overcome—as best he can, and in partnership with the Creator—the endurance of hardship and pain.

But man must know where to stop, and how to control the forces he is able to unleash. Through the weekly observance of the Sabbath, we are reminded that He created "heaven and earth, the sea, and all that in them is" (Exod. 20:11). God offers this reminder by imposing a ban on creative work on one day out of seven. But, strikingly, holy are to be not Sunday, or Monday, or Tuesday—days upon which He created—but the Sabbath, the day on which He *stopped* creating. Greater, as it were, than the God who created the world and its infinite forces is the God who knew when to stop—and thus maintain *mastery* over the forces.

The key to human survival now rests more demonstrably than ever in the capacity to keep under control the forces at man's bidding. This, for instance, applies to nuclear power and its potential for massive destruction by explosion or pollution, as well as, more recently, to cloning. Cloning could presage wonderful progress toward eliminating some of mankind's worst scourges, through, for example, helping to produce organs for transplants. But the cumulative damage of the slightest error or miscalculation could also disturb the fine balance of nature and develop monstrosities beyond man's capacity to repair or control.

Hence, we applaud the president's call for a moratorium on experiments in the artificial generation of life. This will ensure that man will remain master, and not become the victim, of his capacity to exploit the forces of nature.

A Faulty Foundation: The Tower of Babel

Erica Brown, December 30, 1997

The Tower of Babel is presented as a cautionary tale of the dangers of unbridled uniformity.

THE TOWER OF BABEL NARRATIVE, one of the most enigmatic of the foundation stories of Genesis, has intrigued readers of the Hebrew Bible from rabbinic scholars to Franz Kafka to A. S. Byatt. On one level it is an etiological tale—a story about the birth of different languages. Yet, this multivalenced text reveals far more than the etiology of language alone. It is a tale of people wanting to stay together, to build a like-minded community with a striking edifice as its centerpiece. What crime lay in their innocent expression of unity? "Go to, let us build us a city and a tower, whose top may reach unto heaven; and let us make us a name, lest we be scattered abroad upon the face of the whole earth" (Gen. 11:4).

One of the classic explications of this narrative is as a tale of hubris. Man built a tower to get to God—maybe to reach Him, maybe to surpass Him. Ancient man desired to make a name for himself, as the verse explicitly states. In so doing, he used all of the latest advances in construction. Rather than sun-dried bricks, which were weak and would crumble under the weight of a lofty structure, clever man reached the heavens with "[burned] brick for stone and slime [tar] . . . for mortar" (Gen. 11:3). These building materials are not extraneous details but conceal, between the lines, man's devious intent—to show God the vast technological expertise of the human being, and with it, to challenge the Divine. God then showed humanity its frailty by destroying not only the frame of the building, but the framework of society—unified speech.

Another competing theory is that this narrative is a mockery of idol worship. Babel, a center of paganism, was filled with ziggurats, tall sanctuaries that were monuments to polytheism. Archeologists have uncovered these buildings and have found the biblical text a fairly accurate description of the construction process. This was no mere tower, but a temple meant for man's petitions to reach the gods of man's own making. Yet God confused their speech, and in so doing, He confounded their prayers and knocked down their temple. With little effort, the God of monotheism won the battle of faith.

In order to truly grasp the significance of this tower, we have to put it in its biblical context. It comes not long after the Flood. It is a repopulation story that follows the mandate to Noah and his sons given in Genesis; to build this new world, Noah, like Adam and Eve, is told, "Be fruitful, and multiply, and replenish the earth" (Gen. 9:1). He and his sons set out to do that, and the account of their regrowth is offered in chapter 10. But in chapter 11, we have the darker side of repopulation. We have only half the mandate fulfilled. Man was fruitful. He multiplied, but he refused to fill the world. Instead, "the whole earth was of one language" (Gen. 11:1), and the people journeyed together to Shinar [Babylonia]. Man built a tower as a tribute to homogeneity. God looked down upon this act of unity as a deviance from man's stated purpose, indeed blessing. Consequently, He scattered the fledgling community of Shinar and scrambled their speech.

It is not only the content that reflects this message, but the very craftsmanship of the wording. One scholar calls this passage a piece of "narrative art," and takes the first four verses and the last and shows how they oppose one another. Man says, "Let us build," and God says, "Let us destroy." Man says, "Let us live together lest we be scattered," and God responds by scattering them. Even the words, not only the sentences, reflect the Divine reversal of human desire. The word for "brick" in Hebrew is *L-B-N* [the word "brick" in Hebrew is composed of the Hebrew characters L-B-L—*lamed, beit, lamed*], and the word for "confound" is *N-B-L*. Whatever man's plans, God set about to reverse them. The words and sentence structure mirror the message, and, as with a piece of art, the more closely we look, the more we see.

This new post-Flood world was not to be an Orwellian enclave that valued diversity of neither speech nor geography. It was not enough to populate the world. The command was to fill it with as much diversity of place and character as possible. The rudimentary steps of gathering, speaking, and building only in unison would not have a good ending: "Nothing will be restrained from them, which they have imagined to do" (Gen. 11:6). Their plan was stopped early on through Divine intervention.

The message to the inhabitants of Shinar was no less resonant then than it is for us now. To be spiritually—not only architecturally—sound, diversity must be the cement of everlasting structures.

The Message of the Rainbow

Ahron Soloveichik, April 20, 1998

Lessons on limitations and diversity are culled from God's covenant with Noah through the rainbow.

IN GENESIS (9:15), we are told of the covenant that God made with Noah, who acted on behalf of mankind after the Flood. Noah was the first man with whom God made a covenant. Much more is involved in a covenant than in a mere promise. A promise does not imply a mutual relationship, while a covenant does. In order to understand this particular covenant, we must understand the symbolic significance of the rainbow, with which it is associated.

A covenant employs an already-existent natural phenomenon as a token of the relationship established. In the case of the covenant between God and Noah, the rainbow was employed. This does not mean that the rainbow was created at that point . . . just that it was utilized as a sign of the covenant.

What does the rainbow symbolize? First, it is indicative of the idea that the rays of sunlight can penetrate even the most ominous clouds, and that man should not become desperate when he sees members of his society deviating from the right path. Second, it symbolizes the diversity of mankind. The rainbow is the result of the refraction of the sun's rays. Through this process, a single white light is divided into its components and the entire spectrum of colors becomes visible. We find this sight so beautiful that on Yom Kippur, when describing the appearance of the High Priest after he had completed the service of the day, we declare, "Like the appearance of the rainbow in the midst of the clouds, so was the appearance of the Priest" (Liturgy for Yom Kippur). The rainbow is symbolic of diversity. Hope for mankind does not lie in strict uniformity. It is true that every man is created as a pure, white ray. As time passes, however, he is forced into various predicaments and clashes that bring about differences between him and his fellow man. The beauty of life lies in these very differences. There is a comment of Rashbam, one of the early biblical commentators [d. 1158], stricken from most editions [of Hebrew Bible commentary], that explains why God was so indignant with the generation of the Tower of Babel (see Gen. 11). Viewed from the actions [of the people] alone, they seem only to have conspired to build an extremely tall edifice, a tower. If, as we are accustomed to understand, the people were building the tower with the intention of reaching God, they certainly did not deserve to be punished. They were merely stupid!

From the time of Creation, God wanted man to conquer all of the world and to spread throughout the whole of it; as He told Adam, "replenish the earth, and subdue it" (Gen. 1:28), yet He did not will strict uniformity. The sin of the generation of the Tower of Babel was that the people endeavored to be homogeneous. In other words, they built their tower to symbolize their unity, but it was a unity of totalitarianism, as in the former Soviet Union. It was a unity of conformity, and, as a result, the members of the human race would soon be reduced to machines. To counteract this movement, God confused and dispersed the people so that they could not succeed in their attempt. This, then, is precisely the message of the rainbow's diversity.

Aside from its dazzling array of colors, the rainbow is also characterized by its semicircular shape. The nineteenth-century sage Rabbi Yehoshua of Kutna, focusing on this aspect of the rainbow, offers another reason for God's selecting it as the token of His relationship with mankind. Prior to the Flood, he says, God did not impede man from doing whatever he pleased. However, after the Flood, God limited man's free will. He did not want man to have the ability to cause so much harm and evil as he previously had. This is symbolized by the semicircular arch of the rainbow. While in a complete circle, one can revolve around and around ad infinitum, a semicircle imposes a limit.

God, recognizing the nature of His world, utilized the rainbow—a phenomenon stressing both the beauty of diversity and the concept of limitation—as the token of His covenant with mankind. Just as the rays of the sun manage to penetrate through the clouds, so shall the word of God penetrate all souls. Until that time, however, the survival of mankind depends upon recognizing the importance of diversity rather than demanding absolute uniformity.

Personal Privacy and Balaam's Donkey

Menachem Genack, July 15, 1998

Our society relishes the exposure of all things private, but Judaism sees privacy as a basic human right that flows from our unique creation.

THE MIDRASH, a collection of rabbinic traditions, comments that God gave speech only to man and not to any of the animals, for had animals been able to speak, no human would survive. The ubiquitous animal, if verbal, would destroy any semblance of privacy. If able to speak, animals would unmask our foibles, our pettiness, our inevitable failings. Man was created imperfect. Concomitant with his grandeur and majesty is a seamy, ugly side. God, recognizing man's bifurcated nature, protected him, and made the beast mute. The only animal granted the gift of speech was the donkey of the prophet Balaam, who revealed Balaam's obtuseness and sins (Num. 22:28–33). Even a prophet would be diminished and ultimately destroyed by exposure to total scrutiny. . . .

Justice Louis Brandeis, dissenting in *Olmstead v. United States*, declared:

> The makers of our Constitution undertook to secure conditions
> favorable to the pursuit of happiness. . . . They sought to protect
> Americans in their beliefs, their thoughts, their emotions, and
> their sensations. They conferred, as against the government, the
> right to be let alone—the most comprehensive of rights and the
> right most valued by civilized men.

The Midrash's point goes even beyond that of Justice Brandeis, who saw the rights of privacy as inherent to civilization. The Midrash saw these rights of privacy not only as a constitutional endowment or a social right, but as an existential need related to the nature of man; built into Creation, these rights even predate the development of civilization. The rabbis of the Talmud point out that man was created alone, for the universe was created for the individual. The biblical story of the creation of Adam affirms the Jeffersonian notion that the individual is preeminent and superior to the rights of society. The right of privacy flows from the creation of man alone.

Man's Image Transcends Death

Esther Wachsman, July 22, 1998

In October 1994, Nachshon Wachsman, a dual citizen of Israel and the United States and a soldier in the Israeli Defense Forces, was kidnapped and killed by terrorists. This horrifying incident united Israel in prayer. In this letter, his mother reflects on the unifying quality of brotherhood that allows us to transcend death.

WE HAVE JUST CELEBRATED the Jewish holiday of Shavuot, literally translated as "Weeks"; [it is] given this name since the holiday falls exactly seven weeks after the holiday of Passover. On Passover we celebrate our redemption from Egyptian slavery, and we are commanded to then count the days and the weeks until Shavuot, when the two holy tablets were handed to Moses and received by the Children of Israel at Mount Sinai. Those two tablets were two symmetrical halves, with five commandments engraved on each half. Five address our obligations to our "friends." Not "mankind" or "fellow men," but "friends." You knew this, Mr. President, when you said "Shalom, *chaver*"—goodbye, friend—in your brilliant eulogy to the late Prime Minister Yitzhak Rabin. One might assume that it is unnecessary to be commanded not to kill a friend, but God knew that it is specifically toward the friend—or even the brother (the first murder in the Bible is of a brother; Cain killed Abel)—that passions are most fierce and can even lead to murder.

If we start from the beginning, we learn that man was not created like all other creations—in pairs—but rather, man was created alone, and "in the image of God." Man's image, his face, is unique and individual; no two faces, or opinions, are the same. But man can only fully see himself, his image, by seeing others. Only when I look at my friend do I see myself, my own being, my "image"—my individuality and uniqueness. No one else can be me or stand where I stand, and each and every individual is commanded by Jewish tradition to believe that the world was created for him alone, and that the world's continued existence depends on him (Babylonian Talmud, Sanhedrin 37a). The Hebrew words for "alone" and "one," and "together" or "united," have the same root. There is no contradiction between *achad* [or *echad*], one, and *yachad*, together; for only by appreciating the great worth and value of our own individuality can we see the reflection of that value in others, and thus strive for brotherhood, togetherness, and unity (*achdut*).

Man's image cannot be wiped out by death. The impression of his face, which is God's image, continues to exist. That is my personal comfort and revenge against those who tried to wipe out the image of my son, Nachshon. His impression lives on in the hearts and memories of all who knew him, and we await the fulfillment of the prophet Isaiah's words: "He will swallow up death in victory; and the Lord God will wipe away tears from off all faces" (Isa 25:8).

Man's Dual Personality

Joel B. Wolowelsky, July 29, 1998

Great leaders have many moments of conquest and success, but times of failure and submission cannot be avoided. This is not due to any personal flaw, but rather to the nature of man. Realizing this allows one to see darker moments in perspective, knowing that the brighter light will follow.

THE BIBLE TELLS US that after God created man, He saw that "It is not good that the man should be alone; I will make him an help meet for him" (Gen. 2:18). But then, instead of immediately creating woman, God brought all the animal world before Adam for him to name: "And Adam gave names to all cattle, and to the fowl of the air, and to every beast of the field; but for Adam there was not found an help meet for him" (Gen. 2:20). It was only then that God created Eve. What possible connection could there be between Adam's loneliness and his naming all of God's creatures? Could one have thought that Adam could have found a fitting helper among the cattle, birds, and wild beasts?

The answer, I believe, is to be found in Rabbi Joseph B. Soloveitchik's analysis of the apparent duplication in the narration of the creation of man in the first two chapters of the Bible. He argues that each chapter describes a different topology of man. Separated in the biblical narrative, they are combined in every human.

Adam of the first chapter is created "in the image of God"—that is, he possesses God's power of creativity—and is therefore commanded to "Be fruitful, and multiply, and replenish the earth, and subdue it." In carrying out this Divine mandate and achieving the human dignity that comes with it, Adam looks for utilitarian partners to assist him in achieving his practical goals; hence he was created with a companion—"male and female created He them" (Gen. 1: 26–28).

But Adam of the second chapter is formed "of the dust of the ground" (Gen. 2:7) and charged with tilling and tending God's universe (Gen. 2:7; 2:15). He finds his humanity not in conquering, but in fitting into the Divine plan, in seeing himself as but a speck of dust who submits to God's will. A full human being is one who actualizes both dimensions of his human existence—but to do so, he must be aware of both aspects of his personality. God senses Adam's loneliness, his inability to feel fulfilled as a complete person. But how could God explain to Adam the cause—and the cure—of his predicament?

God brings all of Creation to Adam to name. In the Bible, knowing and changing someone's name signifies having power over them. What could be more fulfilling to Adam the First than to have power over all? But the man had already been transformed into Adam the Second by his confrontation with God's moral voice restricting his access to some of the trees of the garden (Gen. 2:16–17). For such a person, power did not suffice; he still remained lonely.

Having taught Adam that his old strategies would not suffice, God then taught him the power of submission and sacrifice: "And the Lord God caused a deep sleep to fall upon Adam, and he slept: and he took one of his ribs . . . and the rib, which the Lord God had taken from man, made he a woman" (Gen. 2:21–22). It is only through such unselfish gestures that Adam the Second can find himself.

To discover his humanity, man must know both sides of himself. Searching for fulfillment exclusively through conquest or submission can yield only failure, frustration, and loneliness. Understanding the dual nature of one's self and the methodologies appropriate for each aspect of his personality is the only hope for actualizing one's full humanity.

The Creation of Man

Menachem Genack, January 8, 1999

The biblical account of man's creation highlights the primacy of man's individual rights.

MAN, UNLIKE ALL THE OTHER ANIMALS, was created alone. Rabbinic tradition, recorded in the Talmud, interprets the reason for Man's lonely emergence as follows:

> Man was created singly to teach that whoever destroys a single life is considered by Scripture as if he had destroyed an entire world, while one who preserves a single life is considered by Scripture as if he had preserved an entire world. And for the sake of peace among people, so that no man would tell his fellow man, "My father is greater than yours." And to teach the greatness of God. For a man mints many coins from one mold and they are all similar one to the other, but God minted all men from the mold of Adam and not one of them is like his fellow man. Therefore, each person must say, "For my sake was the world created." (Babylonian Talmud, Sanhedrin 37a)

Man was created alone to indicate his uniqueness and irreplaceability. Unlike the other creatures, which emerged at Creation as species, man was created alone. While in the animal kingdom, each creature is but a representative of its species, man is singular, significant in his own right. He has infinite potential and a Divine mandate to conquer and subdue the world.

The Talmud, therefore, indicates that, remarkably, while all humans are made from Adam's mold, they are all different one from the other. For the defining dimension of Adam is his distinctiveness; the essence of his mold is his uniqueness. Consequently, it is that quality which he imprints upon his progeny—they, too, are all different. In contrast to the rest of Creation, Man is not defined merely as part of the class, but as a being in and for himself. Maimonides believed, as did Thomas Aquinas, that God's Providence relates to each person, but is limited in the animal kingdom only to the entire species.

Man's rights do not devolve from the group or from society as a whole, but rather are the inherent endowment of each individual. In the age-old conflict between the rights of the individual and those of society, the depiction of man's creation clearly favors the Jeffersonian notion of the preeminence of the individual, as opposed to society. After all, the group or society only came forth subsequent to the creation of the individual.

The biblical story of Creation celebrates the transcendence of the human spirit. Like God, Man is lonely and alone; his majesty is manifest in his loneliness and singularity. His uniqueness is his defining quality. As such, each person is of infinite worth, a world in his own. We may therefore affirm, as we acknowledge the dignity and individuality of our fellow man, "For my sake was the world created."

The Blessings of Adam and Noah

Menachem Genack, January 13, 1999

Mankind and nature must live in harmony, not dissonance.

THE BIBLICAL BLESSING and mandates given to Adam, the first man, and Noah, the survivor of the Flood and progenitor of a new world, are very similar in some points, but markedly different in others.

Let's compare the biblical blessings of Adam and Noah.

Adam	Noah
And God blessed them, and God said unto them, Be fruitful, and multiply, and replenish the earth, and subdue it; and have dominion over the fish of the sea, and over the fowl of the air; and over every living thing that moveth upon the earth. And God said, Behold, I have given you every herb bearing seed, which is upon the face of all the earth, and every tree, in the which is the fruit of a tree yielding seed; to you it shall be for meat. And to every beast of the earth, and to every fowl of the air, and to every thing that creepeth upon the earth, wherein there is life, I have given every green herb for meat. (Gen. 1:28–30)	And God blessed Noah and his sons, and said unto them, Be fruitful, and multiply, and replenish the earth. And the fear of you and the dread of you shall be upon every beast of the earth, and upon every fowl of the air, upon all that moveth upon the earth, and upon all fishes of the sea; into your hand are they delivered. Every moving thing that liveth shall be meat for you; even as the green herb have I given you all things. (Gen. 9:1–3)

The late Professor Nehama Leibowitz, a renowned biblical scholar [d. 1997], points out the glaring omission in Noah's blessing of the mandate to *subdue* the earth, as was said to Adam. Also, while Adam was permitted to eat only vegetation, Noah is permitted to eat the flesh of living beings as well. Why the distinction?

Mankind, through its iniquity and violence, had corrupted all of nature. With his fall, all of nature was correspondingly diminished. To cleanse the Creation, and stop the contagion that man had wrought and which had contaminated the world, God brought the Flood, and the harmony that had previously existed was shattered. In its place was enmity, and a Creation torn asunder into different opposing camps. Man had not fulfilled his moral mandate to subdue the world with care and concern, orchestrating it for the benefit of all Creation, as any responsible ruler would do for the good of his dominion and those placed in his charge.

That harmony having been lost, Noah is not given the mandate to subdue Creation. In the place of the previous amity is enmity and fear. This is most dramatically demonstrated by the new sanction to Noah, permitting him to eat meat—that which was previously forbidden to Adam.

Adam was introduced into a natural order of peace and harmony, with a spiritual congruity throughout Creation. Thus man was forbidden to take the life force of other living creatures. With a deep divide between man and other creatures after the Flood, a concession is made, permitting man to eat the flesh of animals. Man's moral failings have changed the dynamics within the Creation, and changed his relationship to it.

The ultimate goal remains to restore the pristine environment that existed when man was introduced into Eden, and to usher in an era of reconciliation, when man will be one with nature and not at odds with it. That is the prophetic vision of Isaiah: "And the wolf also shall dwell with the lamb, and the leopard shall lie down with the kid; and the calf and the young lion and the fatling together; and a little child shall lead them" (Isa 11:6).

One God—Two Sexes

Benjamin Blech, January 19, 2000

A fusion of the masculine and feminine qualities of spirituality is needed to truly emulate godliness.

THE BIBLICAL TEXT makes clear that man and woman were both designed to be human replicas of their Creator: "So God created man in His own image, in the image of God created He him; male and female created He them" (Gen. 1:27).

The question that begs to be asked is why, if God is One, are His human counterparts two? Reproductive needs clearly don't constitute sufficient reason to justify dividing mankind into male and female. Surely God could have devised a form of asexual procreation—a kind of reproduction already found in nature—either for man or for woman.

What God wanted was someone "in His image." Since God is noncorporeal, His kinship with Adam and Eve has nothing to do with physical characteristics. Human beings are somehow like God. Yet men and women are different. Which of these two, then, is *more* like Him? And why, in a religious tradition of monotheism, *can't* a woman be more like a man—or a man like a woman?

The answer is rooted in a remarkable and daring insight of Jewish sages into the nature of God. For although Judaism posits that God is One, it acknowledges that His names are two. The Bible is not troubled by the duality implicit in the two different Hebrew words for the Almighty—the tetragrammaton, the holy four-letter name that in English translates as "Lord," and Elokim, rendered in English as "God." Names emphasize different aspects of one and the same individual. . . ..

Whenever the Torah speaks of "God," we encounter the Creator in His aspect of stern and strict judge. It is "God" who "in the beginning . . . created the heaven and the earth" (Gen 1:1). Nature is guided by unbending law, by a seemingly cruel principle that cares only for survival of the fittest, and not for those most in need of compassion. "God" in His subsequent relationship with the world is the Lawgiver, teaching the value of justice and the requirement for compliance with Divine imperatives.

Yet "God" knows that He must temper His concern for strict justice with the forgiving and merciful quality of love expressed by His other name, "Lord." Blessed be the name of the "Lord"—for that is the name with which He so abundantly blesses us. When the Almighty reveals to Moses that He is about to redeem the Jewish people from slavery, the Bible records: "And God spake unto Moses and said unto him, I am the Lord" (Exod. 6:2). The "God" of law announces His intention to become the "Lord" of love.

"The Lord, our God" is the perfect partnership of these two ideals. Without the strictness of law, God's children would soon become undisciplined brutes. Without the compassion of love, the Lord's creations would be doomed by their imperfections. A stern Father in Heaven is at the same time our merciful Mother above.

No wonder, point out the scholars of the mystical tradition known as the Kabbalah, that the two different names of the Lord, God, in their original Hebrew, have grammatical suffixes that identify the first one as feminine and the second as masculine. . . . .

The biblical verses describing the creation of human beings are now clear in their references to gender. "*God* created man in *His* own image." That is not a politically incorrect statement that refuses to acknowledge a feminine dimension to the Divine. The text simply states that the male characteristic of God as strict Father brought into being a *man*—to represent that aspect of His image. In Genesis 2:18, the Bible adds: "And the Lord God said, It is not good that the man should be alone; I will make him an help meet for [opposite] him." As long as only Adam existed, it was but "God" who had His image reflected below. The "Lord" needed "Her" image as well. Eve would serve as Adam's "opposite" on earth so that together, man and woman might mirror the dual attributes of their Creator.

True, the Almighty is able to merge the masculine/feminine traits into one harmonious whole. Humans require two different sexes to express what the Lord God can accomplish alone. Yet we all, men and women, must know that we each represent half of the Divine image. We were both created so that together we could make the presence of our Father/Mother in Heaven manifest here on earth.

Emet

Menachem Genack, May 2, 2000

Truth requires breadth of vision, while falsity is a product of insistent myopia.

DEAR MR. PRESIDENT,

You have said many times that the great battle we are engaged in revolves around what one thinks about the nature of truth. We believe, as part of our human limitation imposed on us by God, that no one has the whole truth. Because we don't possess the whole truth, we believe life is a journey and everyone counts.

A beautiful passage in the Talmud conveys the same idea, by offering insights on two Hebrew words. The word for "truth" is *emet* אמת. The first letter, *aleph* א, is the first letter of the alphabet. The second letter, *mem* מ, is in the middle of the alphabet, and the third letter, *taf* ת, is the final letter of the alphabet. The word for "falsity" is *sheker* שקר, and it is also three letters. Unlike the letters in the word *emet*, however, the letters in the word *sheker* are adjacent to one another.

Sheker, or falsity, results when someone with a narrow perspective claims he has the whole truth. But truth for us humans is diffused. Each of us can never capture the full truth because we are existentially limited; each of us reflects only part of God's whole truth. Thus truth must be linked to humility. Genuine truth, *emet*, is the result of bringing different points of a spectrum, in this case the Hebrew alphabet, together.

WILLIAM JEFFERSON CLINTON

May 13, 2002

Rabbi Menachem Genack
Rabbinic Administrator
Union of Orthodox Jewish
    Congregations of America
11 Broadway
New York, New York 10004

Dear Rabbi Genack:

I was fascinated by your account of the
Hebrew words for "truth" and "falsity," and
how their formation fits in with what I've
been saying in my speeches regarding people
who think they have the whole truth. You
were kind to remember how interested I am in
this idea, and I appreciate your taking the
time to write to me about it. Thanks for
always keeping me in mind.

Sincerely,

Bill

Community

Those who isolate themselves lose themselves. You can find yourself only if you know where you came from and where you are going. This search is meaningful only in the context of community.

The relationship of the individual to the community is a recurring theme in the Bible. In this chapter, the writers of the missives look to the Bible for guidance in navigating the complex dynamic between individual and community and explore how we can express our innate humanity and divinity in the context of the world that we all share. Which is more important, care for others and interaction with the community or personal realization through monastic isolation? What are the essential elements of a free society? What role do education, justice, and social concern play in God's plan for how we should live our lives? Does the Bible speak to our responsibility to the environment? How significant is the family unit?

Every human being is created in the image of God and possesses an aspect of holiness. In one letter, I make the point that the Bible teaches us that the holiness found in each individual is qualitatively different than the holiness of the Almighty. God's holiness is manifest in His separation from the world, in His infinite transcendence. Human holiness, however, is achieved not through isolation but through engagement, not by adopting the monastic life but by taking the much riskier approach of confronting the world and its imperfections.

In one of my other missives in this chapter, I explore a variation on this theme of engagement with the world. The Suharto regime in Indonesia fell in 1998 amid turbulent demonstrations led by the country's youth. During that period, my thoughts turned to the Nazirite, the enigmatic figure who piously separates himself from society. The asceticism of the Nazirite, disillusioned with a hedonistic world and frustrated with the established order, is the mark of a young person. With passion and courage, the youth are in the forefront of revolts against oppressive regimes. But the Bible views the Nazirite ambivalently. The Bible crowns the Nazirite with glory for his sanctity, selflessness, and youthful zeal, but requires him to bring a sin offering for his impetuousness and isolation. God wants us to be holy, but also wants us to be tolerant, compassionate, and engaged with society.

Chief Rabbi Lord Jonathan Sacks notes that when Moses led the Jewish people out of Egypt to freedom, he spoke not of military triumph, nor of the perilous journey that lay ahead across the desert, nor even of the land of milk and honey awaiting them at the end of the journey. He spoke instead of children and the duty to educate future generations about the Exodus. "To defend a land you need an army. But to defend a free society, you need families, and an educational system in which ideals are passed on from generation to generation."

Continuing with the notion of the family's critical role in education, one of the missives observes that the iconic biblical passages that speak of teaching the Divine message refer to parents teaching children, not to wise men and elders teaching students. In the Bible, education is entrusted to the family unit. In our push-button culture, we too often look to technology for the quick fix or seek others to do what we find too time-consuming to do ourselves. We should not look to educational institutions to play the role of the family. Knowledge can be taught, but the *love* of knowledge needs to be imbued. Values are not taught but inculcated. This is the job of the family.

Several of the missives celebrate human diversity. In the biblical narrative of the Tower of Babel, God dispersed the society of Babel and splintered their language into a multilingual cacophony. In one letter, I point out that God's goal is not a monochromatic society that stifles the individual, but a multicolored world that fosters diversity and enhances and ennobles each unique individual, created in the image of God. In my missive on the splitting of the Red Sea, I quote the Midrash that the sea did not split in one place, but in twelve distinct places, creating a path for each of the Twelve Tribes of Israel. The message of the Midrash is that there is not just one path to God, but many. These thoughts resonated with President Clinton, who constantly and consistently sounded the theme of the diversity of the human experience, and how without this diversity we are diminished.

In 2002, a new wave of vicious anti-Semitism began to sweep through Europe. The Jewish communities, most notably of France, were suddenly forced to live in fear of vandalism, harassment, and violence. President Clinton had long championed the importance of community, and I reached out to him to call to his attention the urgency of this emerging insidious trend in advance of his trip to Europe. The recent escalation of anti-Semitism, I wrote the president, unlike its previous incarnations, was fed by rampant Israel bashing. I implored the president "as a witness to the historic Camp David negotiations, and as a close friend of the great hero of peace Yitzhak Rabin. . . . You know how deeply and painfully Israel as a nation has yearned for peace, and still does, and the great sacrifices it is prepared to make at Camp David with your encouragement." The president's response was a reassuring testament to his commitment to the communal legitimacy of the Jewish people in the land of Israel:

WILLIAM JEFFERSON CLINTON

July 5, 2002

Rabbi Menachem Genack
129 Meadowbrook Road
Englewood, New Jersey 07631

Dear Rabbi Genack:

Thank you for your letter and for the article by Gabriel Schoenfeld. I'm glad you followed up on our discussion. The upsurge of anti-Semitism and anti-Israel sentiment that countries in Europe have been experiencing is, indeed, profoundly troubling. I do know how much the Israeli people seek -- and have been willing to sacrifice for -- a lasting peace with their neighbors. Please be assured that my commitment to peace in the Middle East, and to replacing ignorance with understanding everywhere in the world, remains undiminished and enduring. I stand ready to help in whatever ways I can.

Thanks again for taking the time to write.

Sincerely,

Bill

In our generation, perhaps more than any other, we have come to realize that issues of concern to the community cannot be divorced from their
impact on the environment. The Jewish view is that God has put the natural
world at humanity's disposal, but our relationship with nature must be one
of stewardship, not exploitation. This notion, however, that there is a moral
imperative that imbues our relationship with the environment, is by no means
theologically trivial, and there are serious theologians whose views as to the
Bible's message on our responsibility to the environment vary across a wide
spectrum. In September 2005, I attended the first Clinton Global Initiative
forum in New York City. President Leonel Fernández of the Dominican
Republic powerfully brought forward the urgent nature of global warming with his observation that if the warming of the atmosphere continues
unabated, the melting of the polar ice caps and the subsequent rise in ocean
level would inundate the Dominican Republic. In the following session, as
Senator Hillary Clinton was delivering an address about climate change, my
thoughts turned to the Torah portion of that week, which contains the biblical injunction against cutting down fruit trees. In my missive entitled "Tree
of the Field," I focus on the Bible's message to humanity that God bequeathed
to Adam dominion over the earth, but, ultimately, the earth belongs to God.
Humanity's mandate is to develop the world, not destroy it, and this entails
sensitivity to the environment.

Thomas Jefferson once said, "A debt of service is due from every man
to his country proportioned to the bounties which nature and fortune
have measured to him." President Clinton repeated this quote in a speech
about national service given at the University of New Orleans on April 30,
1993. As he announced his proposal for the program that came to be called
AmeriCorps, he encouraged each American citizen to become an "agent of
change" by volunteering and making a difference in the community.

Freedom's Defense

Jonathan Sacks, October 21, 1997

Chief Rabbi Lord Sacks eloquently notes, "In a free society the true defense secretary is the secretary of state for education.

IT WAS THE MOMENT for which they had been waiting for more than two hundred years. The Israelites, slaves in Egypt, were about to go free. Ten plagues had struck the country. The people were the first to understand; Pharaoh was the last. God was on the side of freedom and human dignity. You cannot build a nation, however strong your police and army, by enslaving some for the benefit of others. Somehow, history will turn against you, as it has against every tyranny ever known.

And now the time had arrived. The Israelites were on the brink of their release. Moses, their leader, gathered them together and prepared to address them. What would be the content of his speech at this fateful juncture, the birth of a people? He could have spoken about many things. He might have rallied them to cheer at the breaking of their chains. He might have talked about the land flowing with milk and honey that awaited them in the future. He might have spoken, somberly, about the journey that lay ahead, the trek across the desert and the dangers they would face. Any one of these would have been the predictable speech of a great leader sensing a historic moment in the annals of his people. Moses did none of these things. Instead he spoke about children, and the distant future, and the duty to pass on memories to generations yet unborn. Three times he turned to this theme:

> "When your children shall say unto you, What mean ye by this service? That ye shall say . . ." (Exod. 12:26–27)

> "And thou shalt shew thy son in that day, saying, This is done because of that which the Lord did unto me when I came forth out of Egypt." (Exod. 13:8)

> "When thy son asketh thee in time to come, saying, What is this? that thou shalt say unto him . . ." (Exod. 13:14)

About to gain their freedom, the Israelites were told that they now had to become *a nation of educators*. This is what made Moses not a great leader, but the greatest. Freedom is won not on the battlefield, nor in the political arena, nor in the courts, national or international—but in the human imagination and will. To defend a land you need an army. But to defend a free society, you need families, and an educational system in which ideals are passed on from generation to generation, and never lost, despaired of, or obscured. In a free society the true defense secretary is the secretary of state for education. Its citadels are schools. Its heroes are educators.

Moses taught that freedom is more than a moment of political triumph. It is a constant endeavor, throughout the ages, to teach those who come after us about the battles our ancestors fought, and why, so that my freedom is never sacrificed to yours or purchased at the cost of someone else's. . . .

Schools are the strength of a civilization, the guardians of its heritage and hope. That is why, when Jewish tradition conferred upon Moses the greatest honor, it did not call him "our hero," "our prophet," or "our king." It called him, simply, Moshe Rabbenu, "Moses our Teacher." For it is in the arena of education that the battle for the good society is lost or won.

THE WHITE HOUSE
WASHINGTON

October 24, 1997

Rabbi Menachem Genack
333 Seventh Avenue
New York, New York 10001

Dear Rabbi Genack:

Thank you for continuing to pass along to me the "missives." I was particularly impressed with Chief Rabbi Dr. Jonathan Sacks' "Freedom's Defense," in which he focuses on children and our responsibility for properly educating them. We should take to heart Moses' example in that respect.

All the best to you.

Sincerely,

Shabbat Behar and Justice Benjamin Nathan Cardozo

Judith S. Kaye, November 12, 1997

For Justice Benjamin Nathan Cardozo (1870–1938) of the U.S. Supreme Court, law and justice were synonymous. Like Hillel, Cardozo recognized that innovation in the law is at times necessary so that the law may better serve the common good.

Today's Torah portion, Behar, is from the Book of Leviticus (25:1–26:2), which is in a sense a manual, a guidebook of detailed instructions that enabled the priests and Levites to perform the various rites required of them. The oldest name for the Third Book of Moses, in fact, is Torat Cohanim—The Law of Priests.

Yet within this painstaking recitation of rules and procedures about subjects such as sacrifices and *mitzvot* [meritorious acts], this portion sounds a strikingly different note. It deals instead with matters of broader social, commercial, and even environmental ethics—how we must treat our land, our relatives, our servants, our neighbors. The verses of Behar, when read against the technical passages that surround them, are unique in their deep concern about, for lack of a better term, the "underdog"—the slave, the indigent, the stranger. Indeed, words taken from Behar—"Proclaim liberty throughout all the land unto all the inhabitants thereof" (Lev. 25:10)—appear on this nation's Liberty Bell in Philadelphia.

It is, of course, not possible to speak of liberty without also speaking of justice. How many times have we recited the Pledge of Allegiance, concluding "with liberty and justice for all"? A central lesson of Passover is that there is no justice without liberty. And indeed Benjamin Nathan Cardozo—who bore the title "Justice"—through his words and deeds has become the very embodiment of the term.

My own review of Cardozo's work leads me to conclude that in his heart he truly believed that law and justice are synonymous, that—in his own words—"the final cause of law is the welfare of society. The rule that misses its aim cannot permanently justify its existence." Justice, according to Cardozo, "is so much of morality as the thought and practice of a given epoch shall conceive to be appropriately invested with a legal sanction." Cardozo believed that as the law evolves, "the moral norm and the jural [are] brought together, and are one."

The verses of Behar contain instructions concerning the observance of two sanctified years: the Seventh Year, or Shemittah, when the land was to rest and lie fallow, and the Fiftieth, or Jubilee Year, when all Hebrew slaves were to be emancipated and property returned to its original owners. One peculiar feature of the Shemittah was the requirement of a remission of debts, with the outstanding principal due on loans among the Israelites released and remitted to the debtor.

As one might expect, however, because of this strict requirement, as the seventh year approached, potential creditors became increasingly reluctant to lend funds, since the loans would soon have to be forgiven. The first-century sage Hillel, realizing that this unfortunate state of affairs was causing those in need to suffer, devised a solution whereby on the year of the Shemittah, the debt was assigned to the court—which, since it was not "a fellow" of the debtor, could continue to hold the loan, thus preserving the incentive to make loans to the needy. As the classical rabbinic tradition explained in the Talmud: "The rabbis have power to expropriate property should it be for the general public good" (Talmud, Tractate Gittin 36b).

Like Hillel, Cardozo recognized that innovation in the law is at times necessary so that the law may better serve the common good, and he did not hesitate to say so. In a time when the proper role of judges was perceived to be merely to apply existing legal rules, such candid expressions by a sitting judge were startling, even revolutionary. Cardozo believed that in each case, a court "must consider the reason of the rule and the evils which it aims to remedy." Or, as he explained in an essay he called "The Growth of the Law": "'Law must be stable, and yet it cannot stand still.' Here is the great antinomy confronting us at every turn. Rest and motion, unrelieved and unchecked, are equally destructive."

What lesson does Cardozo's life, for all its brilliance and distinction in the law, have for the Jewish people? One answer is that as a people we are of course defined by our history. It therefore is entirely fitting that we study our distinctive past and take pride in the outstanding contributions of one of our own. This great man, who through the Nathan and Cardozo families also brings together so much of the history of Jews in America, has surely earned a special place of honor in our thoughts and in our memory.

But there is more. It seems to me that the same "little, unassuming, unobtrusive" yet ultimately life-defining choices described by Cardozo—choices of right and wrong, of compassion and logic; choices that summon us, often "slyly and craftily," toward heroism or venality—present themselves to every one of us every day, whether we're sitting in a courtroom, in an office, or in our own homes. To prepare ourselves for those unannounced yet critical moments, so that we can recognize them and know how to make the good and the right choices, is a reason both for studying Torah and for seeking justice through law.

But even that sentiment Cardozo expressed best. As he told a class of graduating rabbinical students:

> You will find mockery and temptation on the highways, and for
> the values that you hold to be eternal many a tinsel token will
> be offered in exchange. . . . Then will be the time when you will
> need to bethink yourselves of the values that were chosen by the
> prophets and saints of Israel, and by the goodly and noble of every
> race. . . . . When the course is finished, when the task is ended,
> when the books are closed, may the last appraisal of all values
> reveal [their] choice as yours.

Justice, Justice You Shall Pursue

Bernard Lander, November 17, 1997

Justice is surely one of the great human ends. Yet, while justice and the rule of just law are necessary to achieving the human good, they are not sufficient, as righteousness is also surely necessary.

ONE OF THE MOST FAMOUS injunctions in the Torah, *tzedek, tzedek tirdof* (Deut. 16:20), is generally translated into English as "Justice, justice you shall pursue." [King James Version: "That which is altogether just shalt thou follow, that thou mayest live, and inherit the land which the Lord thy God giveth thee.]

While this ringing phrase has shaped the evolution of the best of Western jurisprudence, it fails to capture the true meaning of the original Hebrew, which is accurately translated as "righteousness, righteousness you shall pursue."

The Torah itself, in verse 18 of that chapter, draws a distinction between the two. The judge is enjoined to administer what the Torah calls *mishpat tzedek*, or "righteous justice" ["they shall judge the people with just judgment"]. There are, then, two kinds of justice, one righteous and the other not. But if pure justice is the ideal, as suggested in the standard English translation of our famous injunction, then what sort of justice fails to meet the extra standard of righteousness?

The answer to these questions is, I believe, wonderfully illustrated by a rabbinic commentary on the biblical law governing a person found murdered between two cities. If diligent inquiry fails to reveal the murderer, then, says the Torah, it behooves the elders of the two closest cities between which the corpse was discovered to determine by measurement that is the closer to the scene of the crime. The elders of the closer city are then obligated to undergo a dramatic ritual of expiation for their responsibility for the crime, asserting publicly "our hands have not shed this blood" (Deut. 21:7).

The rabbis in the Babylonian Talmud (Talmud, Tractate Sotah 45b) ask the obvious question: Is it even conceivable that the elders of the city are murderers? That they themselves committed this crime? Why then must they deny wrongdoing?

The rabbis' answer: Is it not possible that this slain person visited the city and asked for shelter or food, but no one was there to provide for him? Is it not possible that he asked for employment, but no one was there to assist him? And did anyone take the trouble to show him warmth, to accompany him to the city gates as he continued his travels? The elders of the city, representing their city, must therefore atone for their failures and expiate their sin.

But surely the elders would not be found guilty in a court of law. Nevertheless, there is a sense—a biblically mandated sense—in which they are guilty. This is because moral responsibility is not captured by the criteria of justice as embodied in the rule of law. The Torah establishes a higher standard, what we can call, following Deuteronomy 16:18, the standard of "righteous justice." From the perspective of righteousness, God's own perspective, they are guilty as if they had murdered the victim in cold blood. The standard of righteousness calls humankind to a bar higher, and more sublime, than that of justice.

A stark rabbinic tradition reveals the sons of Jacob debating exactly this point. When the brothers finally return to Egypt, the rabbis envisage them studying this chapter in the Torah concerning the responsibility of the elders of the city. They were deeply engaged in intensive legal debate about their responsibility for Joseph's sale as a slave.

Some of the brothers maintained that they were innocent of any charge of wrongdoing against Joseph. They maintained that they, themselves, had not sold Joseph into slavery, had not directly wounded him in any way. By the strictest legal standards of justice, then, they were not culpable.

Other brothers disagreed. They chose to hold themselves to the standard of righteousness, to the implicit standards of the laws governing the elders of the city. They maintained that they were indeed culpable for Joseph's fate, responsible by the bar of righteousness and decency, if not by the bar of justice. It was exactly this view that predominated in the end. The brothers admitted their wrongdoing, and so made healing possible.

The standard of righteousness is embraced in classical Jewish sources not only as an instrument of blame for the past, but also as an instrument to transform the future. This is perhaps most evident in the laws of charity as formulated by Maimonides. All Jews are obligated by law to give charity, the Hebrew word for which also means, interestingly, "righteousness." Nevertheless, some forms of charity, or righteousness, are of greater value than others, and Maimonides ranks them on a scale of one to ten.

The lowest form of "righteousness," says Maimonides, occurs when you give charity to a poor person directly upon his request. The highest expression of charity obtains in a society in which poverty is abolished and every family can provide comfortably for itself. This represents righteousness, *tzedek*, in its highest form—an ideal to transform society.

The standard of righteousness applies not only to the ends but to the means as well. So observed Philo, the great Alexandrian Jewish philosopher, some two thousand years ago.

When the Torah enjoins "righteousness, righteousness you shall pursue," why, after all, is the word "righteousness" repeated twice? One usage, explains Philo, refers to the ends of our actions. Our goals, what we seek to achieve, must be righteous. But that is not enough. Even if we seek righteous ends, we must employ righteous means as well. That is what the second "righteousness" teaches us.

Surely individuals, and even great civilizations and societies, can affirm noble, inspiring goals. Greek civilization sought justice, and Plato's *Republic* gives eloquent expression to Greek moral ideals. But, in the pursuit of justice, Plato sanctioned the murder of handicapped children. Communism, too, in its early history, sought inspiring goals, in which all humans would be treated with absolute equality, in which all would receive according to their needs. Yet communism came to embrace ignoble, totalitarian means to achieve its noble ends. The means we choose must remain as sacred, as righteous, as the ends to which we devote our lives.

Justice is surely one of the great human ends. Yet, while justice and the rule of just law are necessary to achieving the human good, they are not sufficient, as human history woefully reveals. If one phrase were to echo through the grand chambers of civilization, would not that phrase be "righteousness, righteousness you shall pursue"?

Holiness

Nahum M. Sarna, December 24, 1997

Religious philosophers have paid much attention to the idea of the holy, and have encountered great difficulty in analyzing, defining, and interpreting it. But the rabbis understood that to be a holy person is to imitate God's holiness, which they took to mean to imitate the Divine qualities of loving-kindness, righteousness, and justice.

ONE OF THE DISTINGUISHING characteristics of the Book of Leviticus is the repeated demand to strive for the achievement of that state of being described as "holiness." "Ye shall be holy: for I the Lord your God am holy," says Leviticus (19:2). This call for holiness is known to theologians as *imitatio dei*, imitation of God. The prophet Isaiah (6:3) saw a vision of angelic beings proclaiming one to another: "Holy, holy, holy is the Lord of hosts." This threefold repetition expresses the superlative, the absolute, supreme, unsurpassable, ineffable quality of the Divine holiness.

Strangely, the biblical texts offer no direct definition of holiness. Religious philosophers have paid much attention to the idea of the holy, and have encountered great difficulty in analyzing, defining, and interpreting it. They have discovered that the concept is very complex, with some of its aspects being quite elusive. Philologists have delved into the etymology of the Hebrew term *kadosh*, holy, and its equivalents in ancient Semitic languages, and have surmised that the primitive root meaning is "separation." It has to do with that which is apart, unique, totally extraordinary. Phenomenologists of religion have noted that the human response to what is regarded as holy is often ambivalent, a combination of fear and fascination, of trust and terror, of repulsion and attraction. All seem to agree that the idea of the holy constitutes the quintessential reality of the religious life, and that the holiness of God expresses itself in His remoteness, His transcendence, His exaltedness, and His awesomeness.

Now this raises the obvious questions: Why does the Torah repeatedly urge one to strive for holiness in imitation of Divine holiness? Is not this demand inherently contradictory? How can a human being possibly imitate qualities that are exclusive to God, that are intrinsically His, that constitute the very essence of His being, that distinguish the Divine from the human?

These questions clearly agitated the rabbis of olden times, and it is clear that they would not have agreed entirely with the verdict of modern scholars. For they understood the prescription to imitate God as meaning that a human being is really obligated to imitate the Divine qualities of loving-kindness, righteousness, and justice. As stated in the Talmud (Tractate Sotah 14a), Rabbi Hama, son of Rabbi Hanina, explained in reference to the phrase "Ye shall walk after the Lord your God" (Deut. 13:4) that it means to imitate His attributes: to clothe the naked, to visit the sick, to comfort mourners, to bury the dead. Put another way, holiness is attained in a social context, not in isolation and withdrawal from society. That is why the injunction to be holy is formulated in the Hebrew plural form: *you,* collectively, shall be holy. The command is addressed to all the people, not just to special individuals. The plural expresses the interdependence of all society in their joint and common obligations.

A second characteristic of the biblical appeal for holiness is that the injunction is introductory to a series of laws and regulations, ritual, ethical, and moral, as a glance at Leviticus chapter 19 demonstrates. Variegated obligations are indiscriminately woven together. Yet underlying the surface lack of cohesiveness is the unifying concept that bounds must be set to human behavior, that human desires and drives must be weaned away from the destructive level of sordid self-interest, and that ritual plays an important role in this disciplinary process.

A third characteristic of the biblical concept relates to time and space. The Bible, uniquely in the ancient world, gives priority to the holiness of time over the holiness of space. By the holiness of time is meant the sanctifying of specific segments of time. It may be pointed out that the very first usage of the word "holy" occurs in relation to the Sabbath day (Gen. 2:3), in striking contrast to the Mesopotamian viewpoint, in which the culmination of the cosmogonic process is the sanctification of space—specifically, the building of a temple. Time is universal; the sanctification of segments of time can be enjoyed by everyone, rich and poor, high and low, slave and free, as the Ten Commandments prescribe in regard to the Sabbath. The sanctification of a place, in contrast, is restrictive spatially and geographically, and is limited by reason of the need for specialized sacerdotal personnel; the temples in the ancient Near East were generally not accessible to the common lay personnel.

A Hasidic rabbi was asked: Is it not so that a person who pursues holiness in this life goes to paradise? The rabbi responded: You do not understand; one who lives a life of holiness has paradise in *this* life.

You Shall Be Holy

Menachem Genack, 1998

Contrary to popular belief, holiness does not require a monastic lifestyle. In fact, holiness demands communal engagement.

"AND THE LORD spake unto Moses, saying, Speak unto all the congregation of the children of Israel, and say unto them, Ye shall be holy: for I the Lord your God am holy'" (Lev. 19:1–2).

The collection of classical rabbinic wisdom known as the Midrash comments on the phrase "I the Lord your God am holy"—my holiness is different from yours! But would we have imagined that a human can rival God's holiness? Could we think that mortal, finite man could achieve the sanctity of Almighty God?

This section from Leviticus continues with a number of directives that can be understood as a reformulated presentation of all the Ten Commandments. The Commandments were said by Moses to the entire assembly, for the Bible calls the giving of the Law the "day of the assembly" (Deut. 9:10). But in the Hebrew, the Ten Commandments (Exod. 20:1–17) are addressed [to "thou"] in the singular form. It is Leviticus that uses the plural form, representing a charge to the community as a whole.

This distinction indicates that much more is demanded of the community than of the individual. While the Ten Commandments require one to "honour thy father and thy mother" (Exod. 20:12), the plural form in Leviticus requires the more elevated commandment, "Ye [the congregation] shall fear every man his mother, and his father" (Lev. 19:3). Exodus's "Thou shalt not kill" (Exod. 20:13) is transposed in Leviticus to the more demanding "Neither shalt thou stand against the blood of thy neighbour" (Lev. 19:16). "Thou shalt not covet" (Exod. 20:17) emerges as the more exalted "Thou shalt love thy neighbor as thyself" (Lev. 19:18).

Loving-kindness is the essence of the ethical imperative. For this, there must always be a "you," an object of one's kindness. God, however, is holy independent of the universe. His holiness is manifest in His separation, loneliness, and isolation. God is holy in that He is totally "other," beyond the universe, hidden by clouds of transcendence, shrouded in infinity. The rabbis in the Midrash feared that man might try to emulate God and attempt to achieve holiness in the same fashion—by being insulated and aloof, cloistered from the world's temptations and potential cruelty and vulgarity. They insisted, therefore, that we achieve holiness within the context of society, involved and engaged with the community. Coupled with the plural form, the higher ethical standard in Leviticus's reformulated Decalogue calls us to holiness, for only by being involved with our neighbors, carrying their burdens, feeling their pain, and rejoicing in their triumphs, can we come close to God.

Human holiness must be achieved not through negation, but through affirmation; not through isolation, but through engagement; not by abjuring the world and adopting a monastic life, but by the riskier approach of confronting the world and its imperfections. This approach chances failure, but it brings us to the path of redemption.

God of the Earth

Walter Wurzburger, March 25, 1998

God left the world unfinished to give us all the opportunity to function as His partners in completing the work of Creation.

WITH A SEEMINGLY TRIVIAL change in wording, the Bible succinctly sums up the achievement of our patriarch Abraham. When Abraham dispatches his loyal servant, identified in rabbinic tradition as Eliezer in Genesis 15:2, on an important mission, he makes him take an oath by "the Lord, the God of heaven, and the God of the earth" (Gen. 24:3). A few verses later, Abraham reassures Eliezer that his difficult mission will be crowned by success, because "the Lord God of heaven, which took me from my father's house . . . shall send His angel before thee" (Gen. 24:7).

A famous Midrashic comment explains why the second verse omits any reference to the God of the earth. . . . Before Abraham embarked on his life's work, God was not as yet recognized as the God of the earth. It was because of Abraham's tireless efforts that God was ultimately acknowledged as the God both of heaven and of the earth (Midrash Rabbah, Gen. 59.11).

Unfortunately, nowadays, many religious circles are still tempted to consign God to the heavens. It is, indeed, comforting to declare, in the words of the poet Robert Browning, "God's in His heaven, all's right with the world," and close one's eyes to the harsh realities of injustice, oppression, and brutality, that are rampant on earth. But Abraham did not seek an escape from his earthly responsibilities by a flight into transcendental realms. His faith prompted him not to reconcile himself to the prevalence of evil, want, and suffering, but to struggle against it with all his might. . . .

According to Rabbi Joseph B. Soloveitchik, the Almighty purposely left the world in an unfinished state so that human beings, who bear the image of God, should be given the mission to function as His partners in completing the Creation process.

Our task is not to affirm that "all's right with the world" because there is a God in heaven. Instead, our faith in Him should galvanize us into actions designed to make the world more "all right" than we found it.

Transcending Limits

Barry Freundel, April 14, 1998

The growth of cities constituted a blow against the desert. Judaism instructs us to extend our cities—outposts of civilization—and overspread their boundaries to endorse the human need to transcend.

THE BIBLICAL BOOKS of Exodus through Joshua describe how, in the Iron Age, the Jewish people began to give up their nomadic lifestyles and settle in cities. They learned how to forge iron into plows that could till the rocky soil of the Middle East, allowing humankind to raise sufficient crops to settle in one location, and they were no longer required to forage from place to place for food. Humankind was no longer at the whim of sun, wind, and very occasional rain. Instead, a measure of control of one's life and one's environment had been achieved.

The protective space of the city was extended in Numbers, chapter 35, where the Levites, lacking land holdings in the land of Israel, are granted forty-eight cities scattered throughout the land of the other tribes (Num. 35:7). Their grant included a *migrash*, that is, an area of 2,000 square cubits (approximately 4,000–4,500 square feet) stretching in all directions around the border of the city (Num. 35:5). It served to pasture the flocks in biblical times, and later in Jewish history, as recorded in the Talmud, it developed into an environmentally protected area.

Each city constituted a blow for civilization and against the desert. But the *migrash* that extends our city reminds us that there is more to do, and that the benefits of civilization in its best sense must be extended to all.

Jews built sanctuaries of space in cities, and sanctuaries of time in their holidays—and then went about expanding those temporal boundaries. The Day of Atonement falls on the tenth of the month of Tishrei, but the fast exceeds its natural time frame and must begin on the ninth. The shofar, the ram's horn, is associated with the first day of the Jewish year, but is blown each morning for thirty days before the Jewish New Year. The day after major holidays is considered a minor festive occasion. These extensions ensure that the message of each holiday is not cut short by its boundary on the calendar. The rabbis similarly extended one's personal space. The area within four cubits (six to eight feet) of a person is considered part of him or her. In some cases, an object within that distance is considered legally to belong to that person, simply because it has entered their territory.

When taken together, space, time, and civilization remind us of something even more fundamentally human. Jewish law allows one's body to extend past its physical limits; requires our most sacred holidays to transcend the limits of time; and instructs us to extend our cities—outposts of civilization—and overspread their boundaries. In this way, we enshrine in all dimensions of human experience something fundamentally human—the need to transcend. To be human is to want to go beyond, to touch the sky, to climb the mountains, to cross the sea, to walk on the moon. America too was founded by such a vision, and the dream of reaching beyond gives us all reason to do our work today and to hope for an even better tomorrow.

Separation of Powers
and the Dead Sea Scrolls

Lawrence H. Schiffman, May 19, 1998

The ancient writers of the Dead Sea Scrolls believed in a division of power, a concept derived from the biblical notion that ancient Israel was to be governed by both kings and priests.

THERE HAS BEEN so much talk about the Dead Sea Scrolls, but hardly anyone bothers to read them. They are supposed to reveal secrets of ancient wisdom, but for years they remained in the possession of but a few scholars. Yet these ancient texts divulge much wisdom, even for modern government and society. Now that the scrolls are fully available and the veil of secrecy has been lifted, perhaps some of their wisdom may help guide us today.

Of course, the ancient sectarians who composed these texts, considered by most scholars to be the Essenes, did not live in a democratic society. But they did live in a society in which the basic freedoms that we cherish so greatly were regarded as having been vouchsafed by the word of God as recorded in the Bible. Writing in the pre-Christian era, these ancient religious separatists understood the Bible to require a system of government that included a separation of powers between what we would consider the secular and religious authorities. Both, however, were regarded as arms of the same government. It is not that these ancient writers believed in a division of church and state, but rather that they saw the need, on the one hand, to appoint officials responsible for maintaining the religious and ethical character of the people, and on the other hand, for secular authorities charged with collecting taxes, protecting the populace from foreign invasion, and governing the day-to-day affairs of the nation.

The sectarians derived these concepts from the biblical notion that ancient Israel was to be governed by kings and by priests. Indeed, this was the system of administration in the period of the United Monarchy, circa 1020–922 BCE, when David and Solomon ruled over the people and the high priests Zadok and Abiathar conducted the nation's religious affairs. But the sectarians who occupied the ruins at Qumran, near the shore of the Dead Sea

where the Scrolls were found, surely believed that the priestly, religious officials were to be the highest rulers of the nation. For this reason, a text known
as the Temple Scroll puts forward the notion that the king may not go to war
except with the permission of the high priest. Further, this same text, pro-
posing a utopian government for the Jewish people in the pre-Christian era,
suggests that the king should be assisted by a council of thirty-six—twelve
priests, twelve Levites, and twelve laypeople.

What are we to learn from such texts, since we live in a society that
cherishes the division of church and state? The truth is that in the biblical
period, the priests of the Temple were subservient to the royal power. Just
take a look at the architecture of Solomon's palace and his temple. The temple
he built was actually a small appendage of his palace complex, a sort of royal
chapel. When he was displeased with his high priest Abiathar, he simply ban-
ished him to Anathoth, Abiathar's ancestral home. Clearly, in First Temple
times, under the kings of Judah and Israel, religion was subject to governmen-
tal interference, even control. This same situation existed in Greco-Roman
times, and the sectarians of Qumran keenly felt the need to redress this balance. But they were unable to cut the Gordian knot. They had no concept of
the division of church and state. The only solution for them was for the state
to be subservient to the authority of religious leaders.

Our society, as we all know, has chosen to solve this problem by divorcing
the two estates—government and religion—and thus guaranteeing the same
freedom from political dominance that the religious leaders of the Jews in pre-
Christian times sought to create.

Education and the Family

Simon Posner, June 2, 1998

While schools and learning aids are surely necessary weapons in the struggle for educational excellence, the battle cannot be won without the resolve of the parents.

WHEN LOOKING AT SCRIPTURE, one cannot help but notice the numerous references to education and the teaching of the tradition. To cite only two examples:

Deuteronomy 6:4–7: This passage contains one of the central statements of Jewish faith, and, in fact, these words were often on the lips of Jewish martyrs as they sacrificed their lives for their religion:

> Hear, O Israel: The Lord our God is one Lord: And thou shalt
> love the Lord thy God with all thine heart, and with all thy soul,
> and with all thy might. And these words, which I command
> thee this day, shall be in thine heart: And thou shalt teach them
> diligently unto thy children.

Proverbs 1:8: This verse expresses the responsibility of transmitting the teachings of one generation to the next:

> My son, hear the instruction of thy father, and forsake not the law
> of thy mother.

What is striking about these central biblical precepts is the absence of references to teachers, professional educators, or schools. One would have expected that the people would be exhorted to follow the teachings of the wise men, the leaders, and the elders. And yet, in these critical passages, the message is clear: The Bible does not speak of teachers and students, but of parents and children. Education is entrusted to and conducted through the family unit. The parents must teach the children, and the children are admonished to heed the instruction of the parents. It is the family unit that is the most effective vehicle for communicating knowledge.

Perhaps underlying this message of Scripture is the notion that while schools can communicate knowledge and individual teachers can be inspiring, the family setting is the most ideal setting in which the love of knowledge is instilled, respect for learning is nurtured, admiration for scholars is fostered, and intellectual curiosity and inquisitiveness are encouraged. And each of these is accomplished not by a specific lesson plan, but through the osmosis of the ordinary interchange of daily life. Values are not taught but inculcated. Knowledge can be taught, but the love of knowledge needs to be imbued. How do you encapsulate the cluster of messages that is conveyed to a child when the parent says, "It's time to turn off the TV and do your homework; I'll help you with it"?

For values to be transmitted, context is essential, and for transmission of the love of knowledge and the respect for education, our experience teaches that the family is the ideal context. There are no shortcuts or easy answers in this process. In our push-button culture, we have become accustomed to look to technology to come up with the quick fix, or to seek out others to do the tasks that we find too unpleasant or time-consuming to do ourselves. But if we want to instill love of learning in our children, we have to be prepared to do the job ourselves, and we should not look to formal educational institutions to play the role of the family. The old saying is "When I clean up the yard it takes me two hours, and when my kids help me it takes me four hours." But the truth is that we are not really interested just in cleaning up the yard. We intuitively feel that we need to connect with our children to convey to them the values of cooperation, education, and responsibility. This takes an ongoing investment of time, effort, and personal commitment.

Professional educators cannot be expected to do the job of parents, and computers cannot take the place of family interaction. While schools and learning aids are surely necessary weapons in the struggle for educational excellence, the battle cannot be won without the resolve of the family. Scripture teaches us that this commitment is rewarded with a love of learning and a reverence for education that are transmitted across the generations.

The Nazirite

Menachem Genack, June 12, 1998

While God calls us to holiness, He wants us to be open to and engaged with society, and to be tolerant and compassionate.

THE NAZIRITE IS a mysterious and enigmatic figure. He is enjoined from cutting his hair, imbibing wine, and coming in contact with a dead person. The Bible has an ambivalent view of the Nazirite. On the one hand, he is declared as holy: "All the days of his separation he is holy unto the Lord" (Num. 6:8). Yet at the conclusion of his Naziriteship he is required to bring a sin offering to the Temple (Num. 6:14). He is both saint and sinner simultaneously. Rabbinic tradition in the Talmud suggests that his sin is not in concluding his Naziriteship, but in initially refraining from drinking wine and living an isolated ascetic existence rather than enjoying and sanctifying the permissible pleasures of God's creation.

The Nazirite is forbidden to come into contact with a corpse, even of his closest relatives:

> All the days that he separateth himself unto the Lord, he shall
> come at no dead body. He shall not make himself unclean for his
> father, or for his mother, for his brother, or for his sister, when
> they die: because the consecration of his God is upon his head.
> (Num. 6:6–7)

Similarly, a priest is forbidden to come into contact with a corpse, but in his case, a dispensation is given for members of his immediate family:

> And the Lord said unto Moses, Speak unto the priests the sons
> of Aaron, and say unto them, There shall none be defiled for the
> dead among his people: But for his kin, that is near unto him,
> that is, for his mother, and for his father, and for his son, and for
> his daughter, and for his brother, and for his sister a virgin. (Lev.
> 21:1–3)

In both cases, immediate family members are listed, but the two lists are not the same. Why does the Bible, as it enumerates the kin for whom the Nazirite may not defile himself, not list the son and daughter, as it does in Leviticus when addressing the priests?

Who is the Nazirite? He is a person who is idealistic and enthusiastic, though disillusioned with a hedonistic world and frustrated with the established order. By rejecting the pleasure of the grape and the convention of the well-kept appearance, he achieves holiness through withdrawal. That enthusiasm, idealism, impatience with the world, and uncompromising standard is the mark of a young person. "And I raised up of your sons for prophets, and of your young men for Nazirites" (Amos 2:11). We often see that the element in society most sensitive to a corrupt, existing system is the youth. With great passion and courage, they have led student revolts against oppressive regimes. The Bible does not list son and daughter among the kin of the Nazirite, suggests the late Rabbi Yaakov Kamenetzky, for the Nazirite is typically young and unmarried, and has not yet established his own family.

The Bible crowns the Nazirite with glory for his sanctity, self-sacrifice, and youthful zeal. But it requires of him to bring a sin offering for his impetuousness, isolation, and aloofness. While God calls us to holiness and demands of us exacting standards of behavior, He wants us to be open to and engaged with society, and to be tolerant and compassionate.

Jacob's God

Mark Dratch, March 16, 1999

When faced with godlessness, Jacob persevered and insisted on finding godliness.

"HEAR, O ISRAEL: The Lord our God is one Lord" (Deut. 6:4) begins the Jew's daily declaration of faith. When recited as part of the liturgy, it is followed not by the biblical verses that come after it, but by the words "Blessed be the Name of His glorious Kingdom forever."

The Talmudic sages explain that the recitation of "Blessed be the Name of His glorious Kingdom forever" has its origins in a moving exchange between Jacob and his sons, as Jacob was about to die.

> And Jacob called unto his sons, and said, "Gather yourselves together, that I may tell you that which shall befall you in the last days" (Gen. 49:1). Jacob wished to reveal to his sons the "end of the days," whereupon the Divine Presence departed from him [and he was unable to do so]. Said he, "Perhaps, Heaven forefend!, there is one unfit among my children . . ." [But] his sons answered him, "Hear, O Israel [for Jacob's name was also Israel], the Lord our God, the Lord is One: just as there is only One in your heart, so is there in our heart only One." In that moment our father Jacob opened [his mouth] and exclaimed, "Blessed be the name of His glorious kingdom forever and ever." (Talmud, Tractate Pesachim 56a)

This explanation is as mysterious as it is moving. Imagine the scene. Jacob, as he approached death, called his children around him in order to bid farewell. He did so as a father, in order to say good-bye and to express to them his personal feelings. He also did so as a patriarch, in order to pass on to them the strength of his religious convictions. He intended to reveal to them the End of Days, the secrets of faith and of history. He wanted to give structure, meaning, and purpose to their existence—but the Divine Presence abandoned him. Precisely at that moment when he wanted to cement his sons' relationship with God with a prophetic explanation of the meaning of their lives, the purpose of their future sufferings, and the Divine role in their history, the presence of God departed from him and Jacob had to speak of other things. He could not offer them understanding. He was only able to pray, to offer them blessings instead.

This alienation from God was not a new experience for Jacob. In fact, Jacob suffered the absence of the Divine Presence for long periods throughout his life. For the twenty years that he spent in the house of his father-in-law, Laban, in Paddan Aram—one of the most vital times of Jacob's life, as he built his family and his wealth—God was not with him. And during the twenty-two years that Joseph was missing, God was also not with Jacob (Gen. 45:27).

Why had God deserted Jacob at these critical times of his life? The biblical commentator Rashi points out that God abandoned Jacob in the house of Laban because as long as he lived in the evil, devious, and hostile milieu of his father-in-law, there was no room for God (Gen. 31:3). And Maimonides suggests that God abandoned Jacob during his mourning for Joseph because of Jacob's sorrow and anxiety. It was not until he was brought news that Joseph was alive that Jacob's spirit was restored and he found God again. The irony and tragedy of it is that at precisely those times that he needed God most, God was not there! Precisely during the challenges of life in Laban's house when he most needed moral support and encouragement; precisely during the loneliness and anguish of mourning for a lost son when he most needed God's broad shoulder to lean on to assuage his grief and despair; and precisely while facing his own death, the future of his family, and the fate of his faith, Jacob most needed God—and each time, God was not there for him. How tragically ironic that it was at those times in his life when he was bone-tired, emotionally weary, and psychologically dreary that he felt so spiritually spent.

Yet, strangely, it was precisely at one of these moments of spiritual crisis that Jacob blessed his sons. Most strangely, it was precisely at this moment of Divine silence that Jacob's children declared to their father their faith in God. "Hear, O Israel . . ."

How had Jacob succeeded in passing on his faith to his children? What had Jacob taught them? His secret lay in the fact that despite God's absence, Jacob persevered; despite the immoral influences of Laban's house, he refused to yield; and despite his grief at Joseph's loss, he refused to surrender. Jacob's secret lay in the fact that, despite it all, he refused to accept a godless reality. On his deathbed when the Divine Presence departed from him, he invoked the Name of God and offered blessing and prayer. It was because of his pain and it was despite his pain that he continued to believe. The greatness of Jacob's spiritual character was that he was able to reach out to God, and leave his hand extended—even if it remained empty, even if his gesture remained unanswered. It was not only what he said and what he did that made Jacob the man of faith that he was, but it was especially *when* he said it and when he did it: during moments of despair and trouble. Jacob taught his children, by personal example, that it is at those moments when it is hardest to pray that true prayer is needed the most and the best prayers are formed. Jacob taught his children, by personal example, that it is at those moments when it is hardest to believe that true belief is needed and true convictions are formed.

Thus, Jacob's persistence did not go unrewarded; his prayers and beliefs sustained him through long and difficult times. Jacob's persistence did not go unanswered; after each lapse he reunited and reconciled with God. And Jacob's persistence did not go unnoticed; his children, specifically at a time of Divine absence, declared, "Hear, O Israel!" They were able to sustain this conviction because they had a role model, a great man of faith; a man who relied on the potential of God's greatness, even though it seemed remote and unattainable; a man who continued to pray and live according to God's will, even when he felt estranged and cheated and deceived; a man who was able to believe in God, even in His absence—and who was therefore able to pass on that relationship to his children.

The Two Midwives and the World's First Recorded Act of Civil Disobedience

Joseph Telushkin, March 24, 1999

In the course of civil disobedience, much must be risked, but not necessarily everything. Presciently, this letter was sent to President Clinton the same day as the launch of Operation Allied Force, which helped to facilitate the end of the Yugoslav Wars.

PHARAOH'S INITIAL GOAL in enslaving and oppressing the Hebrews is to limit their growth. This scheme fails; as the Bible records, "The more they afflicted them, the more they multiplied and grew. And they were grieved because of the children of Israel" (Exod. 1:12).

The Egyptian ruler decides on a more savage method to achieve his goal. He summons the two chief midwives working with the Hebrew women and instructs them to kill all newborn baby boys. Infant girls, he adds, are to be spared; presumably, in the absence of Hebrew males, they will marry Egyptians, assimilate, and so bring an end to the Hebrews.

The next verse (Exod. 1:17) informs us that "the midwives feared God, and did not as the king of Egypt commanded them, but saved the men children alive."

The midwives' refusal to obey Pharaoh's murderous edict on grounds of conscience constitutes history's first recorded act of civil disobedience. Most people who live under monarchic dictatorships (such as prevailed in ancient Egypt) or in totalitarian regimes (such as Nazi Germany or the Soviet Union) obey immoral laws, if for no other reason than fear of being executed. From where then did the midwives derive the moral strength to disobey Pharaoh's decree?

The Bible tells us: they feared God. While the other inhabitants of Egypt feared Pharaoh more than anyone else, the midwives' fear of God liberated them from the fear of the Egyptian tyrant. And while the concept of fear of God antagonizes many people, bringing to mind primitive images of punishment and damnation, in actuality, fear of God can be liberating—liberating people from fear of human beings.

When Pharaoh learns that newborn male babies are still alive, he summons the midwives. "Why have ye done this thing, and have saved the men children alive?" he rails at them (Exod. 1:18).

Although courageous enough to disobey Pharaoh's edict, the midwives have no wish to be martyrs. They tell Pharaoh a contrived story: they wished to carry out his decree but, unfortunately, "the Hebrew women are not as the Egyptian women; for they are lively, and are delivered ere the midwives come in unto them" (Exod. 1:19).

This untruthful response contains an important lesson in biblical morality. Although a human being is obligated to resist a murderous order, he or she is not obligated to speak truthfully to a murderer and die on account of this truth telling. The Bible notes (Exod. 1:20–21) that God subsequently rewards the midwives for their courageous behavior, thereby indicating biblical approval both for their initial behavior and for their untruthful response to Pharaoh.

Obvious though this lesson might seem to us, some of the greatest figures in Christian theology and Western thought have argued that lying is always wrong, even when life is at stake. St. Augustine argued that lying bars one from eternal life: "Since then, eternal life is lost by lying, a lie may never be told for the preservation of the temporal life of another [presumably including one's own life]." Some fifteen hundred years after St. Augustine, Immanuel Kant, in an effort to establish a universally binding secular ethic, also condemned all lying, whatever the circumstances. Thus, Kant taught that if a man fleeing for his life is hiding in our house, and the would-be murderer asks whether "our friend who is pursued by him has taken refuge in our house," we are forbidden to lie or mislead him. From Judaism's perspective, one who would tell a truth that would enable a would-be murderer to kill an innocent person would bear grave moral responsibility.

Adam and Cain

Menachem Genack, June 1, 1999

It is not only evil itself that diminishes humanity, but indifference to evil, a sad trait that has historically plagued humankind.

IF WE ANALYZE the responses of God to Adam's sin of eating from the Tree of Knowledge and to Cain's sin of the murder of Abel, we will find extraordinary parallels in the language of the Bible.

Adam	Cain
They heard the voice [*kol*] of the Lord God walking in the garden. (Gen. 3:8)	And He said, What hast thou done? the voice [*kol*] of thy brother's blood crieth unto me from the ground. (Gen. 4:10)
And the Lord God called unto Adam, and said unto him, Where art thou? (Gen. 3:9)	And the Lord said unto Cain, Where is Abel thy brother? (Gen. 4:9)
Thy desire [*teshukatech*] shall be to thy husband, and he shall rule over thee. (Gen. 3:16)	If thou doest well, shalt thou not be accepted? and if thou doest not well, sin lieth at the door. And unto thee shall be his desire, and thou shalt rule over him. (Gen. 4:7)
Unto Adam He said, Because thou has harkened unto the voice of thy wife, and hast eaten of the tree, of which I commanded thee, saying, Thou shalt not eat of it: cursed is the ground for thy sake. (Gen. 3:17)	And now art thou cursed from the earth, which hath opened her mouth to receive thy brother's blood from thy hand. (Gen. 4:11)
Thorns also and thistles shall it bring forth to thee; and thou shall eat the herb of the field. (Gen. 3:18)	When thou tillest the ground, it shall not henceforth yield unto thee her strength; a fugitive and a vagabond shalt thou be in the earth. (Gen. 4:12)
And He drove out the man. (Gen. 3:24)	Behold, thou hast driven me out this day from the face of the earth. (Gen. 4:14)

The Bible's use of strikingly similar language in these two stories of sin and retribution indicates that the stories are related. And indeed, one may view the murder of Abel as both an indirect and a direct consequence of Adam's sin. As the first man to violate the word of God, Adam set the stage for others by shattering the authority of God's rule. Were it not for Adam's sin, which diminished humanity for all generations, Cain would not have fallen so deeply as to kill his brother. And as the one to bring the punishment of mortality upon all humanity, Adam, and not Cain, may also be viewed as the one who committed the first murder, as it was Adam's sin that made all humans mortal and subject to death. Adam was thus directly, as well as indirectly, responsible for the murder of his own son, Abel.

In our contemporary context, while Hitler and his agents were the murderers of millions of victims of the Holocaust, it was Stanley Baldwin and Neville Chamberlain's amoral policy of appeasement, which winked at evil and at the terrible plight of the Jews, that made the Holocaust possible. Though they were not the murderers, they were morally culpable, as they idly stood by as their neighbor's blood was shed.

The lesson must be learned well, whether it be Kosovo, Rwanda, or any other place on the globe that has been forsaken by God, for indifference can make us unwilling accessories to murder. That indifference will turn back on ourselves when we become the victims in an uncaring, cold, and harsh world.

The Tower of Babel

Menachem Genack, 1999

Society unchecked can hinder individual expression and the diversity of human experience, a theme President Clinton constantly emphasized.

THE STORY OF THE TOWER OF BABEL is shrouded in mystery. What was the purpose of building the enormous tower that stretched to the heavens? What was the sin in its construction, to which God responded by confusing the language of mankind and dispersing humans over the face of the earth?

This strange event takes place after the Great Flood. Society at the time of the Flood was characterized by violence, licentiousness, and anarchy. The bonds of civil society had unraveled. God then brought the Flood, which eradicated all humanity, saving but Noah and his family.

We may speculate that the post-Flood generation, seeing the disaster that an anarchistic society had brought, moved in the opposite direction. It created an Orwellian, homogenous, centrally controlled society, substituting the centripetal force of totalitarianism for the centrifugal force of anarchy. The individual was of little value; only the faceless mass was significant. The pithy description of the devaluation of the individual, reported by the Jewish Midrashic tradition, is noteworthy. If a brick fell from the top of the Tower, the Midrash states, people would mourn, for it involved so much effort to get it to the top. But if a *person* fell from the Tower, it was of no consequence. Only in the cohesiveness of the whole, the people thought, could they avoid the fate of the generation of the Flood. . . .

God's dispersal of the society of Babel was not a punishment or retribution as much as it was a plan to free the individual from the bonds of a stifling society and affirm the diversity of the human experience, now represented and enhanced by the multilingual cacophony. No longer enslaved by a society of the Tower, which crushed the individual, the human experience would spread to new places and climes, precipitating new cultures and new mediums of human expression. . . . What God seeks is not the monochromatic world of the valley of Shinar, but a multicolored one, in which the diversity of the human experience enhances and ennobles man, created in the image of God.

The Splitting of the Sea

Menachem Genack, May 4, 2001

The biblical imagery of the splitting of the Red Sea serves as a reminder that no one approach is the exclusive avenue toward godliness.

OUR IMAGE of the splitting of the Red Sea is emblazoned in our minds from the Cecil B. DeMille movie *The Ten Commandments*. But Jewish Midrashic tradition has a different version. According to the Midrash, the sea did not split in one place, but in twelve distinct places, creating a path for each of the tribes. In addition, the Midrash says, the water froze and was crystal clear, so that each tribe could see the other tribes as they traversed the Red Sea.

In the Passover Haggadah, which contains the story of the Exodus and which is read on Seder night, we read that the miracle of the splitting of the sea was multitudes greater than all the miracles and plagues that God brought upon the Egyptians in Egypt.

Based on the Haggadah, we often think of the splitting of the sea as the climax of the Exodus. The paths through the sea were the exit tunnels from Egypt. But in fact, the splitting of the sea is not only the route from Egypt, but also the entryway to the experience of Sinai. Sinai represents the ultimate revelation of God to man, when God revealed His Ten Commandments. According to tradition, this revelation was preceded by an earlier revelation at the Red Sea. The rabbis said that what a simple maidservant saw at the Red Sea was greater than what the prophet Ezekiel saw in his visions. The experience of revelation at the Red Sea may be why God chose to give the Jewish people some of His commandments already at Marah, before they reached Sinai: "There he made for them a statute and an ordinance, and there he proved them" (Exod. 15:25). According to tradition, this "decree and ordinance" included the laws of the Sabbath, respect for parents, and civil law.

What the Midrash means to communicate is that there is not just one path to God—that is, to Sinai—but many paths. Each of the tribes, therefore, had to be cognizant and respectful of the various traditions, customs, and outlooks of the other tribes. As the members of each tribe crossed the sea, imbued with religious ecstasy, they also had to gaze through the clear waters and glimpse the equally valid approaches of the other tribes.

WILLIAM JEFFERSON CLINTON

May 28, 2001

Rabbi Menachem Genack
Rabbinic Administrator
Union of Orthodox Jewish
    Congregations of America
11 Broadway
New York, New York 10004

Dear Rabbi Genack:

Thank you so much for sending me a copy of "The
Splitting of the Sea." What a wonderful way of
looking at that miraculous event. In my
speeches abroad, I have been talking about the
fact that each of the great monotheistic
religions teaches that we cannot ignore our
neighbors or turn our backs on them -- that we
are all members of one human family. Your
missive is a great illustration of that. It
reminds me of how the Muslims say Allah put
different people on the earth, not that they
might despise one another, but they might know
and cherish one another.

You were kind to offer to study the Bible and
Talmud together. I know that doing so would be
an enriching experience, and I've alerted my
schedulers about the possibility.

Thanks for keeping in touch. All the best to
you.

Sincerely,

Bill

Cities

Jeremy Dauber, August 30, 2001

Following the establishment of the Clinton Foundation's headquarters in the Harlem neighborhood of New York City, this letter reflects on the biblical concept of the city and the unique qualities of New York.

Mr. President:

Several years ago, I received a letter from you congratulating me on my election to a Rhodes Scholarship, a letter that meant a great deal to me. Thanks to Rabbi Genack, I'm delighted to have the opportunity to return the favor.

In your letter, you spoke of your warm memories of the city of Oxford, and given that we share not just one, but two cities in common (I'm now a professor at Columbia University), and in light of your recent moves and transitions, I began thinking about the role cities play in the Hebrew Bible in general and the Pentateuch in particular. Though some of the evidence is scattered and disparate, I think the Bible has real lessons to teach on the theme, lessons I hope might be helpful as you settle into your new life as a New Yorker.

From the very first mention of cities in the Bible, we see that they are the product of a mixed heritage: Cities are founded by Cain, the man cursed to wander the earth eternally:

> And Cain went out from the presence of the Lord, and dwelt in the land of Nod, on the east of Eden. And Cain knew his wife, and she conceived, and bare Enoch: and he builded a city, and called the name of the city, after the name of his son, Enoch. (Gen. 4:16–17)

The irony, is of course, intentional: out of motion may come stability; out of evil, good. Even from the worst cities in the Bible, mentioned early in Genesis, we may at least take moral lessons, if nothing else: Babel's hubris and rebellion against Divine rule result in the linguistic diversity and multiplicity that modern readers and thinkers cherish today. Even Sodom and

Gomorrah, those cities hated by God, allow Him to demonstrate not merely His hatred of injustice, but His love of human prayer and argument: were it not for the example of Sodom, we would not know that Abraham had the power to change God's mind, an episode whose theological consequences are revolutionary.

As the Genesis account of patriarchal history continues, an interesting narrative strategy is revealed: accounts of the founding of cities seem to provide the clearest overt appearances of the biblical narrator. That is, the narrator takes pains to emerge from the narrative to note that the small well or tiny encampment of a patriarch is the root of a contemporary flourishing settlement. For example, the narrator notes in Genesis 26:33 that Isaac gives the name Sheba to the area surrounding the well dug by his servants, and adds that "therefore the name of the city is Beersheba *unto this day*"—that is, the day of the narrator. In doing so, the narrator concretizes the thematic approach adumbrated throughout Genesis—that individual acts by great men have deep consequences, consequences affecting many, and that, as the rabbis put it, *ma'aseh avot siman lebanim* (literally, "acts of the fathers are a sign to the sons"). It can hardly be coincidental, then, that many of the foundational acts of these patriarchs are ones of hospitality, peace, and kindness. Abraham plants his tent on the plains of Mamre and acts charitably and hospitably to strangers who approach; not merely do those strangers turn out to be angels, heralding the miraculous birth of Isaac, but the place of that kindness becomes the thriving town of Hebron (Gen. 13:18). Isaac's pact of peace with Abimelech, king of Gerar, becomes the later Beersheba, as alluded to earlier (Gen. 26:27–34). And, of course, Abraham's ultimate act of sacrifice and devotion to God, the binding of Isaac, takes place on Mount Moriah, which, according to Jewish tradition, becomes the center of Jerusalem (see Gen. 22:14 and the comments of the Midrash, esp. Midrash Rabbah, Gen. 56:11). The panchronic approach taken by the narrator here, spanning past and present, emphasizes once more these stories' contemporary relevance.

As the Pentateuch shifts from primarily a recitation of Jewish history to primarily a catalog of Jewish law, we see that, legally speaking, cities themselves have a transformative power as well. Most obviously, the Cities of Refuge, mentioned in Numbers 35, have the power to effectively negate a death sentence placed on the head of an accidental murderer; once inside these spaces, the blood avenger is forbidden from touching the individual. In an analogous case, farmers are forbidden from eating certain consecrated agricultural tithes until they enter the walls of Jerusalem, where the tithes can be consumed (Deut. 14:22–26).

In other words, the establishment of and move to cities in the Bible is seen as an essentially optimistic act; acts of great men have the power to create and rejuvenate cities, and cities have the power to transform men in fundamental ways. The biblical author does not wear rose-colored glasses; there are deep problems in many cities, problems that may be beyond one man's capacity to repair, even if that man is Abraham. But even then, the Bible does not excuse us from the effort to do so, and it acknowledges that such an effort can have fundamental and deep-rooted effect, even if that effect is not apparently obvious; though God destroyed Sodom and Gomorrah and scattered Babel, this does not mean Abraham's intervention was in vain.

As a New Yorker, I, like many others, am excited about your decision to work in the greatest city in the world, and particularly your choice to work on 125th Street (just blocks away from my office). There has been much made in the newspapers of the potentially transformative effect your presence will have on Harlem. In light of the biblical views regarding cities and those who move to them, I think this advice is well justified. My hope for you, and for the city, is that you will be able to live these biblical lessons to the fullest: to be fully aware of the effect that your small actions here will have not just in the present, but for the future, too, and to allow the city and its residents to work their subtle and not-so-subtle magic upon you. Though we may never be able to convince you to drop the Razorbacks for the Lions, it's my hope that New York provides you with a place to figure out what comes next as gracefully and easily as possible.

WILLIAM JEFFERSON CLINTON

September 28, 2001

Rabbi Menachem Genack
Rabbinic Administrator
Union of Orthodox Jewish
    Congregations of America
11 Broadway
New York, New York 10004-1303

Dear Rabbi Genack:

Thank you very much for the missive by
Jeremy Dauber. I've written to Professor
Dauber directly to let him know how much I
appreciated it. I'm grateful that you
continue to think of me.

I hope you and your family and friends are
all well.

Sincerely,

President Truman
and the Weekly Address

Menachem Genack, November 4, 2002–June 5, 2007

On November 4, 2002, I sent a letter about President Truman and the Jewish Sabbath to historian and author David McCullough, who wrote the noted biography *Truman*. In January 2003, I forwarded the letter to President Clinton; several years later I forwarded it to Senator Hillary Rodham Clinton. The letter and their responses follow:

DEAR MR. McCULLOUGH,

A few weeks ago there was a story in the Israeli press about President Truman that I thought you might find interesting.

DAVID McCULLOUGH

January 30, 2003

Dear Rabbi Genack,

I can't thank you enough for taking the time to send me the story about President Truman. It is one I had not heard before, and certainly it speaks for his fundamental good will and fairness.

As probably you know, Harry Truman was the only president of the twentieth century who never went to college. But he also exemplifies in many ways how much about life that matters does not come necessarily from education. Somewhere along the line, somehow or other, possibly from his mother, he acquired a resilient, basic sense of right and wrong, and an ability to put himself in the other person's place.

He could also, as I expect you know, use expressions in private correspondence, and apparently in private conversation, that were clearly anti-Semitic. Judged by such slurs, he is understandably diminished. I once asked someone who knew him well about this. I was told that they were "old habits of the mouth," and my own feeling is that there's much truth in that, and largely in view of so many of his actions, both private and official, which are exactly to the contrary.

Sincerely,

President Truman's advisors had urged him to address the American people each week. After deliberations with communications experts, the weekly speech was scheduled for Friday nights. A Mrs. Berl heard of this decision and was disturbed. There would be many Orthodox Jews who would like to hear the president's speech, but who would not be able to because it would be broadcast on the Jewish Sabbath. She wrote a letter to the president describing her patriotism, but regretted her inability to hear him speak because she could not operate an electrical appliance on the Sabbath. "As a result," she wrote, "I request that you reschedule the broadcast." Amazingly, a week later, Mrs. Berl received a letter in the mail informing her that President Truman read her message and was seriously considering its contents. Two weeks later the president gave his usual speech on Friday night, but announced that for various reasons it would thereafter be broadcast on Tuesdays.

I think this short anecdote speaks volumes about Harry Truman . . .

WILLIAM JEFFERSON CLINTON

May 16, 2007

Rabbi Menachem Genack
Rabbinic Administrator
Union of Orthodox Jewish
  Congregations of America
11 Broadway
New York, New York 10004

Dear Rabbi Genack:

Thank you for passing along your
correspondence with David McCullough -- it
is very interesting. President Truman
brought a unique, dynamic perspective to the
White House and led our nation through
challenging times. I will actually be
speaking about his legacy alongside David
this summer at the Truman Library in
Missouri, and I'm looking forward to it very
much.

As always, I appreciate your thoughtfulness
and insight. All the best to you.

Sincerely,

HILLARY RODHAM CLINTON
NEW YORK

United States Senate
WASHINGTON, D.C. 20510-3204

June 5, 2007

Rabbi Manachem Genack
The Orthodox Union
11 Broadway
New York, New York 10004

Dear Rabbi Genack:

Thank you for sharing your exchange of correspondence
with historian David McCullough about President Truman's
weekly addresses to the nation. Mrs. Berl's letter proves the
difference one individual can make, even at the highest levels of
government. I hope my own letter finds you well and I look
forward to seeing you again soon.

With appreciation and best regards, I am

Sincerely yours,

Hillary Rodham Clinton

Tree of the Field

Menachem Genack, September 20, 2005

This missive reflects on the divine imperative to cultivate and protect our natural environment. In 2005 President Clinton established the Clinton Global Initiative, of which a major focus is environmental issues.

A PASSAGE IN DEUTERONOMY articulates the biblical mandate to protect the environment. In the King James edition the passage reads:

> When thou shalt besiege a city a long time, in making war against it to take it, thou shalt not destroy the trees thereof by forcing an axe against them: for thou mayest eat of them, and thou shalt not cut them down (for the tree of the field is man's life) to employ them in the siege. (Deut. 20:19)

The striking phrase "for the tree of the field is man's life" affirms that man's life is dependent on the trees. The King James translation follows the understanding of this verse according to the medieval biblical commentator Abraham Ibn Ezra.

Rashi, another commentator, renders the phrase differently: "For you may eat of them, but you shall not cut them down; *for is the tree of the field man*, that it should be besieged of you?" According to this reading, the Bible tells us that even in times of war, we must remember not to go to war against nature, against the trees, as they are not our enemies; the trees are not part of the enemy city that is besieged.

According to both readings, the Bible admonishes us that even in a time of battle, we must not destroy the fruit trees and defile nature.

This point is elaborated in the next verse: "Only the trees which thou knowest that they be not trees for meat, though shalt destroy and cut them down" (Deut. 20:20). The phrase "the trees which thou knowest" is an allusion to the Tree of Knowledge, which Adam and Eve were enjoined not to eat. When Adam was created he was given a Divine mandate to have dominion over all the earth and to subdue it (Gen. 1:28). But as man develops technological prowess and subdues the earth, he must remember that the earth is not his, but God's. That was the message inherent in the original commandment to Adam and Eve not to eat of the Tree of Knowledge: *Though I give you the world for cultivation and development, it is only on loan to you; it still belongs to me.*

This idea is expressed in the ancient Midrashic tradition. When God made Adam, the Midrash states, He took him and showed him the trees of the Garden of Eden. God said to Adam, "See my world, how beautiful and praiseworthy it is. I made it for you. Be mindful that you do not destroy it!" (Midrash Rabbah, Eccles. 7:13).

Thus our sensitivity to the environment is not only a utilitarian concern, but also a sacred mission.

WILLIAM JEFFERSON CLINTON

October 25, 2005

Rabbi Menachem Genack
Rabbinic Administrator
Union of Orthodox Jewish
    Congregations of America
11 Broadway
New York, New York 10004

Dear Rabbi Genack:

Thank you for writing to me about the Global
Initiative. I thought it was a great
success.

As you saw at the conference, I believe the
future of the environment is one of the most
pressing concerns of the 21st century, which
the missive you sent me perfectly
demonstrates.

I'm glad you were able to attend the event.
Hillary and I send our best wishes.

Sincerely,

V

Faith

At the height of the Civil War, Abraham Lincoln said, "I have been many times driven to my knees by the overwhelming conviction that I had nowhere else to go." Faith begins with the recognition that, although we can choose our destinies as good and decent people, we cannot control events. All of us must appreciate this lesson. Those entrusted with positions of political power, perhaps even more than the rest of us, must have the humility to understand that their power is limited; that their aspirations may not materialize the way they envisioned; and that ultimately, the way events turn out is in the hands of God. This message must be heard often, and therefore it was a focus of the letters to the president.

Professor David Shatz sees a profound model for American life and society in the narrative of the twelve spies dispatched by Moses to survey the land of Canaan. The ten spies who argue against launching the conquest of Canaan, were fearful, in Professor Shatz's view, of leaving the wilderness, where all their needs were provided by God. To launch the practical initiative in the new land, they thought they would have to forfeit the special relationship the Children of Israel had with God. Only Caleb and Joshua realized the truth, that God's providence does not require the rarified passive existence of the wilderness, but is most fully realized in the thick of political, economic, and military decisions and initiatives. So, too, many Americans are people of deep religious faith, but America's is not a faith that counsels quietism and frowns upon human effort; rather it is the faith of Caleb and Joshua. We affirm, "In God we trust," but we trust our own judgment and ability too.

I sent my missive on the ten plagues, "For I Shall Be with You," in 2001, shortly after President Clinton left office. I suspect that this was a particularly stressful time for the president given the rush of events at the end of his administration, including his granting of pardons, some of which aroused controversy. I hope that the missive helped give him some measure of solace.

Elyakim Rubinstein, who currently serves as a justice on the Israeli Supreme Court, contributed a letter about the crucial role that history and memory play in sustaining the Jewish people through the long Diaspora. In our own time, collective memory is especially important in asserting the historic link of the Jewish people to the land of Israel. Mr. Rubinstein shared with me a remarkable story that occurred during President Clinton's attempt to create sustainable peace in the Middle East before he left office. Mr. Rubinstein, who was attorney general of Israel at the time, participated in the negotiations between the Israelis and the Palestinians in July 2000 at Camp David. One of the critical issues in the peace talks was the status of Jerusalem, with its Jewish and Moslem sacred sites. While discussing the competing claims to the Temple Mount, Yasser Arafat refused to acknowledge any historical Jewish link to the Temple Mount. The president, in frustration, asked Mr. Rubinstein to collect many of the biblical citations that mention Jerusalem and the Temple Mount. The next morning, with noticeable annoyance, Clinton handed Arafat the list of citations. Remembering history is important, and Arafat, in this circumstance, was guilty of forgetting.

Although faith begins with a recognition that we cannot control events, there needs to be a realization that faith is a balance of humility and initiative. We must have the humility to see that, ultimately, we are not in control. But we must also recognize that faith is linked to hope. God has granted us the opportunity to seize the initiative, and faith compels us to take up that God-given opportunity and inscribe our signature on history's canvas. Abraham Lincoln, more than any other U.S. president, possessed a faith that achieved this balance. Lincoln, who preserved the Union by dint of his indomitable will and valiant leadership, was able to write, in complete sincerity, "I claim not to have controlled events, but confess plainly that events have controlled me. Now, at the end of three years' struggle the nation's condition is not what either party, or any man devised, or expected. God alone can claim it."[1]

---

[1] From a letter Abraham Lincoln sent to Albert G. Hodges, editor of the Kentucky newspaper the *Frankfort Commonwealth*, April 4, 1864.

Exodus

Menachem Genack, April 15, 1997

Historic greatness often emerges from seemingly insignificant acts of hope.

THE STORY IN EXODUS of the redemption from Egypt begins with the inconspicuous verse "And there went a man of the house of Levi, and took to wife a daughter of Levi" (Exod. 2:1). Generally the Bible, when introducing major figures, delineates their genealogy, yet here the parents of Moses are introduced anonymously. According to classical Jewish tradition (Talmud, Tractate Sotah 12a), Amram had separated himself from his wife, Jochebed. "Why bring children into the oppressive bondage in Egypt?" he asked. Yet his daughter Miriam prophesied that the redemption would come, and she cajoled her father to remarry her mother—and from that union was born the redeemer, Moses. Miriam . . . never gave up hope, and communicated that hope to her parents. The Bible wants to emphasize that one couple rebuilding their family—what at the time seemed insignificant and with such little prospect of success—sowed the seeds for the ultimate redemption. Courage and faith can infuse unnoticed events with historical significance. There are never impossible hurdles, only man's limited dreams; for behind the veil of history is God's hidden, loving hand, shaping and driving the human chronicle.

THE WHITE HOUSE
WASHINGTON

April 23, 1997

Rabbi Menachem Genack
129 Meadowbrook Road
Englewood, New Jersey   07631

Dear Rabbi Genack:

Your letter to me was wonderful and its message
inspired. I will try to take the lessons of
Exodus to heart and will continue with courage
and faith to do the job the American people
sent me here to do.

Thank you for your prayers, your counsel, and
your friendship. I cherish them all.

Sincerely,

Bill Clinton

The Almighty Has His Own Purposes

Menachem Genack, July 28, 1997

Joseph played a pivotal role in consolidating Pharaoh's power. While Joseph was focused on preventing famine within Egypt, he was also unwittingly hastening God's plan for Israel's story of enslavement and redemption.

IN GENESIS 47, the biblical narrative of the reconciliation of Joseph with his brothers and his reunion with Jacob is interrupted for a lengthy record of all of Joseph's dealings with the people of Egypt:

> And when that year was ended, they came unto him the second year, and said unto him, We will not hide it from my lord, how that our money is spent; my lord also hath our herds of cattle; there is not ought left in the sight of my lord, but our bodies, and our lands. Wherefore shall we die before thine eyes, both we and our land? buy us and our land for bread, and we and our land will be servants unto Pharaoh: and give us seed, that we may live, and not die, that the land be not desolate. And Joseph bought all the land of Egypt for Pharaoh; for the Egyptians sold every man his field, because the famine prevailed over them: so the land became Pharaoh's. And as for the people, he removed them to cities from one end of the borders of Egypt even to the other end thereof. (Gen. 47:18–21)

Joseph's policy of storing grain during the years of plenty to provide for the years of famine is central to the larger narrative. However, the redistribution of Egyptian land, as well as the negotiations that produced it, has no evident bearing on the destiny of the Children of Israel, and gives the appearance of an irrelevant digression.

The medieval biblical commentator Nachmanides [d. 1270] suggests that the Bible elaborates on Joseph's dealings in order to indicate Joseph's integrity and loyalty to Pharaoh. Joseph not only saves Egypt; he acts as a true servant of Pharaoh by transferring vast properties into the hands of the ruler, with nothing going to Joseph himself. The next Pharaoh was to repay this loyalty by anticipating that Joseph's people would be guilty of sedition (Exod. 1:8–10). This expectation completes a recurring pattern in Joseph's life, which sees him repeatedly and groundlessly suspected of perfidy. His brothers suspect that he plots to tyrannically rule over them. Though ever faithful to his master, Potiphar, Joseph is falsely accused of adultery with Potiphar's scheming wife. Consequently, the Bible makes a point of affirming Joseph's loyalty and integrity.

There is, I believe, another reason for the Bible to dwell upon the details of Joseph's buying all the land in Egypt. Egypt, before Joseph, was a feudal society. While Pharaoh was preeminent, he was not all-powerful. There were other centers of influence within Egypt, including private owners of land and capital, a powerful clergy, an aristocracy, and different regional centers of power. Joseph, by acquiring all the land and inhabitants on behalf of Pharaoh, transforms Egyptian society from a feudal system to a totalitarian one. By dislocating the population, he eliminates the various regional power bases. Now all economic and political power is vested in Pharaoh.

Unbeknownst to the players in this drama, Jacob and his children are inexorably being drawn to Egypt to realize God's prophecy to Abraham that "thy seed shall be a stranger in a land that is not theirs, and shall serve them; and they shall afflict them four hundred years" (Gen. 15:13). As it describes the creation of the totalitarian system, the Bible tells us that Joseph is not only the Divine instrument for bringing the Israelites to Egypt; he also creates the system that ultimately enslaves them.

Joseph appropriately centralized control so that the collection and distribution of food would be done effectively and efficiently. Thus Egypt survived the brutal famine. But the seeds of God's plan for the Israelites' bondage in Egypt—the cauldron in which a new nation was forged—were also being sown.

Abraham Lincoln recognized the infinite distance between God and man. Sensing our limited perspective, he commented in his second inaugural address, "The Almighty has His own purposes." It is that sense of irony and humility that the Bible teaches in the unfolding of the Joseph narrative.

God Unfair to Cain?

Shalom Carmy, October 6, 1997

A belligerent conviction of what constitutes fairness in life can lead to inconsolable anger when life's experiences do not reflect those certitudes.

CAIN WAS A FARMER; Abel was a shepherd. Cain offers to God the fruits of his labor; so does Abel. God favors Abel, whereupon Cain is wroth and his face falls. God tells Cain that if he will do well, his face will be lifted, but that sin crouches enticingly at his door, though it is within Cain's power to rule over it (Gen. 4:2–7). Cain subsequently kills his brother. He is punished by being uprooted from the land; an exile, he builds the first city (Gen. 4:8, 12–17).

Why did God turn to Abel's offering, but not to Cain's? One traditional approach (familiar from the classical Midrashic tradition and from Rashi's commentary) discovers a deficiency in Cain's sacrifice: Abel brought the best of his flock; Cain did not choose the best of his vegetables. Therefore Abel's superiority was deserved, as was the Divine rebuke delivered to Cain. Perhaps this justification is implied by the biblical story, but it is not an obvious reading. The reader might understandably conclude that God's preference for Abel is not clearly motivated in the biblical text. What does this say about Divine fairness as expressed in this episode?

Sympathy for Cain's outlook turns up in many authors of the Romantic period. Fascinated by exile, alienation, and evil, men like Samuel Taylor Coleridge, Lord Byron, and Charles Baudelaire fancied themselves of Cain's party. In the Spanish philosopher Miguel de Unamuno's remarkable novel *Abel Sánchez* (1917), the title character, an easygoing, popular, lucky artist, dies at the hands of the work-driven, ever-responsible doctor, Joaquin, whom he had always effortlessly outshone.

Among traditional commentators, the Netziv [Rabbi Naftali Zvi Berlin, head of the famed Volozhin Yeshiva, d. 1893] confronted most explicitly the possibility that Cain did not deserve to have his offering rejected. Cain's reaction to the lack of Divine response reflects his bewilderment. "Cain was very wroth"—that is to say, he resented the apparent injustice. "And his countenance fell," meaning that he came to doubt his own worth. He is confused because he regarded himself as more deserving than Abel. His struggle to make the earth fruitful was more laborious than his brother's cultivation of the sheep, and the aim of his toil was to yield necessary food, rather than the luxurious products provided by Abel. In Cain's opinion, then, his adoption of the simple life made him the more pious brother; it was he who merited God's favor.

According to the Netziv, Cain is wrong in his conviction that only his Spartan way of life is pleasing to God. Life is not always fair in the sense that Cain defines fairness. Both the hard-working farmer's frugal comfort and the shepherd's leisurely lavishness can accommodate a life devoted to the service of God. It all depends on the spiritual orientation of one's efforts at work, and the manner in which the individual uses or abuses his or her nonlaboring time. This is what God seeks to communicate when He tells Cain that if he does well, his face will be lifted. But Cain remains with his envy and avenges himself on its object.

The first murderer, as the Netziv resurrects him from the text, is not a one-dimensional figure, wicked from the womb. He is a human being very much like us, possessed of a keen sense of what is fair and what is not, and quick to feel hurt and humiliation when his vision of himself and his position in relation to others is confounded.

The Ram in the Thicket

Gail (Giti) Butler Bendheim, November 5, 1997

Both God and man are involved in the efforts of communicating and unifying temporal perspective with Divine aspirations.

AT THE CLIMACTIC MOMENT of the story of the binding of Isaac, Abraham, his hand stretched forth over the beloved son whom he is about to slaughter, is commanded by a heavenly voice to stop. We are then told the following: "And Abraham lifted up his eyes, and looked, and behold behind him a ram caught in a thicket by his horns" (Gen. 22:13).

What are we to make of this ram in the thicket that appears so arrestingly at the climax of this moving story? Should we consider the ram to be preserved in the thicket—an offering from God to Abraham, which will allow Abraham to maintain his humanity—or is the ram trapped there, a victim of conflicting impulses and ensnaring complications?

According to the Jewish Midrashic tradition, this particular ram was one of ten miraculous entities that were fashioned during dusk on the sixth day of creation. These entities were held in their dusk-like state—out of space and out of time—until their moment of usefulness arrived. According to this interpretation, the ram is preserved in the thicket by God for just this very moment, in order to be taken as a substitute for Isaac. This is the ram's purpose in the world, and both the ram and the thicket are passive agents, playing out the will of God.

But there is something not quite passive about this ram. He is, after all, "caught," implying some kind of resistance. Sensitive to this nuance, the Midrash offers another very different scenario that contradicts the traditional notion of an inert and passive creature awaiting its sacred destiny: it was running toward Abraham, but Satan caused it to be caught and entangled among the trees.

This image of a running ram, evoking images of Abraham himself as he runs to welcome a guest, collides with the image of the thicket. The thicket becomes an intervening obstacle that, far from playing out the will of God by preserving the ram, is, instead, an agent of Satan. The ram, eagerly bounding forward to take action in the world, perhaps trying to get to Abraham even before he binds his son, is suddenly and completely routed by the entangling power of evil.

This is a very different story, and it has very different implications for the way man lives his life on earth.

In the first story, God, the omnipotent Creator, runs the world with precise timing, unfailing control, and total engagement, watching over His creatures and choreographing a masterpiece of perfect balance. This is a world of true and simple faith, in which the players are assigned the roles they will play, and in which they play these roles with predictability and precision.

The second story is the more complicated one, and perhaps the one that is truer to the complexities of modern reality. The second story introduces the element of conflict, and the possibility that man is vulnerable to forces in the world from which God may not protect him. In fact, God seems to allow even Himself to be subject to the vagaries of fortune. God sends the ram, but Satan blocks his way, thus changing the course of history.

Who is this Satan who is possessed of such compelling power? Perhaps Satan is emblematic of Abraham's own mistaken understanding of what God has asked of him, and thus of all those aspects of man that can confuse him and distort his sense of purpose as he attempts to act responsibly in the world. Life, in all of its convoluted density, can get in the way of even God's intentions, because life includes the formidable presence of negative forces that challenge man's judgment and his understanding of what God wants of him.

Between God's sending of the ram, and man's receiving it, lies a terrain rich in the potential for productive communication, and rife with opportunities for the breakdown of that link. Both man and God share the overwhelming job of trying to get past all of the obstacles that life places in the way. Often, it must seem to God that man is not trying hard enough; often, man wonders in turn why God seems to have hidden His face. Perhaps the knowledge that, in some way, God and man are partners in this challenge can encourage us, and our leaders, to do our best to prune our side of the thicket.

The Royal Conflict: King David and Michal

Emanuel Feldman, December 3, 1997

This letter advises that differing approaches to Divinity must complement one another, rather than compete for exclusivity.

ONE OF THE CLASSIC domestic disputes in the Bible takes place in the story of King David and his wife Michal (2 Sam. 6:12–23).

David, king of Israel, has finally established Jerusalem as the Holy City, the capital of the land. Many years earlier the Philistines had captured the Holy Ark. King David has now brought the Ark back to Jerusalem, and he leads a great celebration in honor of the event. He is ecstatic, and as verses 14–15 tell us, he dances in the streets "with all his might," leaping and shouting to the sounds of the shofar trumpet. But not everyone is happy. Michal, the queen, watches from the palace window, and as David hops and springs before the populace, she despises him "in her heart."

Finally, the Ark is placed in its special tent. David offers up sacrifices to God, distributes cakes and bread to the people, and returns to his own household to give them blessings.

In verse 20, Michal greets her husband the king with bitter words:

> How glorious was the king of Israel to day, who uncovered himself to day in the eyes of the handmaidens of his servants, as one of the vain fellows shamelessly uncovereth himself! (2 Sam. 6:20)

It is unseemly, unbecoming, unworthy, undignified to behave in such a manner. King David replies:

> It was before the Lord, which chose me before thy father, and before all his house, to appoint me ruler over the people of the Lord, over Israel: therefore will I play before the Lord. And I will yet be more vile than thus, and will be base in mine own sight: and of the maidservants which thou hast spoken of, of them shall I be had in honour. (2 Sam. 6:21–22)

That is, one's own self and one's dignity count for naught when one serves the Lord; only God is noble and has greatness and dignity; man exalts God by humbling himself. And on this note the story ends, with the laconic statement that Michal bore no children.

It is tempting to dismiss Michal out of hand: shrewish, concerned with status, position, and appearances. But Michal is no ordinary person. She is, after all, the daughter of the anointed one, King Saul. She was raised in his palace, and knows something about giving proper honor to the Creator. Surely there is more to this story than its surface reveals, more than a queen angry at her royal husband for dancing in the streets. Perhaps we can hear in this powerful narrative a distant reverberation and echo of something we experienced long before the times of King David.

For the source of this echo we must look at the genealogy of the protagonists: David is a direct descendant of Judah, whose mother is Leah. Michal is the daughter of Saul, who descends from Benjamin, whose mother is Rachel. As we see in the Joseph stories, the children of Rachel and Leah represent two prototypes, two diverse though equally legitimate approaches to God. And in the words that ring out between David and Michal there is somehow an echo of the ancient differences between the children of Rachel and the children of Leah.

The first manifestation of these differences takes place in the conflict between Joseph and his brothers: Joseph, son of Rachel, against the leader of the brothers, Judah, son of Leah. Their dispute concerns the proper way to serve God—not merely the symbolic dispute concerning the cloak of many colors. Is the primary service of God to be open, outward, public—or is He to be served inwardly, quietly, in a hidden way?

Elsewhere we have suggested that Joseph represents the mind, the intellect. He is otherworldly, remote, distant, removed from the mundane things that for him detract from the service of God. Joseph represents the worship of God by solitude, withdrawal, reserve, reflection. By contrast, Judah and the brothers represent the qualities of heart and emotion. God is to be served from within the world, by community, by a coming together, by utilizing and elevating the world.

For Joseph it is enough to love God, to serve Him in quiet ways, concealed behind a veil. It is not necessary to demonstrate to others this love for Him; but for Judah, the love of God is so overwhelming that it must be shared and demonstrated to all, so that others may join in reaching for Him and loving Him. How can love of God, so powerful, be kept to one's own self? As we have already seen, this philosophical conflict has never been resolved throughout Jewish history. It appears here once again, a distant echo of that ancient struggle, in the personalities of Michal and David.

David is the "sweet singer" of Israel. He will serve God in all ways: by composing and singing his psalms, by studying God's word, by prayer. And, if the occasion demands it, he will serve God by dancing, springing, jumping, hopping. He cannot contain his exuberant joy; his inner fire and his enthusiasm know no bounds. And if this king dances together with the commoners, with the servants, with the rabble, what of it? Before God we are all rabble, we are all servants. David's love of God is so overwhelming that it must be shared with others: it cannot remain private, hidden in a quiet corner.

Saul, on the other hand, is contemplative, brooding. Even after Saul is appointed king by Samuel, Saul "hath hid himself among the stuff" (1 Sam. 10:22) (Is this why Saul initially finds David so intriguing and refreshing?) And Michal, the daughter of Saul, tracing her lineage to Joseph and Rachel, approaches God with reserve, thought, inwardness, quiet: God is served in a whisper, just as Rachel whispered her secrets to her sister Leah on the wedding day (Talmud, Tractate Megillah 13b). And when Michal sees her husband the king dancing wildly in public, the ancient dispute erupts once again, and we hear David's angry retort. (There is an interesting echo of the Joseph story here as well: according to Jewish Midrashic tradition, one of the charges that Joseph leveled against Judah and the brothers was that they treated the children of the servant-wives as inferiors. But now King David [Judah] is accused of behaving before the servants as if they were equals. Is this a correction of Judah's mistakes? Or is it an indication that Joseph's original accusation was wrong?)

It is an issue which will remain unresolved until the end of days, when the way of Leah and the way of Rachel, the way of Joseph and the way of Judah, the way of Michal and the way of David—heart and emotion, mind and intellect—all will be seen to be part of the way of God, whom we serve in private and in public, with heart and with mind, in concealment and in openness.

Leaving the Wilderness:
The Sin of the Spies

David Shatz, 1998

Faith and human initiative are often incorrectly presented as an either/or proposition. This letter, within the context of the Jewish people's transition from the wilderness to the land of Israel, considers the balance between man's resourcefulness and God's providence.

IN CHAPTER 13 OF NUMBERS, Moses dispatches twelve spies to the land of Canaan and charges them to report back on the nature of the land and its inhabitants. All but two—Caleb and Joshua—return with a counsel of despair. The Canaanites are powerful, say the scouts; their cities are fortified; and so "we be not able to go up against the people; for they are stronger than we" (Num. 13:31). Fearstruck and disheartened, the Israelites refuse to continue on their journey. Their recalcitrance provokes God's anger and leads to that generation's losing the Promised Land.

The people's despair and lack of faith are hard to comprehend. This is a nation that had witnessed the Ten Plagues, the splitting of the Red Sea, the descent of the manna, and miraculous protection from snakes and scorpions. How could they lose faith so quickly? Didn't their experience tell them that the God who had done all this could deliver the fearsome Canaanites to them as well?

Some interpreters propose an interesting explanation, one that cuts to the very essence of religious faith. Yes, the people recognized God's power, as displayed in Egypt and in the desert. But they also sensed that, in the promised new land, they would be living on new terms and in a new context. In the wilderness, whatever they needed by way of food and protection was provided by God through a steady pattern of miracles. The people did not have to labor; they were not charged with managing their own practical affairs. In the new land, though, things would be different: they would need to work the fields, create an economy, establish a government, and mobilize an army. As Rabbi Jonathan Sacks put it in a recent essay, "Canaan meant emergence, practical responsibility, the work of building up a nation."

This is why the people were afraid. Spirituality, they reasoned, is an either/or proposition. Once you undertake practical initiative, as in the new land, you leave no place for God's workings. You forfeit your special spiritual relationship; your labors cannot be holy. Your fate then depends on nature, on ordinary rational probabilities. Reasoning thus, the people feared what lay ahead—and despaired due to the magnitude of the challenge.

This is a fundamental error. Indeed, the lesson of the episode is that it is a sinful error. Only Caleb and Joshua realized the truth, that spirituality and God's providence do not require a perpetuation of the wilderness, a rarefied passive existence. On the contrary, God's work takes place in the thick of political, economic, and military decisions and initiatives. "Let us go up at once, and possess it; for we are well able to overcome it," Caleb insists (Num. 13:30). God helps those who help themselves, and indeed mandates that people shape their own destiny with wisdom and initiative. Religious faith must operate not in a supernatural sphere—but in the nitty-gritty of ordinary existence and its challenges.

This lesson of the episode of the spies affords an understanding of American society. All across America's life—from medicine to economics, from technology to politics—this country embraces an ethic of initiative, what the late Rabbi Joseph B. Soloveitchik called the stance of "majesty." Yet many of our citizens are also people of deep religious faith. America's is not a faith that counsels quietism and frowns upon human effort; it is rather the faith of Caleb and Joshua. We affirm that "in God we trust," but we trust our own judgment and ability too. We know that if the Lord does not "build the house, they labour in vain that build it" (Ps. 127:1). But we recognize that God will bless the builders' labors only if they do their proper share.

Hannah's Prayer

Menachem Genack, February 26, 1998

Prayer that emerges from total despondency has a distinctive ability to change one's circumstances.

HANNAH'S PRAYER serves in the Bible as the model for the silent petition, the unenunciated supplication. "And it came to pass, as she continued praying before the Lord, that Eli marked her mouth. Now Hannah, she spake in her heart; only her lips moved, but her voice was not heard" (1 Sam. 1:12–13).

Hannah prayed for a son, and God delivered her from her tortured state of barrenness. She conceived and gave birth to the prophet Samuel. Why was this particular prayer of Hannah's answered? Why not all the innumerable other times that she undoubtedly prayed for a child? What was unique about this time when she "poured out [her] soul before the Lord" (1 Sam. 1:15)?

Hannah had a loving, caring husband, Elkanah. Upon seeing Hannah's tears and pain and her torment by her rival, Peninnah [Elkanah's second wife], Elkanah tried to console his cherished wife Hannah: "Then said Elkanah her husband to her, Hannah, why weepest thou? . . . am not I better to thee than ten sons?" (1 Sam. 1:8). Hannah immediately arose, "And she was in bitterness of soul, and prayed unto the Lord, and wept sore" (1 Sam. 1:10).

Rabbi Joseph B. Soloveitchik suggested that until that day, Hannah's burden of her barrenness, and her prayerful hope to be fulfilled and bear a child, was carried by both her and Elkanah. But now Hannah realized that Elkanah had given up all hope of having children by her and had resigned himself to Hannah's infertility. "Am I not better to thee than ten sons?"

Hannah in her utter loneliness . . . dependent now only on God, prayed— a silent prayer, heard by no one but God. "Out of the depths have I cried unto thee, O Lord" (Ps. 130:1). That prayer was like none ever heard before. And:

> Elkanah knew Hannah his wife; and the Lord remembered her.
> Wherefore it came to pass, when the time was come about after
> Hannah had conceived, that she bare a son, and called his name
> Samuel, saying, Because I have asked him of the Lord." (1 Sam.
> 1:19–20)

Abraham

Menachem Genack, March 2, 1998

Abraham's life balanced the ideals of logical reasoning and faithful dedication in the service of God.

ABRAHAM IS INTRODUCED to us in the Bible as a man isolated and lonely. He proclaims God and a new monotheistic theology in a world that had completely forgotten Him. That expression of total loneliness comes to its peak at the Akedah, the binding of Isaac. Indeed, *ivri*, the word for "Hebrew" applied to Abraham in Genesis 14:13 ["There came one that had escaped, and told Abram the Hebrew"], according to the rabbis also means "opposite shore"; for Abraham was on one shore, and the entire world was on the opposite shore. This could have precipitated in Abraham a sense of isolation, frustration, bitterness, and misanthropy. But he remains the paradigm of kindness, hospitality, love, and concern—even for the iniquitous cities of Sodom and Gomorrah. Truth and compassion are often mutually exclusive attributes. Abraham represents the bond between the two. In the words of the Psalmist, "Mercy and truth are met together; righteousness and peace have kissed each other" (Ps. 85:10). Tradition teaches that Abraham discovers God through logic. He argues that a universe so perfectly ordered must be created, and that the Author of nature must have a relationship with His creatures. Abraham is so driven by the force of reason that he even argues with God in defense of Sodom, that He must conform to a universal ethical standard: "Shall not the Judge of all the earth do right?" (Gen. 18:25). Yet Abraham is willing to succumb to the Divine imperative to slaughter his only son. . . . In the process, he is willing to sacrifice his concept of reason and justice, in the face of God's terrifying command.

Abraham's greatness unfolds as he lives between the tension of mutually exclusive experiences, and encompasses conflicting emotions and ideas. He is not vanquished or diminished by the anguish of the paradox and contradiction but, on the contrary, is elevated by it. He emerges as the man of faith, thus achieving a heroic existence.

The Expulsion of Ishmael and the Binding of Isaac

Uriel Simon, April 3, 1998

This letter presents a remarkable analytic comparison between Abraham's binding of his son Isaac and his decision to expel his son Ishmael. Clinton invested a great deal of time in trying to bring peace between the Arabs and Jews. He would often note that they both descend from Abraham. This missive emphasizes their common ancestry and parallel biblical experiences.

THERE ARE MANY OBVIOUS AFFINITIES, in both content and language, between the expulsion of Ishmael (Gen. 21) and the binding of Isaac (Gen. 22). In both cases, the patriarch Abraham is commanded to part from a son forever, and this parting carries with it a threat of death—potential death in one case, certain death in the other. In both cases the Bible stresses the magnitude of the loss: Regarding Ishmael and his mother, the Lord says to Abraham, "Let it not be grievous in thy sight because of the lad, and because of thy bondwoman" (Gen. 21:12); while the threefold elaboration in the command to Abraham—"Take now thy son, thine only son Isaac, whom thou lovest" (Gen. 22:2)—serves to underline how precious Isaac is to his father.

On both occasions, Abraham's response is immediate, unquestioning:

> And Abraham rose up early in the morning, and took bread,
> and a bottle of water, and gave it unto Hagar, putting it on her
> shoulder, and the child, and sent her away: and she departed, and
> wandered in the wilderness. (Gen. 21:14)

The wording in Isaac's case is similar:

> And Abraham rose up early in the morning . . . and took two of
> his young men with him, and Isaac his son . . . and rose up, and
> went unto the place. (Gen. 22:3) [And on the third day] Abraham
> took the wood of the burnt offering, and laid it upon Isaac his
> son. (Gen. 22:6)

In both stories the reader is convinced that the young lad's death is imminent: Ishmael seems doomed in view of his mother's profound despair:

> She cast the child under one of the shrubs . . . [and] said, Let me
> not see the death of the child. And she sat over against him, and
> lift up her voice, and wept. (Gen. 21:15–16)

And Isaac likewise appears doomed, as his father seems absolutely determined to go ahead with the sacrifice: "And Abraham stretched forth his hand,
and took the knife to slay his son" (Gen. 22:10).

In both cases, heavenly salvation comes in the blink of an eye: "And the
angel of God called to Hagar out of heaven, and said unto her, What aileth
thee, Hagar? fear not" (Gen. 21:17); and again in the same vein, "And the
angel of the Lord called unto him [Abraham] out of heaven, and said . . . Lay
not thine hand upon the lad" (Gen. 22:11–12).

This message of salvation enhances the parents' eyesight; they suddenly
perceive something they could not see before, and act accordingly: "And God
opened her eyes, and she saw a well of water; and she went, and filled the
bottle with water, and gave the lad drink" (Gen. 21:19). Similarly, "And
Abraham lifted up his eyes, and looked, and behold behind him a ram caught
in a thicket by his horns: and Abraham . . . offered him up for a burnt offering
in the stead of his son" (Gen. 22:13).

Each son now receives a blessing in keeping with the gravity of the previously threatening danger; rather than suffering death and oblivion, Abraham's
progeny will be fruitful and multiply, to become a great nation. God promises
Hagar that "I will make [Ishmael] a great nation" (Gen. 21:18); a similar, but
even greater, future is predicted for Abraham himself, through Isaac:

> That in blessing I will bless thee, and in multiplying I will
> multiply thy seed as the stars of the heaven, and as the sand which
> is upon the sea shore; and thy seed shall possess the gate of his
> enemies; And in thy seed shall all the nations of the earth be
> blessed. (Gen. 22:17–18)

. . . What is the possible meaning of this consistent, obvious parallelism?
First and foremost, we realize that by banishing Ishmael, Abraham was, just
as in the second story, both objectively and subjectively giving up his son.

Thus the binding of Isaac as an offering was preceded by Abraham's giving up his firstborn son; similarly, Ishmael's expulsion was preceded by God's first commandment to Abraham, to give up his parents and kin, to cut off all contact with his origins: "Get thee out of thy country, and from thy kindred, and from thy father's house, unto a land that I will shew thee" (Gen. 12:1). But this last parting, from Isaac, is radically different from the first two: while the first partings had a well-defined purpose—"And I will make of thee a great nation" (Gen. 12:2), on the one hand, and "for in Isaac shall thy seed be called" (Gen. 21:12), on the other—the binding of Isaac is so fearful precisely because it demands that that very purpose be sacrificed.

Common to the expulsion of Ishmael and the binding of Isaac is that, in both cases, the terrible pain of irreversibly giving up a beloved son is compounded by pangs of conscience, aroused by what is basically an immoral act. Commanded to offer up Isaac as a sacrifice, Abraham is required to commit bloodshed; while in regard to Ishmael, the Lord instructs Abraham to obey Sarah—but she is demanding that he disinherit his own son, banishing him and his mother, penniless and helpless, to the forbidding wilderness between Canaan and Egypt: "Cast out this bondwoman and her son: for the son of this bondwoman shall not be heir with my son, even with Isaac" (Gen. 21:10). As explained by the medieval Jewish commentator Abraham Ibn Ezra:

> Many wonder at Abraham—how could he banish his own
> son, also evicting son and mother with nothing? Where was
> his generosity? Indeed, we may wonder at those who wonder,
> for Abraham was simply doing the Lord's bidding, and had he
> given Hagar money against Sarah's will, he would not have been
> observing the Lord's command. In fact, after Sarah's death he
> indeed gave gifts to the sons of Ishmael (Ibn Ezra, Gen. 21:14).

Now, as God had never actually intended Isaac to be sacrificed but intended only to test Abraham, He could not have told Abraham in advance that he would not have to shed his son's blood, and that the lad would live and prosper. As far as Ishmael was concerned, however, Abraham was informed beforehand that the expulsion was necessary in order to accomplish the different national goals that God envisaged for the two sons and, moreover, that the youth would survive his ordeal:

Let it not be grievous in thy sight because of the lad, and because of thy bondwoman; in all that Sarah hath said unto thee, hearken unto her voice; for in Isaac shall thy seed be called. And also of the son of the bondwoman will I make a nation, because he is thy seed. (Gen. 21:12–13)

That the Torah is extremely sensitive to the ethical aspect of the two partings is also indicated by the parallels between the names given the two sons. Isaac's name, derived from a Hebrew word meaning "laughter," commemorates his miraculous birth, as both his parents had expressed, through concealed laughter, their despair of bearing a child: "Then Abraham fell upon his face, and laughed, and said in his heart, Shall a child be born unto him that is an hundred years old? and shall Sarah, that is ninety years old, bear?" (Gen. 17:17). Similarly, "Sarah laughed within herself, saying, After I am waxed old shall I have pleasure, my lord being old also?" (Gen. 18:12). When the promise was fulfilled and the child was indeed born, Sarah expressed her thanks by investing the name with an added meaning: "God hath made me to laugh, so that all that hear will laugh with me" (Gen. 21:6). Ishmael's name too is an expression of thanks—it means "God will hear." For when Hagar was fleeing her mistress Sarah, the angel of the Lord promised her: "Behold, thou art with child and shalt bear a son, and shalt call his name Ishmael; because the Lord hath heard thy affliction" (Gen. 16:11). And now that the angel has come to save the lad from dying of thirst, he too underscores the glad news by giving the name an added twist, also signifying ready response: "Fear not, for God hath heard the voice of the lad where he is" (Gen. 21:17).

Pharaoh's Irony

Menachem Genack, April 7, 1998

God's plans always account for—sometimes in ironic ways—efforts to thwart His plans.

THE ANCIENT JEWISH Midrashic tradition teaches that Pharaoh's astrologers glimpse the future and predict that Pharaoh's ultimate nemesis will be subdued by water. Indeed, Moses, who will redeem the Jews from the bondage in Egypt and bring Pharaoh and his empire crashing down, will be punished by God: He is not allowed to enter the Promised Land, because he hit, rather than spoke to, a rock while trying to get water out of it.

Pharaoh, hoping to sabotage his future antagonist in a way that also fulfills the vision of his astrologers, brutally orders that all male children be drowned in the waters of the Nile (Exod. 1:22).

Moses's parents save their new infant by hiding him in a basket among the reeds at the edge of the Nile, where he is watched over by his sister. Pharaoh's daughter, while bathing in the Nile, finds this baby and adopts him and raises him as her own (Exod. 2:2–10).

The extraordinary irony is that Pharaoh, in his cruel attempt to destroy a future threat, brings that threat even closer to himself. As a result of Pharaoh's terrible decree, Moses is placed in the basket, to be found by Pharaoh's daughter and raised in the royal court. There he learns, as a prince of Egypt, safely ensconced in Pharaoh's house, the skills of leadership needed to ultimately challenge Pharaoh and save his people, the Israelites.

Pharaoh arrogantly tries to force God's hand, but as events unfold, he is entrapped by his own evil devices.

> There are many devices in a man's heart; nevertheless the counsel
> of the Lord, that shall stand. (Prov. 19:21)

Looking Over Serah's Shoulder

Yaakov Elman, July 8, 1998

Many passages in the Bible recount temporal and mundane matters; buried within these litanies lies a comfort of sorts regarding God's compassion and concern for all of life's details.

SCRIPTURALLY, WE ARE ALL second-class citizens—if not worse. Scripture itself testifies of Moses that his like will never arise again (Deut. 34:10). But we are not Abrahams, we are not even Balaams—we are not even at the level of Balaam's donkey, who saw an angel. When was the last time God spoke to one of us directly, face-to-face and not in dreams, in words and not in symbols? When did we last see an angel with a sword raised in his hand? When did the fire descend from Heaven when we opened our mouths in praise? Not to put too fine a point on it, when was the last time anyone added a book to Scripture? Or a chapter to the Koran, for that matter?

We live in an orphaned age, when the word of God is mediated to us by holy texts, enshrined in tradition and traditional understanding.

But the problem goes beyond that. Even those of us who hold the doctrine of *sola scriptura* ["by scripture alone"], and who approach the Bible directly without the mediation of experts or clergy but with the aid of our own religious impulses, must still deal with the cardinal problem posed by Scripture: We are clearly not its intended audience, except at second remove.

Moses is told over and over again: "Speak to the Children of Israel." Not, let it be noted, the Israelites and the Jews of the First Temple period, or of the Second Temple period—Jews of the *land* of Israel—and not the Jews, the Christians, and the Muslims of Spain, nor to us.

Thus, we read in exacting detail of the intricacies of the construction of the Tabernacle, of the sacrificial service offered during the first week of its inauguration—a service that will never be repeated. We read of people who, but for their mention in the Pentateuch, would have been totally forgotten and, but for those of us who study the Bible quite closely, hardly exist.

What did Serah, daughter of Asher, do to have merited a mention in the Bible? Presumably her contemporaries knew, but we do not—but she appears twice in the Bible (Gen. 46:17 and Num. 26:46). Unless we resort to rabbinic tradition, we have no idea of her significance. What lesson does her (unrecorded) life hold for us? Moreover, the broader question must be asked: What lesson is all of the time-bound material in an eternal document meant to teach us? Why must we know, for instance, the names of all the camping spots at which the Israelites stopped during their wanderings in the wilderness?

The first eleven chapters of Genesis form an introduction to universal human history; the rest deals with the history of those Israelites who, saved from the rigors of an Egyptian enslavement, *saw* God's saving hand at the Red Sea, *heard* His voice at Sinai. And even if we cannot see God with our own eyes, or hear Him with our own ears, we are there, standing on the shores of the sea, in terror of the pursuing Egyptians, and trembling before the thunder at Sinai. It is to them that God speaks, for them He legislates, to them He shows Himself. We Jews, Christians, and Muslims are the Johnny-come-latelies, standing on tiptoe, trying to catch a glimpse of what they saw clearly.

But there is hope for us. Despite the Israelites' direct relationship to God, ensured by the presence of the Tabernacle in their midst, by the fire and voice descending from Heaven, they failed in their duty to God, time and again. As proof of their failure we need look no further than that revelation itself. And yet their failures *became* part of that revelation.

There is no universal human being; there are only individuals, mostly acting together, sometimes acting alone, occasionally getting it right, often getting it wrong. Jewish mystics declare that not one, but six hundred thousand revelations were given over at Sinai, each one refracted through the consciousness of one of the individuals who was there. The human race is an abstraction; only human *beings* exist, and the details of their lives, the humdrum concreteness of their existence, are important. According to Scripture, what we eat and how we eat, how we engage in all the activities that make us human, is *important to God*.

There are also no universal generations. God speaks to individual generations, and particular groups—but He allows the rest of us to overhear Him. "And because he loved thy fathers, therefore he chose their seed after them" (Deut. 4:37). As the renowned Jewish philosopher and legal scholar Maimonides noted, God's ways are different from ours. He spoke to the Israelites gathered around the mountain, in their language, to their concerns; but His intended audience was clearly all of humanity. His love for Abraham included his descendants; His concern for those descendants included the entire human race.

Jethro came to witness and went home to Midian with a report of what he had seen. The Scriptural record is *our* Jethro.

The Tabernacle was the concrete embodiment of God's love and concern for those who stood around Sinai. His account of that Tabernacle, carried down the generations, is the concrete embodiment of His love and concern for all of us. Though we no longer have the Tabernacle, nor the pillar of fire, that love and concern is still available to us, as Scripture testifies. The same God Who cared for Serah, daughter of Asher, cares for every one of us—even me. Scripture's mundane, time-bound descriptions comfort me as much as do its eternal verities.

Go Forth

Menachem Genack, December 2, 1998

Faith requires sacrifice—sometimes of one's past, at other times of one's future.

THE BIBLE INTRODUCES two of Abraham's trials—his leaving his homestead in Ur Kaśdim, and the binding of Isaac—with the identical Hebrew phrase, *lech lecha*, meaning "go forth," which does not appear at any other place in the Bible. In both trials, Abraham is told to go to a land not yet designated, but to be revealed later:

> Now the Lord had said unto Abram, Get thee [go forth] out of thy country, and from thy kindred, and from thy father's house, unto a land that I will shew thee. (Gen. 12:1)

> And he said, Take now thy son, thine only son Isaac, whom thou lovest, and get thee [go forth] into the land of Moriah; and offer him there for a burnt offering upon one of the mountains which I will tell thee of. (Gen. 22:2)

Clearly, the Bible means to associate these two dramatic events. In the first trial, Abraham is told to leave his familiar surroundings, the house of his father, the society and civilization of which he has always been part. Abraham does not hesitate; he is willing to uproot himself from his secure, known environment to travel toward an unknown, unrevealed land. In a word, Abraham is willing, at God's command, to sacrifice his entire past.

On the other hand, when Abraham is willing to heed the terrible Divine command to sacrifice his son Isaac, who was born to him and his wife, Sarah, in their old age, and about whom God had promised "in Isaac shall thy seed be called" (Gen. 21:12), Abraham is ready to sacrifice his *future*. Abraham, the ever-obedient servant of God, the knight of faith, is prepared to sacrifice everything for God—even his future and his past.

When Abraham pleads that God save the evil cities of Sodom and Gomorrah, he says, "Behold now, I have taken upon me to speak unto the Lord, which am but dust and ashes" (Gen. 18:27). The nineteenth-century commentator Rabbi Yosef Ber Soloveitchik interprets Abraham's statement as follows: Dust has no past, but has great potential, and can be cultivated and bring forth fruit—and thus, it has a future. Ashes, on the contrary, had a past, but now have no future. Abraham is humbly affirming by his choice of words that without God's grace, he has neither future nor past.

History records that because of Abraham's incomparable faith and heroic existence, the world was endowed with a great legacy—belief in the one God, Creator of the universe—and with a tradition of love and kindness, which inspires us to hope for a better future.

A Book Unto Itself

Maurice Lamm, 1999

This letter examines the nuanced message contained within Israel's prayer when approaching war.

STUDENTS OF THE BIBLE refer to the Five Books of Moses. But the leading jurist in Jewish history, Rabbi Judah the Prince (second century CE), editor of the Mishnah—the collection of rabbinic texts that underlies the Talmud— said that actually there are not *five* books, but seven.

Two verses, Numbers 10:35–36, are the only verses in the Torah scroll bracketed with parentheses, formed by an upside-down Hebrew letter. [The letter *nun*, phonetically like the letter "n," is the fourteenth letter in the Hebrew alphabet. It looks much like a bracket.] These verses by themselves form a separate book of the Bible, with its own integrity. The seven books would then be Genesis, Exodus, Leviticus, the first part of Numbers until the parenthesis, verses 35 and 36, the remaining part of Numbers, and Deuteronomy.

Today, these two verses are chanted at the central moment of the Jewish service—when the congregation rises to greet the Torah scroll as it is taken from the Ark to be read.

Here, then, is the fifth book of the Bible, in its entirety:

> And it came to pass, when the ark set forward, that Moses said,
> Rise up, Lord, and let thine enemies be scattered; and let them
> that hate thee flee before thee. And when it rested, he said,
> Return, O Lord, unto the many thousands of Israel.

Understood in context, the significance of these words does indeed make them worthy of being a separate book. The verses constitute the battle hymn of the nation, sung as the soldiers marched behind the Holy Ark, fully armed and prepared to do combat. But they did not seek blood or vengeance or massacre.

They implored God to "rise up"—to appear so awesome that the enemy would flee rather than fight, scatter rather than do battle. Mobilized for war, the soldiers yet had a deep-seated yearning to find peace, not triumph; to achieve victory, without vanquishing.

It is the war we avoid, not the war we win, that makes us strong. This is the irony: to avoid war, we must already be strong. Only the strong sing the ultimate prayer of the battle hymn: "Return unto the families." Is not this the prayer of America and its commander-in-chief? "Be strong, so that even those who hate us will flee."

The two verses are a book unto themselves.

That this eloquent sentiment still lives was articulated best by the pithiest statement ever made about war. Jan Masaryk [Czech foreign minister 1940–48] said: "I want to go home."

The Two Camps

Menachem Genack, December 16, 1999

Jacob, when faced with destruction, finds strength in God's protection.

"I AM NOT WORTHY of the least of all the mercies, and of all the truth, which thou hast shewed unto thy servant; for with my staff I passed over this Jordan; and now I am become two bands (Gen. 32:10)."

Jacob, returning to the land of Canaan from his sojourn with his treacherous father-in-law, Laban, is fearful of his encounter with his brother, Esau. Jacob splits his camp in two, "And said, If Esau come to the one company, and smite it, then the other company which is left shall escape" (Gen. 32:8). Thus, in a moment of great danger and distress, Jacob splits his camp in two. How then, when he prays to God, and recounts all God's kindnesses to him, does he state that he is now become two camps? The two camps of Jacob are not a result of the waxing of his might, but an indication of crisis and vulnerability.

The answer, I believe, is that Jacob is not referring to the two camps that he has divided, but rather to the two camps of angels he had met upon entering the land of Canaan. "And Jacob went on his way, and the angels of God met him. And when Jacob saw them, he said, This is God's host: and he called the name of that place Mahanaim [two camps]" (Gen. 32:1–2).

At his moment of maximum exposure and danger, as he contemplates his divided camp, Jacob sees in his mind's eye the two camps of angels that he had met earlier. Though isolated and imperiled, Jacob is not forlorn and without hope, for behind his seemingly feeble two camps stand two camps of angels, protecting and defending him and his people. It is that unseen reality to which Jacob refers that gives him—the man of faith—solace and hope.

The Bible thus teaches us a lesson of faith. When we seem most lonely and deserted, God's Providence and protection is always with us, and He never abandons us. "For he shall give his angels charge over thee, to keep thee in all thy ways" (Ps. 91:11).

And Jacob Was Left Alone

Martin E. Marty, September 11, 2000

A brief and powerful lesson from Jacob's lonely battle: With the wound comes the blessing.

"AND JACOB WAS LEFT alone" (Gen. 32:24). Surround himself with as much company as he would like: still Jacob, like so many others, found that the really decisive things in life came when he was "left alone." In Jacob's case, the isolation ended when "a man" came and "wrestled . . . with him until the breaking of the day" (Gen. 32:24). A man: *ish*, in Hebrew, yes, "a man." But also a somehow Divine being, for at the end of the wrestling, Jacob said, "I have seen God face to face" (Gen. 32:30). Some think Jacob was wrestling with Jacob, in an internal struggle—good Jacob versus bad Jacob. We can stay with the economical Pentateuchal version, not needing to resolve an age-old question about the identity of "a man."

Instead the focus falls on the wrestling match itself and its consequences. Strong Jacob (Gen. 29:10, 28:18) could not prevail, nor could "a man." Unfair, we might say, when we hear that Jacob was wounded in the thigh by the anonymous antagonist. But even with that advantage, *ish* was not strong enough to break Jacob's desperate hold.

Morning nears.

"Let me go," *ish* pleads (Gen. 32:26). Jacob: "I will not let thee go, except thou bless me" (Gen. 32:26). Fair enough. And after a conversation about names and a name change for Jacob, "he [*ish*] blessed him [Jacob] there" (Gen. 32:29).

What we take from this encounter in which Jacob sees God face-to-face while wrestling, and because he wrestled, can be this: As with Jacob, you do not get the blessing until and unless you have been wounded. And you are not left alone to cope with your wound. With the wound comes the blessing.

The theme of the interplay of wound and blessing courses throughout the patriarchal stories. It informs those stories and our lives.

And, by the way, the new name for Jacob was, is: Israel.

THE WHITE HOUSE

WASHINGTON

September 19, 2000

Rabbi Menachem Genack
Orthodox Union
Union of Orthodox Jewish Congregations
     of America
11 Broadway
New York, New York 10004

Dear Rabbi Genack:

Thanks for sending the latest missive. I
always appreciate the time you take in
presenting me with important lessons from
Scripture.

I've also written Dr. Marty a note of thanks.
Again, thank you, and best wishes.

Sincerely,

Bill Clinton

For I Shall Be With You

Menachem Genack, February 10, 2001

Through faith we can transcend our obvious limitations and connect to the infinite. On his last day in office President Clinton issued 140 pardons and commutations. He was criticized for some of them and was despondent about the barrage of criticism. On February 18, 2001, he wrote an op-ed in the *New York Times* defending his pardon of Marc Rich (he later stated he regretted granting the pardon). This letter was intended to give him some measure of solace during this period.

> And Moses said unto the Lord, O my Lord, I am not eloquent, neither heretofore, nor since thou hast spoken unto thy servant: but I am slow of speech, and of a slow tongue. And the Lord said unto him, Who hath made man's mouth? or who maketh the dumb, or deaf, or the seeing, or the blind? have not I the Lord? (Exod. 4:10–11)

MOSES, THE MOST RELUCTANT of prophets, feels unworthy to be God's messenger. How can I, Moses argues, a stutterer, be God's spokesman and deliver His message to Pharaoh? God's response is that He who gave speech to man will facilitate Moses's tongue to speak before Pharaoh.

Jewish tradition in the Midrash, quoted by Rashi, interprets God's answer metaphorically as a reference to the time when Moses escapes from Egypt and from Pharaoh's henchmen after killing an Egyptian who was smiting a slave. The Midrash reads:

> Who made Pharaoh mute, that he did not immediately order your execution, and his agents deaf, that they did not hear Pharaoh's order to have you killed? And who made Pharaoh's assassins blind that they did not see you as you escaped? (Rashi, Exod. 4:11)

Moses feels that he is unqualified for his great historic mission. And God tells him that He does not mean to send him alone; "I will be with thee" (Exod. 3:12). Look around, Moses; not only will I be with you, unseen and unbeknownst to you, as you appear before Pharaoh, but I have always been standing next to you. Moses, how do you think you survived Pharaoh and his assassins? It was only because I was ever by your side.

After Egypt had been afflicted with seven plagues, God tells Moses, "Come to Pharaoh" (Exod. 10:1),* and Moses tells Pharaoh of the next impending disaster—the plague of locusts. Rabbi Joseph B. Soloveitchik pointed out the strange phrase in the Bible, "Come to Pharaoh." It more appropriately should have said, "Go to Pharaoh." God, Rabbi Soloveitchik explained, is telling Moses that, when I send you to Pharaoh, I will be there with you in Pharaoh's palace. Indeed, I will be there even before you appear. So, God says not "Go to Pharaoh," but "Come to Pharaoh."

The Bible's message is not limited to Moses, but is directed to each of us. As we are confronted with what seem insurmountable challenges to be met with our very finite abilities, we must remember that God is always standing next to us, giving us the strength to endure, and even the potential to be triumphant.

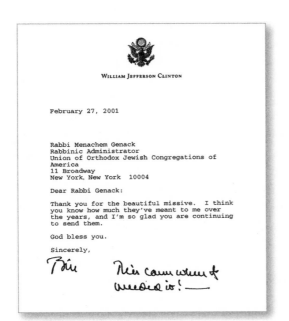

WILLIAM JEFFERSON CLINTON

February 27, 2001

Rabbi Menachem Genack
Rabbinic Administrator
Union of Orthodox Jewish Congregations of America
11 Broadway
New York, New York 10004

Dear Rabbi Genack:

Thank you for the beautiful missive. I think you know how much they've meant to me over the years, and I'm so glad you are continuing to send them.

God bless you.

Sincerely,

Bill

This came when
I needed it!

---

* Although the phrase "Come to Pharaoh" (Exod. 10:1) is typically rendered as "Go to Pharaoh," in the original Hebrew the word used is *bo*, meaning "to come," as opposed to *lech*, meaning "to go," which is used when God commands Abraham (see the first paragraph in the letter titled "Go Forth," page 179).

Remembering History, Remembering Amalek

Elyakim Rubinstein, January 27, 2013

Elyakim Rubinstein sent this missive to President Clinton on International Holocaust Remembrance Day—January 27, the date in 1945 that Auschwitz was liberated. In his cover letter to the president Justice Rubinstein wrote, "Thank God, we now have a Jewish—and democratic—state of our own; never again will wandering Jewish refugees knock on closed doors for a haven."

HISTORY IS CONSTANTLY on the mind of a Jew. On Passover he sits at the Seder table and reenacts the Exodus from Egypt. On Sukkot he sits outdoors with his family in a booth as his patriarchs did in the desert. On Purim and on Hanukkah he reads about and recalls the glorious victories of his ancestors. Few events in the life of a Jew are not in one way or another a *zikaron*, a remembrance, of an earlier event. The Sabbath is called by the prayer book a "remembrance" of the act of creation. God's subtle hand becomes evident through history, and it is by reflecting on history that a Jew renews his faith in God's providence. And it is through *zikaron*, remembering, that the Jews have survived so many difficult periods in their long diaspora.

Early in their life as a nation, the Jews learned of the importance of the concept of *zikaron*. Soon after the Jews left Egypt they were attacked by the people of Amalek. After a difficult battle the Jews defeated Amalek. Afterward God exhorts Moses to "Write this for a remembrance (*zikaron*) in a book and rehearse it in the ears of Joshua: for I will utterly put out the memory (*zecher*) of Amalek from under heaven" (Exod. 17:14).

Who was [the nation of] Amalek and why was it so important that God wipe out all memory of them? And why did Moses have to write it down as a remembrance? After all, Moses wrote down everything God told him— without God's prompting him Moses would have dutifully written down this episode anyway. Amalek, according to many Jewish thinkers, is not only a reference to the biblical/historical people. In ancient times, King Sennacherib of Assyria removed borders and dispersed peoples, and the result was a disruption of historical continuity. We can no longer identify in flesh and blood the descendants of the archenemies of the Jews. But we can identify the spirit of Amalek. Amalek, in biblical times, attacked the Jews for a single purpose: to divert the Jews from their goal, which was to make known the role of God in this world. Because Amalek was the first of all nations to attack the Jewish nation, Amalek became the standard-bearer of any force bent on tearing away at Divine Providence.

For Amalek, rather, the world is anarchic and directionless. History . . . contains no meaningful narrative. In Deuteronomy the language the Bible uses to describe Amalek's encounter with the Jews is [one] of happenstance. "Remember what Amalek did unto thee by the way, when ye were come forth out of Egypt" (Deut. 25:17). Happenstance neatly summarizes the weltanschauung of Amalek: Ultimately there is no real meaning behind events.

God tells Moses that He will wipe out the memory of Amalek. He doesn't say that He will wipe out the nation of Amalek. What God means is that at the dawn of redemption those who attack the concept that there is a God, that there is a Providence, will be eradicated from the world. This is what the Jewish people should remember.

Because this point is so important in sustaining the Jewish people through the long period before God will carry out the promise conveyed in the verse, God tells Moses, "Write this for a remembrance in a book.". . . But as a father relates a story to his son and yet, in the middle, tells him to remember this, so too God tells Moses to take this point, above everything else, to heart.

28 Feb. 2013

Dear Elyakim,

Thank you for your article on Remembrance and the Jewish ethos which I found fascinating.

And thank you for your service to Israel and the cause of peace during and after Prime Minister Rabin's tenure. I miss him still.

Sincerely,

Bill Clinton

Dreams and Vision

President Clinton's appreciation of the importance of vision for a society in transition was one of the factors that inspired me to begin our correspondence. Throughout his tenure, the contributors stressed vision as a necessary element of leadership. Part of vision means being optimistic even during the bleakest of times. It means having the courage to stick with one's dream despite a chorus of naysayers. It requires the willpower and imagination to see beyond the limitations of the present. As we witness dizzying transformations in our social and economic environment, as methods and speed of communication change dramatically, it is as crucial as ever to have leaders who can anticipate the direction in which our society needs to go.

The Bible is replete with dreams and dreamers, but no biblical account captures so dramatically the compelling need of the leader to dream, and the challenge of translating the dream into reality, as the story of Joseph. Chief Rabbi Jonathan Sacks sees Joseph the dreamer as the paradigm for all great visionaries. He invokes the memory of Theodor Herzl, who dreamed of a homeland for the Jewish people in Israel and overcame skepticism and opposition to found a movement that realized this historic dream. As Rabbi Sacks writes, "Dreams are where leadership is born. Holding fast to them is where it is tested. Those who manage both are those who change the world."

In the summer of 1999, during the deliberations on the federal budget, President Clinton asked me for a biblical perspective on budgetary matters. In my missive "The Seven Fat Years," I noted the observation of Nachmanides that Joseph audaciously went beyond what was requested of him—an interpretation of Pharaoh's dream. After interpreting the dream, he forged ahead and, unsolicited, offered his own economic solution to the coming famine foretold by the dream—the excess produce from the seven fat years must be stored as a reserve for the seven lean years. The essence of leadership is to be able, in years of plenty, to see the challenges beyond the horizon. So too, in our own time and our own country, those who determine fiscal policy must recognize that the cycle will turn, and that we need to husband the wealth generated during times of prosperity to sustain us during times of economic contraction.

The eminent scientist Professor Samuel Danishefsky closely reads the biblical text and discerns that Joseph's brothers expressed their hatred for Joseph even before they heard the substance of his dreams. The message is that the dreamer faces inherent skepticism and hostility from the nondreamer regardless of the contents of the dream.

The Joseph story is not the only biblical narrative from which we can draw lessons of vision for the future. Abraham received God's promise that his descendants would be enslaved in a foreign country for four hundred years before inheriting the Promised Land. One contributor writes that Abraham's commitment was "right now," but the culmination was generations hence. Every leader is faced with the tension between making a decision that is popular and satisfying in the short run and being responsible to destiny. Abraham was the paradigm of the man of faith and vision, a model for all leaders.

In my missive on the significance of the tzitzit, the four-cornered fringed garment, I note its proximity in the biblical text to the narrative of the twelve spies, leaders of the tribes, sent by Moses to survey the land of Canaan. The spies who counseled against proceeding to the Promised Land were guilty of myopia. All they could see was the challenge of an unforgiving land populated by fierce inhabitants. Shortly thereafter, the Bible records God's commandment to the Jewish people to wear a four-cornered garment with fringes, each fringe containing a blue thread. When gazing upon the blue of the thread, the sages say, one is reminded of the blue of the ocean, and the ocean mirrors the blue of the sky, and the sky reflects the hue of God's throne of glory. Gazing upon the tzitzit is to elevate our vision so it is not limited only to the here and now but perceives that which is boundless and transcendent, and glimpses the distant horizon.

Joseph and His Brothers

Menachem Genack, August 15, 1996

President Clinton has often spoken of the dramatic economic changes that are present and will continue to emerge in the new Information Age. The ensuing changes, representing both great opportunities and dislocations, will be as profound as when America in the last century changed from an agrarian to an industrial society, and people emigrated from rural environments to urban centers. The following missive notes a biblical antecedent to this kind of change.

RABBI JOSEPH B. SOLOVEITCHIK suggested that Joseph's prophetic recognition of impending economic and social changes, and his constant warning to his brothers to prepare to confront a new economic reality, was a source of tension between him and his brothers. Yet Joseph, though misunderstood and despised by his brothers, saved Jacob's household from starvation. Rabbi Soloveitchik once said:

> What in truth had disturbed Joseph's peace of mind? In regard
> to such matters, our sages have said: "A man's dreams bespeak
> his innermost thoughts and feelings." What did Joseph seek? To
> what did he aspire? What foreboding troubled him? The answer
> is: an obscure feeling of insecurity frightened him. What were
> the elements of this insecurity?—the biblical Joseph was not
> persuaded that "and Jacob dwelt in the land wherein his father
> was a stranger" (Gen. 37:1) would endure for long. The words
> "thy seed shall be a stranger in a land that is not theirs" (Gen.
> 15:13) kept tolling in his ears. He saw himself and his brothers
> in an alien environment, far from the land of Canaan, in new
> circumstances and under new conditions of life. In his dream
> he saw "behold, we were binding sheaves" (Gen. 37:7): we are
> no longer in Canaan, we are in the land of Egypt and can no
> longer be shepherds. We are integrated into a new economy, with
> new styles of living, characteristics, and laws. We can no longer
> support ourselves by pasturing sheep. The sons of Jacob have to
> learn new occupations such as farming, building, stonecutting,

and woodwork, and become skilled in gold, silver, and brass, which are adapted to the new conditions. Basically he dreamt of a new framework within which the unity of the family could be preserved, even in the far places where the Creator of the universe would scatter them. His constant preoccupation was the continuation of Abraham's tradition amidst a new economic structure and civilization.

The brothers did not understand him, for they looked upon the future as a continuation of the present. They perceived all problems from within the framework of their life in Canaan, the land of their fathers' wanderings. In the traditional surroundings, in the thoroughly familiar habitat of the patriarchs, they did not need new frameworks or novel economic methods.

The biblical Joseph relates: "and, behold, the sun and the moon and the eleven stars made obeisance to me" (Gen. 37:9)—there is secular culture, great and powerful technology creating wonders and changing the foundations of our life. Even if it is true that in Canaan we can get along without it—this secular culture entails destructive elements, many negative and perverse aspects; it may be a blessing and a curse simultaneously, and thus as long as one can live without it, so much the better for the spirit—finally we will have to relate to it. The confrontation will not take place in Canaan, however, where life flows serenely, but in a new and alien land where the tempo of life is greatly accelerated and fundamental changes occur daily. God's decree "thy seed shall be a stranger in a land that is not theirs" (Gen. 15:13) will be fulfilled sooner or later. In "a land that is not theirs," I fear, we will not be able to maintain a separation between us and the surroundings. If we will not be prepared for new conditions, the environment will swallow us! On the other hand, if we think of the future, we can plan for binding the sheaves, for "the sun and the moon and the eleven stars"—for a new economic and social order. We can render Abraham's heritage triumphant in the alien surroundings too!

Joseph's brothers, however, answered him: "Why do you meddle   in the secrets of the All-Merciful? Why do you get involved with the secret plans of God? We do not know when

God will execute His decree 'thy seed shall be a stranger' (Gen. 15:13). Meanwhile we are in Canaan. We live our lives in holiness and purity; we support ourselves by pasturing sheep. We do not have to worry about the future—we will get by without binding sheaves, without the sun, the moon, and the eleven stars." But Joseph stood fast; he was not at all secure regarding the political and economic status quo of Jacob's house in Canaan, and he never ceased warning his brothers. "And his brethren envied him" (Gen. 37:11)—the more he tried to convince them, the more their stubbornness grew—"and they hated him yet the more for his dreams, and for his words" (Gen. 37:8).[1]

Aug. 21, 1996

Dear Rabbi Genack,
    Thank you for your help on the birthday party and especially for your reflections on Joseph and his brothers. Your insight was profound and very helpful to me.
    Sincerely,
    Bill Clinton

[1] Rabbi Joseph B. Soloveitchik, *The Rav Speaks: Five Addresses on Israel, History, and the Jewish People*, p. 28. New York: Judaica Press, 2002.

Now and Tomorrow

Joseph Grunblatt, November 7, 1997

Leaders in public life are continually faced with the realization that life is a constant tension between instant satisfaction and historical vision. It is by keeping an eye toward the future that our leaders can hope to build a better world for generations to come.

ABRAHAM IS PORTRAYED in the Bible as the biological progenitor and spiritual father of the Jewish people. He enters into a covenant with God. God's commitment to Abraham lies in the future, a future that will bring suffering for his descendants and severely challenge their endurance. Only then will they see the Promised Land.

God says: "Know of a surety that thy seed shall be a stranger in a land that is not theirs, and shall serve them; and they shall afflict them four hundred years. . . . But in the fourth generation they shall come hither [into the Holy Land]" (Gen. 15:13, 16).

Abraham's commitment, his part of the bargain, is right now in his lifetime. When God decides to inform Abraham about the impending destruction of Sodom and Gomorrah, He reasons that He must inform His covenantal partner: "For I know him [Abraham], that he will command his children and his household after him, and they shall keep the way of the Lord, to do justice and judgment" (Gen. 18:19).

Abraham must begin his building program right now, to work for a future he himself will not see, a people whose peoplehood he will not share, and a promised land he will not inherit. The futuristic nature of the Divine promise is brought home to Abraham when his beloved wife Sarah dies, and he must engage in business with the sons of Heth in order to procure a burial ground in the land that would ultimately belong to his descendants (Gen. 23).

A beautiful story is told in the Talmud (Tractate Taanit 23b) about a legendary man of piety, Honi HaM'agel, who saw an old man planting a carob tree. It was believed that it takes seventy years for this tree to produce its first edible fruit. Honi asked the elderly man: "You know, it takes seventy years for this tree to produce fruit. Do you really think that you will live that long?"

"No," answered the man, "but I found fruit on the trees that my grandfather planted; my grandchildren will enjoy the fruit of my labor."

Life is a constant tension between instant satisfaction and historical vision—a vision to build a better world for generations to come. It is by keeping an eye toward the future that we can hope to build a world that will ultimately approach the vision of the prophets.

Leaders in public life—from leaders of small institutions to world leaders—are constantly faced with that tension, that temptation. Do I focus on satisfying immediate needs, that which is popular now and will gain for myself acclaim and approval, or do I have a greater responsibility toward destiny? This is an issue even in more mundane matters, such as: Do I gain popularity with the people by not taxing them, while neglecting the upkeep and repair of bridges and infrastructure; or do I "bite the bullet," lest our grandchildren will, at enormous cost, have to rebuild bridges that are literally falling down?

Abraham was the paradigm of the man of faith and vision; and if we experience the rebirth of the Jewish people in the Promised Land of Israel today, we are eating the fruits from the tree that Abraham planted.

Of Dreams, Dreamers, and Nondreamers

Samuel J. Danishefsky, January 26, 1998

This letter emphasizes that a dreamer must be prudent in projecting the role he plays in his dreams: He may face resentment from the technocrat, who is narrowly bound by linear thought processes. Possible skepticism and hostility from others is a price the dreamer must be prepared to pay for the privilege of having the ability to dream.

THE TORAH PORTION of Vayeishev (Gen. 37–40) carries many fascinating lessons, of particular consequence to those with a bent for original and visionary departures. The portion begins with a one-sentence introduction of Joseph, the next to the youngest of Jacob's offspring. Joseph befriended the relatively less privileged of Jacob's sons, namely those emanating from the maidservants Bilhah and Zilpah. Jacob showed preference for Joseph and outfitted him with a distinctive woolen tunic (Gen. 37:3). Incidentally, the rabbis in the Talmud (Tractate Shabbat 10b) question the wisdom and propriety of this sort of display of favoritism. Not surprisingly, Joseph's brothers took umbrage at this seemingly uneven treatment.

At this point, Joseph seeks to apprise his brothers of a dream which he had dreamed—"Joseph dreamed a dream, and he told it his brethren: and they hated him yet the more" (Gen. 37:5). In the next verse we read of Joseph telling his brothers, "Hear, I pray you, this dream which I have dreamed" (Gen. 37:6). Joseph then reveals the contents of the dream, which involved the symbolic bowing of the sheaves of the brothers to the sheaf of Joseph. The brothers then "hated him yet the more for his dreams, and for his words" (Gen. 37:8).

While we can readily understand the brothers' resentment at the end of this passage, [they expressed] their anger and hatred even before they had heard the contents of the dream. It seems that they not only resented the substance of the dream but the very existence of the dream, and, by inference, of the dreamer. This is in contrast to the reaction of the patriarch Jacob. In verse 10, we read of Jacob's rebuke to a later, but similar dream: "What is this dream that thou hast dreamed? Shall I and thy mother and thy brethren indeed come to bow down ourselves to thee to the earth?" (Gen. 37:10).

Later, in reference to Joseph's attempted goodwill gesture to visit his brothers, we read:

> And when they saw him afar off, even before he came near unto them, they conspired against him to slay him. And they said one to another, Behold, this dreamer cometh. Come now therefore, and let us slay him, and cast him into some pit, and we will say, Some evil beast hath devoured him: and we shall see what will become of his dreams. (Gen. 37:18–20)

There are multiple layers of messages here for the dreamer. First, the dreamer must be particularly circumspect in projecting the role he plays in his dreams: Obviously, any implication of a special advantage for the dreamer is fraught with potentialities for misunderstanding and resentment. However— and this is the key point—the dreamer (the visionary!) faces an intrinsic skepticism and even hostility from the nondreamer, regardless of the contents of the dream. The here-and-now technocrat, himself incapable of the seemingly mystical quantum-level leap from strictly linear thought processes, actually resents this quality in others. It is a price the dreamer must be prepared to pay for the privilege of the mental leap that transcends normative patterns.

In contrast to Joseph's brothers, Jacob the Patriarch himself has a history of dreaming (Gen. 28:12; 31:10–11). Hence, his rebuke is directed not to the existence of the dream, but rather to its contents. The dreamer appreciates the capacity of others to dream. Jacob reacts only to the element of self-aggrandizement inherent in the contents of Joseph's dream.

Closer to our own time, I can well remember the negative reaction of many to the extraordinary Martin Luther King Jr. "I Have a Dream" speech. The reaction of many racists was not only to the idyllic vision of racial harmony projected by M.L.K., but to the fact that he was a proud and unabashed dreamer. It is sad but true that the dreamer exposes himself to hostility for the mere act of dreaming.

The Personalities of Noah and Abraham

Judith Bleich, February 10, 1998

Crises can be catalysts for change. While some people merely survive, others thrive.

THE PERSONALITIES OF NOAH and Abraham are frequently compared and contrasted in rabbinic writings. Noah and his family survived the deluge, and Noah is identified as the progenitor of the human race as it exists today; however, Noah failed to save his contemporaries, and his deportment subsequent to surviving the Flood is not depicted as exemplary. In contradistinction, Abraham is singled out as the great spiritual teacher who proclaimed the existence of a single God, ruler of heaven and earth, and as the spiritual leader who brought blessing to mankind.

In a single two-letter Hebrew word, the Bible gives us an insight into the nature of Noah's tragic flaw. The rain and waters of the Flood covered the earth; the ark alone remained intact. Genesis 7:23 reads:

> And every living substance was destroyed which was upon the
> face of the ground, both man, and cattle, and the creeping things,
> and the fowl of the heaven; and they were destroyed from the
> earth: and Noah only [*ach*] remained alive, and they that were
> with him in the ark.

The word "only" is the literal translation of the Hebrew *ach*. The word *ach* occurs in multiple contexts in the Bible and is always interpreted in rabbinic exegesis as an exclusionary or limiting term (*mi'ut*), i.e., a word whose purpose is to limit the ambit of the phrase it modifies. Use of the term in this context is puzzling. Noah and those who were with him in the ark all survived. How, then, are we to understand limitation in this context?

People react to crises in different ways. Some flounder and are overwhelmed; some cope with adversity and survive; and some few not only manage to remain unscathed but emerge transformed individuals, the better for the experience. Noah lived through a world-shattering cataclysm. He saw the eradication of the civilization of his time. But the awesome devastation he witnessed left no imprint upon him. He did not grow as a result of the catastrophe. He suffered loss and misfortune but became no wiser. Noah survived, but he was *ach* Noah, only Noah, the very same limited and shortsighted individual he had been in the past. A person who is not ennobled by disaster is a lesser person. Such a person certainly cannot be a model of spiritual heroism.

Abraham, the sages tell us, experienced ten trials. The last and most wrenching of all was the binding of Isaac. The Hebrew word for "tested" (*nisah*) also has the connotation of "raised up" or "elevated." These tests had an uplifting effect upon Abraham. Abraham became the towering figure that he was precisely because he was able to turn adversity into an uplifting experience. Only a person capable of learning from trials and tribulations can be an inspiring leader and a source of blessing to all the families of the earth.

The Strength to Dream

Jonathan Sacks, 1999

President Clinton is a dreamer. This is not a sign of naïveté but of leadership. Yet a successful leader must not only dream; he must have the perseverance and the ability to see setbacks as an opportunity to move forward.

PERHAPS JOSEPH WAS ASKING for trouble. As a young man he dreamed dreams. That is the glory of youth. But he did more. He told his brothers about his dreams. They became jealous. They saw him as a danger. And when Joseph came out to see them tending their father's sheep, envy turned to animosity (see verses from Gen. 37:18–20 on page 199). . . .

The irony is that it was just this moment that led to Joseph's dreams coming true. Joseph was thrown into the pit, sold into slavery in Egypt, and eventually rose to prominence and power. He became not only the architect of Egypt's economy, but also the savior and protector of his own family.

A little over a hundred years ago, another visionary, Theodor Herzl, witnessed the rising tide of anti-Semitism in Europe. Almost half a century before the Holocaust, Herzl realized that Europe was no longer safe for Jews. The solution, he believed, lay in the return of Jews to their ancestral home in Israel, and the creation there of a Jewish state.

He faced immense opposition. People believed it could not be done. They said, "The danger is not real. Besides, the task is impossible. After a lapse of two thousand years, Jews are not up to the challenge of sustaining an army, making a desolate land fertile again, and running a sovereign state of their own." Herzl's reply was simple. "If you will it, it is no dream."

Elie Wiesel, in a humorous vein, once pointed out that there was a time when Theodor Herzl and Sigmund Freud lived on the same street in Vienna, but Wiesel noted that it was lucky that they never met. Had they met, Herzl would have told Freud of his dream of a Jewish state. Freud would have asked Herr Herzl how long he had been having this dream. He would have invited Herzl to his consulting room, tracked down his idealism to a disturbed childhood, and cured Herzl of his dreams. Had they met, said Wiesel, there would today be no Jewish state. Fortunately, the United States and the Jewish people were never cured of their dreams.

Leadership is the courage to dream a dream, to be guided by it, and not to be deflected by those who say it cannot be. For those whose imagination is fixed on the distant horizon, obstacles turn out in the end to be opportunities, and setbacks become sources of strength. So it was with Joseph, and with Herzl. So it is in every generation with those who share the twin gifts of vision and persistence. Dreams are where leadership is born. Holding fast to them is where it is tested. Those who manage both are those who change our world.

The Seven Fat Years

Menachem Genack, July 23, 1999

During the summer of 1999, at the peak of more than seven years of unprecedented prosperity in America, President Clinton asked me for a biblical perspective on the budget deliberations. This letter was a reminder that it is important to garner the resources of the fat years in order to preserve the nation during the inevitable lean years that will follow.

PHARAOH HAS A DUAL DREAM. Out of the Nile emerge seven beautiful, robust cows. After them, seven emaciated cows emerge and swallow the fat cows. Then Pharaoh dreams that seven ears of thin grain, scorched by the east wind, swallow seven healthy ears of grain.

Agitated, Pharaoh seeks an interpretation of his dreams. The Hebrew slave, Joseph, who is known as an interpreter of dreams, is brought from his dungeon to appear before Pharaoh:

> And Joseph said unto Pharaoh, The dream of Pharaoh is one:
> God hath shewed Pharaoh what he is about to do. The seven good
> kine [cows] are seven years; and the seven good ears are seven
> years: the dream is one. And the seven thin and ill favoured kine
> that came up after them are seven years; and the seven empty ears
> blasted with the east wind shall be seven years of famine. This is
> the thing which I have spoken unto Pharaoh: What God is about
> to do he sheweth unto Pharaoh. Behold, there come seven years
> of great plenty throughout all the land of Egypt: And there shall
> arise after them seven years of famine; and all the plenty shall be
> forgotten in the land of Egypt; and the famine shall consume the
> land; And the plenty shall not be known in the land by reason
> of that famine following; for it shall be very grievous. And for
> that the dream was doubled unto Pharaoh twice; it is because the
> thing is established by God, and God will shortly bring it to pass.
> (Gen. 41:25–32)

But Joseph does not merely explain the dream; he offers a course of action:

> Now therefore let Pharaoh look out a man discreet and wise, and
> set him over the land of Egypt. Let Pharaoh do this, and let him
> appoint officers over the land, and take up the fifth part of the
> land of Egypt in the seven plenteous years. And let them gather
> all the food of those good years that come, and lay up corn under
> the hand of Pharaoh, and let them keep food in the cities. And
> that food shall be for store to the land against the seven years of
> famine, which shall be in the land of Egypt; that the land perish
> not through the famine. (Gen. 41:33–36)

Nachmanides was puzzled by Joseph's audacity. Joseph, a slave, had been summoned to interpret Pharaoh's dream, but not to become Pharaoh's minister of economy or offer unsolicited advice. Nachmanides therefore suggested that Joseph offered his advice because the advice itself was part of the Divine plan, and of the interpretation of the dream. The swallowing of the fat cows and of the healthy ears of grain represented the need to store the abundance from the prosperous years for use in the lean years. Thus the dream itself indicated the course of action and was not Joseph's independent advice.

The essence of leadership is to be able, in years of plenty, to see the challenges beyond the horizon of the yet unseen, but inevitable, years of famine, and to garner the resources of the fat years to preserve the nation during the lean years.

These past seven years have been unprecedented years of plenty and prosperity in America. Inevitably, however, the cycle will turn, and lean years will be upon us. We must be disciplined enough, and in Joseph's phrase "discreet and wise," not to squander the produce and wealth of the fat years, but rather husband that abundance to sustain us in the lean years of economic contraction.

The First Blessing of the Day

Menachem Genack, September 22, 1999

The requirement to say a blessing each dawn, to give thanks for being able to distinguish between day and night, reminds us that even in the midst of a dark, bitter night we must be aware of the boundless opportunities for redemption in the future.

THE FIRST OF THE MORNING BLESSINGS, which are the prologue to the daily prayers, is a praise of God: "Who gives the rooster [*sechvi*] the understanding to distinguish between day and night." The word *sechvi* in this blessing has a dual meaning, denoting both the rooster and the human heart, in terms of the heart's capacity to understand the distinction between day and night. In either case, why is the crowing of the rooster *or* the human response to the rooster of such importance that it should be the subject of the initial blessing of the day?

The text of our blessings and prayers was formulated by the members of the Great Assembly, led by Ezra, in the period between the destruction of the First Temple [by the Babylonians] and the building of the Second Temple (sixth century BCE). This period was one of despair and disorientation in the wake of the destruction of the Temple and the loss of Israel's sovereignty. So bleak was the situation that classical Jewish tradition tells us (Talmud, Yoma 69b) that the prophet Jeremiah was unable to declare God to be *gibbor* (mighty). "Where," he challenged, "is His might to be seen when gentiles raucously and blasphemously dance in His Temple?" Yet when the members of the Great Assembly formulated the liturgy, they were able to see God manifested as *gibbor*, even in that dark time. God's might is expressed in His Divine discipline, they explained, in His toleration of even those who blaspheme against Him. The omnipotent God does not vent His power and anger at man's iniquity—and He even permits the invader, in the playing out of free will, to desecrate the Temple. This is an expression of God's forbearance and, indeed, His might.

Rabbi Joseph B. Soloveitchik has pointed out that *gibbor* in this context means an expression not of power, but of heroism. Thus, the blessing "Who girds Israel with might," which is part of the series of the morning's blessings, means not that Israel is crowned with power—Israel was never a powerful nation—but rather that Israel has been afforded a heroic existence. Heroism is inversely proportional to brute strength and power. The more one is powerful, the less he is required to exhibit heroism.

Ezra was the prophet of faith. In past historical periods, the Jew was required to maintain faith in Jewish destiny and to persevere against all odds; that is, he was required to live heroically. It was this faith that enabled Ezra to return from exile with only a small portion of the Jewish population, and to rebuild the Temple and reconsecrate the land.

THE WHITE HOUSE
WASHINGTON

November 29, 1999

Rabbi Menachem Genack
Rabbinic Administrator
Union of Orthodox Jewish
    Congregations of America
11 Broadway
New York, New York 10004

Dear Rabbi Genack:

   Ann Lewis passed along your beautiful
missive. I appreciate your sharing your
insights about the crowing of the rooster and
the profound lessons it teaches us about hope
and heroism. As we prepare to meet the challenges of the 21st century, messages like this
can strengthen and inspire us for the work ahead.
I thank you for sharing your wisdom and for all
you do to foster an atmosphere of compassion
and fellowship in our country.

   Hillary and I send our best.

Sincerely,

Bill Clinton

Though the sanctity of the land had been canceled by the Babylonian conquest, Ezra's courageous resettlement sanctified the land for all time. The root of that eternal sanctity was Ezra's heroism: his undiminished vision of the future. Without this heroic posture, Jewish existence would have been impossible in an environment of unlimited hostility.

The dawn of our salvation, both personal and national, will break—even though we are in the midst of a dark, bitter night of exile—if our vision is not limited to the present and immediate circumstances, but rather encompasses the boundless opportunities for redemption in the future. If our view is not riveted to current historical circumstances, but rather glimpses our future destiny, salvation is at hand. From this universal view flows religious fortitude in the face of all obstacles, and serenity even when confronted with chaotic, difficult times.

It is this essential worldview, I believe, that the rabbis perceived in the crowing of the rooster. In utter darkness, the rooster is able to sense the dim, indiscernible streak of light on the horizon. To the members of the Great Assembly, who saw Jewish history entering an epoch of instability and darkness, the rooster heralded the streak of light in the distant historical firmament. It is thus appropriate that the members of the Great Assembly required each Jew to articulate this quintessential message of faith as the first blessing of the morning service.

Where There Is No Vision, the People Perish

Menachem Genack, December 4, 2000

The biblical requirement to wear tzitzit (fringes) on one's garment requires that we see them (Num. 15:39). The tzitzit is meant to elevate our vision so it is not limited only to the here and now but also glimpses the distant horizon. The princes of a nation need such elevated vision to serve their people.

JUST BEFORE THE JEWISH PEOPLE were to enter the Land of Israel, they suffered a terrible setback. Moses sent twelve princes, each the leader of a tribe, to survey the land. The princes returned with a crisis of confidence. "Nevertheless the people be strong that dwell in the land, and the cities are walled, and very great" (Num. 13:28). "We be not able to go up against the people," they concluded, "for they are stronger than we" (Num. 13:31).

Here God was calling them to the Promised Land, a land of sanctity and majesty, a land in which "the eyes of the Lord thy God are always upon it, from the beginning of the year even unto the end of the year" (Deut. 11:12). Yet they were able to see only a "land that eateth up the inhabitants thereof" (Num. 13:32). As a result of their misgivings and the widespread lament their misgivings prompted, God delayed the Jewish people's entrance to the Land of Israel for forty years.

A passage at the end of Shelach, the Torah portion in which this episode appears, describes the commandment to wear the fringed garment, and provides a beautiful endnote to the episode of the princes. God tells Moses, "Speak unto the children of Israel, and bid them that they make them fringes in the borders of their garments." Each Jew should "put upon the fringe of the borders a ribband of blue" (Num. 15:38). According to the sages, the blue of the tzitzit conveys the lesson of the tzitzit. The blue, the sages say, reminds the wearer of the blue of the boundless ocean, and the ocean mirrors the blue of the sky. And the sky, the sages say, reflects the hue of God's throne of glory. As the verse states, "And there was under his feet as it were a paved work of sapphire stone, and as it were the body of heaven in his clearness" (Exod. 24:10).

The sin of the princes lay in their myopic view, and the tzitzit are meant to rectify this sin. Indeed, this idea is implied by the biblical text. Earlier, Moses exhorted the princes that they should "see the land, what it is" (Num. 13:18). Because the princes faltered, the Jewish people are encouraged to behold the inspiring tzitzit: "And it shall be unto you for a fringe, that ye may look upon it, and remember all the commandments of the Lord, and do them" (Num. 15:39).

Rashi also suggests that the commandment of the tzitzit is related to the sin of the princes. The term the Bible uses to describe the spying by the princes is *latur* (Num. 13:16), a word scarcely used in the Bible. And yet the word appears, in a different form, in the passage on the tzitzit, to emphasize that "ye seek not after your own heart and your own eyes, after which ye use to go a whoring" (Num. 15:39). Rashi makes subtle reference to the episode of the spies in his commentary on this verse. Why should one resist straying after his heart and his eyes? Because "the heart and the eyes are *spies* for the body," leading a person to transgress.

The requirement to wear tzitzit, which etymologically comes from the Hebrew word meaning "to glimpse," is an antidote to the myopia of the princes. The tzitzit mean to elevate our vision so it is not limited only to the here and now, riveted only on the ephemeral moment, but perceives that which is boundless and transcendent, and glimpses the distant horizon.

THE WHITE HOUSE

WASHINGTON

12-11-00

Dear Rabbi Genack,

Thank you so much for your latest letter on vision.

I look forward to them and hope you will write from time to time after I leave office. —

Sincerely,

Bill Clinton

12-11-00

Dear Rabbi Genack,

    Thank you so much for your latest letter
on vision.

    I look forward to them and hope you will
write from time to time after I leave
office.

                              Sincerely,
                              Bill Clinton

Holidays

n Judaism, holidays are not only opportunities for family camaraderie and joy; they also provide profound theological lessons that inform our world views. The calendar directs and elevates our thoughts to fundamental truths. The missives in this section cull some of the teachings encountered throughout the year.

Notwithstanding the lofty significance of the holidays (including the Sabbath), their onset is often fraught with tension, sometimes with a tinge of frantic comedy, for the observant Jew in the public sphere. In the Jewish calendar, the Sabbath begins at sundown every Friday, and the other holidays similarly begin at sundown. By sundown, the observant Jew should be at home with his or her family, ready to greet the holiday and be enveloped by its sanctity. This can have serious implications for anyone who is not on vacation, retired, or independently wealthy. At any Friday afternoon meeting at the office, the person looking at his or her watch with increasing frequency and anxiety is probably mentally calculating just how long it will take, given rush hour traffic, to get home by sundown, and weighing how much longer they have before needing to bail out of the meeting.

I remember the occasion of the signing of the 1998 Wye Accord between the Israelis and Palestinians; it was signed on Friday afternoon, October 23, without too much time to spare before the onset of the Sabbath. I was watching the proceedings on television, and President Clinton was waving people on to expedite the process, saying, "The sun is setting; it's almost Shabbat." A few days later, I saw the president and told him how impressed I was that he was concerned about the timing. He told me that he knew that the documents had to be signed quickly out of respect for the Israeli delegation because it was Friday afternoon, and the Sabbath was approaching. He said that he was well aware of the schedule and was trying to keep to it, but Yasser Arafat, oblivious to the time exigencies, kept speaking and completely threw the proceedings off schedule. Jack Lew, currently U.S. Secretary of the Treasury and formerly President Obama's chief of staff—and a Sabbath observer—shared with me a similar reminiscence of Mr. Clinton's awareness and sensitivity. Mr. Clinton had called Mr. Lew by telephone. It was a Friday afternoon, and the president told him, "Don't worry Jack, I know when sundown is, and I'll be off by then."

President Clinton's sensitivity to observance of the Jewish holidays set the tone for his administration, but sometimes things got carried a bit too far. The president was scheduled to meet with Pope John Paul II at the White House on October 4, 1995. That day happened to fall on Yom Kippur, the most sacred day of the Jewish High Holy Days, and some time before the event, I received a call from the White House inquiring if it would be offensive to the Jewish community if the meeting were held on Yom Kippur. I responded that the president was not Jewish, and the Pope was clearly not Jewish, so I was at a loss to see any issue.

The president's interest in the Jewish holidays extended beyond the High Holy Days and the Sabbath. In August 1993, I got a call from the White House inviting me for a meeting of New Jersey leaders with President Clinton. The president was meeting with delegations from various states to get them to lobby their members of Congress to support his budget. In fact, those meetings were the key to the success of Clinton's five-year economic program, which passed by one vote in the Senate—Vice President Al Gore's tie-breaking vote. As he would quip, "When I vote, we win."

The initial scheduled date for the meeting was the ninth day of the Hebrew month of Av, the date that commemorates the destruction of both the First and Second Temples in Jerusalem and the most somber day of the Jewish calendar. I explained to the aide that on that day I would have to wear sneakers because, according to Jewish tradition, one does not wear leather shoes on a day of mourning. He listened and then told me, "I hope you don't come, because the president is chronically late and he's going to ask you why you are wearing sneakers, you'll tell him, he'll be curious, he'll undoubtedly be interested, and that will further set back his schedule."

As it happened, the meeting was postponed one week, so the problem with the sneakers never occurred.

During this period in 1993, at the beginning of his presidency, there was doubt expressed in some quarters as to Mr. Clinton's ability to exercise effective leadership. But the president wasn't the only one with problems. That week my five-year-old son, Moshe, had his brand-new bicycle, which he had left on a baseball field, stolen. He was very distraught about this loss. When my wife tucked him in that night, with Barney the dinosaur under his arm, she told him that Daddy was going to the White House tomorrow to meet with the president. He looked up and asked, "Could Daddy tell the president about my bicycle?" After the meeting at the White House the next day, President Clinton asked for comments, and when he called on me, I told him about my son's request. I said, "Mr. President, there is still someone who thinks you are omnipotent, but he is only five years old." This elicited a big laugh from the president . . . but no bicycle.

Moshe Genack meets the president and the first lady at the White House, June 10, 1999, at a reception celebrating the New York Yankees and their 1998 World Series win.

The Fourth Commandment

Cynthia Ozick, September 26, 1997

Sabbath, the Jewish people's treasure of time, is given new meaning in this moving missive.

> Remember the sabbath day, to keep it holy. Six days shalt thou
> labour, and do all thy work: But the seventh day is the sabbath of
> the Lord thy God: in it thou shalt not do any work, thou, nor thy
> son, nor thy daughter, thy manservant, nor thy maidservant, nor
> thy cattle, nor thy stranger that is within thy gates: For in six days
> the Lord made heaven and earth, the sea, and all that in them
> is, and rested the seventh day: wherefore the Lord blessed the
> sabbath day, and hallowed it. (Exod. 20:8–11)

THE SABBATH is not only not in nature, it is against nature. In nature, all the days are alike—the birds continue to fly, the fish to swim, the grass to grow, the beasts to forage. But the Sabbath enters human history as a creation, an invention, a transcendent *idea*: an idea imposed on, laid over, all of nature's evidences. The Greeks and the Romans derided the Jews for observing the Sabbath—conduct so abnormal as to be absurd, and economically wasteful besides. From the pagan point of view, there was no profit in such idleness; Sabbath rest promoted both a household and a communal laziness that extended from the cookstove to the cowshed, from the employer to the most insignificant employee. For the Greeks and the Romans, all days were weekdays. Both master and slave were slaves to a clock that never stopped.

It was the biblical Sabbath that divided time and made the week. The Sabbath altered the world and how we perceive it. Without the Sabbath, time in a crucial sense has no reality—it simply rolls on, one sunrise after another, meaninglessly. Without the Sabbath, human toil is no different from the toil of an ox. But the injunction to hallow the seventh day honors labor by honoring rest from labor, just as the Creator—lavishing generative fervor on the fashioning of the universe in six days, stopping on the seventh to contemplate the perfection of the Divine work. And so we do as the Creator did.

The Sabbath stands for liberation—and not only human liberation. Even the ox is liberated from toil on the Sabbath. Every creature, human or animal, is respected for its individual essence and given a day of peace. The Sabbath stands for the brotherly peace of paradise; it sanctifies by seizing perfection out of the ragged flow of ordinary time. It conveys an understanding of distinctions: that the sacred departs from the everyday, and therefore can never bore us; and that, as the Sabbath is unique in the week's row of days, all beings are unique and not to be regarded as drones or robots or slaves of any system.

Holiness *means* separateness: *kadosh*, the Hebrew word for "holy," is rendered as "set apart." The Sabbath is set apart from routine so that the delights of being alive can be savored without the distractions of noisy demands, jobs, money, and all the strivings of ego. Both power and powerlessness become irrelevant; on the Sabbath equality and dignity rule. The Sabbath denies outsiderness. Only a life in danger can override the Sabbath's focus on spiritual and moral elevation—elevation achieved through tranquillity, fellowship, study, song, beauty, cleanliness, family intimacy. Every festive Sabbath meal is a holiday of thanksgiving. The Sabbath inspires us all—every woman, child, and man, and every stranger—to become the best that we can be. Every Sabbath day is a sacred fulfillment. Every Sabbath is a completion of Genesis: a Divine creation in itself, fashioned, through human dedication, in the image of God.

Sound the Shofar

Menachem Genack, November 6, 1997

Evoking the timeless message etched on Philadelphia's Liberty Bell, this letter presents a message of freedom heard from the shofar.

> Blow up the trumpet in the new moon, in the time appointed, on
> our solemn feast day. For this was a statute for Israel, and a law
> of the God of Jacob. This he ordained in Joseph for a testimony,
> when he went out through the land of Egypt: where I heard a
> language that I understood not. I removed his shoulder from the
> burden: his hands were delivered from the pots. (Ps. 81:3–6)

IN PSALM 81, the command to sound the shofar directly precedes Joseph's going forth in Egypt; the rabbis derive from this juxtaposition that Joseph was freed from prison on Rosh Hashanah, the Jewish New Year, when the shofar is traditionally sounded. As the shofar announced freedom for Joseph, who was incarcerated by Potiphar [a slaveowner] in Egypt, so it is for all: the clarion call of the shofar heralds the termination of servitude. Part of the verse describing the call of the shofar during a Jubilee year [the Sabbath year that comes after a period of seven cycles of seven years, see page 226], when the Bible commands that all slaves are to be set free, is inscribed on the Liberty Bell: "Proclaim liberty throughout all the land unto all the inhabitants thereof" (Lev. 25:10).

But wherein lies, in the blast of the shofar, freedom's sweet sound? The answer, I believe, is that the sound of the shofar—a prayer without words— is intended to wake us up from our slumber, from the lethargy of time, from the vanity of our small pursuits, and remind us that God has endowed each of us with a great mission. It is, therefore, a transcendent message of freedom.

The shofar means to free, therefore, not only the slave from economic bondage, but all of us, who are to a degree enslaved and ensnared by the routine of life, and by the pressure of earning a livelihood—encumbrances that deflect us from focusing on our true mission. The shofar severs not only the external bonds of political and economic slavery but, more fundamentally, the internal bonds that incarcerate us psychologically and spiritually. Its call is to awaken the internal spirit within us that is pure, pristine, and eternally free. A person can be externally enslaved, but spiritually free—as he can be externally free, but internally enslaved. Everything depends on one's will and one's sense of perspective and purpose.

The shofar awakens the real persona, the soul that is ever free. While its light may be diminished, it is never extinguished.

Qualitative Time

Menachem Genack, January 29, 1999

We often seek quantity in life, while ignoring the significance of the quality of life. This letter, based on a powerful essay by Rabbi Joseph B. Soloveitchik, shares the significance of being conscious of the quality of time versus the quantity of time.

GOD SPOKE TO MOSES and Aaron in the land of Egypt, saying, "This month shall be unto you the beginning of months: it shall be the first month of the year to you" (Exod. 12:2).

The first Divine commandment given to the Israelites in Egypt was to establish a new lunar calendar whose first month would be Nisan, the month of the redemption from the bondage in Egypt. Why was it so essential as a precursor for redemption to establish the new calendar?

The answer, I believe, is not only that the new calendar represented a new way of marking and recording time, but more fundamentally, that it instructed the Israelites on how to view and relate to time. Under the old solar calendar, time and history were static, immutable, and inexorable. Mankind was limited and incarcerated by chronology. The new lunar calendar represented a new concept in time. The phases of the moon, its waxing and waning, represent time that is changeable, creative, and dynamic. Man is no longer merely the slave of time, but can be its master.

Were this new concept of time not introduced, the new Jewish nation could not have emerged from the gloom of subjugation to the light of emancipation, and the great experiment in freedom would have been stillborn. Under the preexisting laws of history, this slave people would have been crushed under the centuries of bondage and oppression by the mightiest civilization of the ancient world. The new calendar afforded a new vision of redemptive, creative time that brought with it hope and limitless possibilities of change, growth, and freedom. Thus was shattered the deadening stoicism that wedded a person to "fate" and prevented one from molding his own destiny.

Rabbi Joseph B. Soloveitchik, in a wonderful essay, "Sacred and Profane," speaks about the enormous influence noted French philosopher Henri Bergson (1859–1941) had on modern philosophy with his formulation of a new concept of time—the so-called *durée*, duration:

[Bergson] contrasted this concept of time with that of the physicist, which is pure chronometry, time quantified and frozen in geometric space, time associated with space in motion and, in modern physics, with the time-space continuum.

Thus, Bergson speaks of fleeting time, living and immeasurable, beyond the scientist's mesh. No clock can be applied to this qualitative time, which is transient, intangible, and evanescent, and, on the other hand, creative, dynamic, and self-emerging. In this "time" there are no milestones separating past, present, and future. It is not unidimensional, as is physical time, but multidimensional, compenetrating and overlapping past, present, and future.

With this qualitative time, Bergson contrasts quantitative time. This is time measured by the clock, by the rotation of the earth on its axis, and by its revolution about the sun. This "time" is uniform, empty, and noncreative.

While Bergson limited himself to a philosophical and metaphysical analysis of time, we may proceed further and posit this dualistic time concept as the prime norm of human life that carries with it practical implications and ethical aspects. Man encounters the alternative of molding time in a quantitative or qualitative pattern.

There are some people who live in quantitative, dead time. They measure time by the clock and by the calendar. For them there is no merger of the past and the future. The present itself is a lost moment. A year is endless. How much more so centuries and tens of centuries! These people are deprived of an historical consciousness; for history is the living experience of time.

The man, however, who lives in qualitative time has a different criterion for the experience of time than the quantitative experience. He measures time, not by *length-extensio*, but by pure quality, creativity, and accomplishment. While for the man with a quantitative apprehension, all fractions of time are equal because all represent physical "t's"; for the man of qualitative apprehension, there is no equality among temporal fractions of time. Moments are heterogeneous. One may live an entire lifespan quantitatively, not having lived even a moment qualitatively. And, contrariwise, one may have lived a moment quantitatively and have lived through an eternity qualitatively. The alternative is up to man himself. *The time norm is the highest criterion by which man, life, and actions should be judged.* . . .

The individual who measures time in purely quantitative terms is an essentially passive personality. He is a recipient and not a giver, a creature rather than a creator. His prototype is the slave. The slave has no time-consciousness of his own, for he has no time of his own. . . .

The basic criterion which distinguishes freeman from slave is the kind of relationship each has with time and its experience. Freedom is identical with a rich, colorful, creative time-consciousness. Bondage is identical with passive intuition and reception of an empty, formal time stream.[1]

Without this Bergsonian time consciousness that transforms quantitative into qualitative time, the glorious story of the Exodus would have been impossible, for the path of liberation leads through the medium of time. As we approach the new millennium, with its risks and opportunities, we might well contemplate the meaning of time, its urgency and possibilities.

[1] Rabbi Joseph B. Soloveitchik, "Sacred and Profane," *Gesher*, Vol. 3, No. 1.

Tu B'Shevat

Menachem Genack, January 6, 1997

In President Clinton's 1993 inaugural address, he noted that although the inaugur-ation ceremony is held in the depths of winter, through "the words we speak and the faces we show the world, we force the spring, a spring reborn in the world's oldest democracy that brings forth the vision and courage to reinvent America." What follows is a reflection on the obscure Jewish holiday Tu B'Shevat and the elements required to "force the spring." (Note: I had originally intended these reflections to be published in a newspaper as an op-ed piece, but instead ended up handing them to the president as a letter reflecting on the inauguration.)

I TOOK MY CHILDREN TO WASHINGTON to watch President Clinton being sworn in a second time. I was prepared to brave the frigid temperatures so that my children could witness this historic occasion and the glory of the American political system, which for more than two hundred years has affirmed peacefully the transfer of power from administration to administration. But the cold snap ended, and on inaugural day, the temperatures were moderate, the city was drenched with sun, and the president even doffed his coat while delivering the inaugural address. The change in weather from the bitter cold of the day before to the relative warmth of inaugural day was almost a metaphor for the inaugural ceremony, which, to paraphrase John Kennedy, signifies change as well as renewal.

The warm weather brought back to me the words from Bill Clinton's inaugural address four years earlier, which summoned America to a new sea-son of renewal, to "force the spring" even in the midst of the winter, and my mind wandered to a short story I had once read.

The classical Hebrew author, I. L. Peretz, in an apocryphal story enti-tled "Between Two Mountains," describes the encounter of two rabbis. The rabbi of Brisk [Brest-Letovsk] had a profound analytical mind: contemplative, logical, and devoid of undisciplined emotion. A disciple of his had become a Hasidic rebbe, filled with passion and religious fervor, and had cajoled his master, Rabbi Soloveitchik, to come to visit at a gathering of the rebbe's fol-lowers. As Peretz tells the story, from the song and warmth of the Hasidic rebbe, surrounded by his Hasidic adherents, the snow outside melted, the trees bloomed, and the birds began to chirp. The cold Russian winter twilight, through the ecstasy of the Hasidim, had been transformed into a bright spring day. As sunset approached, the rabbi of Brisk looked at his watch and interrupted the song to remind the assembly that it was getting late. Suddenly, the glorious spring faded and changed again to the previous winter scene.

"To force the spring" requires imagination, vision, and faith.

In February 1991, I met with then-senator Al Gore, together with some of my colleagues. At the conclusion of the meeting, as I stood to leave, Senator Gore turned to me, and said, "Rabbi, don't forget that today is Tu B'Shevat." I smiled and was indeed impressed with his knowledge of this minor Jewish holiday.

Tu B'Shevat, the fifteenth day of the Jewish month of Shevat, is the Jewish Arbor Day, the "New Year" for trees, which is relevant in Jewish law to certain laws of tithing. Yet Tu B'Shevat has a transcendent message. The Talmud says that Tu B'Shevat represents the day that sap begins to flow through the veins of the tree. Though the season is still frigid and blustery, the first stirrings of spring in the depths of the tree trunk go undetected. Though the tree's limbs are barren, Tu B'Shevat proclaims the coming of the season when the trees will be laden with fruit and foliage. It is the harbinger of the coming of spring and the redemption of the land from the cold bonds of winter.

It is our national capacity for reinvigoration, our rededication to traditional time-tested ideals and values in a constantly changing modern context—ever optimistic and undaunted by new challenges—that we celebrate every inaugural day. It is America's Tu B'Shevat.

Purim

Menachem Genack, February 26, 1999

Purim is often associated with merriment. Beneath the surface, however, Purim embodies the providence to be found even in life's seemingly happenstance events.

IN THE BOOK OF ESTHER, the series of events described [in Persia] seem to be chaotic, ironic, and undirected. The king orders the execution of his queen on the advice of his minister. . . . An entire people is doomed to be exterminated throughout the Persian Empire on the fourteenth day of the month of Adar—a day callously chosen by Haman, based on his casting lots. That cruel lottery, the *pur*, epitomizes the quixotic happenstance, the nihilistic nature of existence of the time.

Esther is the only book of the Bible in which God's name is not mentioned. The Bible thus teaches that what on the surface seems to be only a story of ambition, lust, and political intrigue, in fact has a deeper, unseen reality. The deeper reality is that God, though hidden from view, is ever-present, and is molding and controlling events. Indeed, the root of the name Esther, in Hebrew, means "hidden." According to rabbinic tradition recorded in the Midrash, wherever the Book of Esther mentions the king, it refers explicitly to Ahasuerus—and implicitly, to the King of Kings, Who, though unbeknownst to Ahasuerus, is moving the saga to its inexorable conclusion.

The book of Jewish mysticism known as the Zohar comments that Yom Kippurim, the biblical name for the holiday of Yom Kippur, can be read *Yom k'Purim*—a day "like Purim." Yom Kippur, in its temple service, also revolves around a lottery, which determines the destiny of two identical sacrificial goats—one to be offered in the Holy of Holies, the other to be ignominiously thrown over a precipice in a barren desert (Lev. 16:8–10).

Although Purim and Yom Kippur are very opposite in tone—Purim being a day of frivolity and feasting, Yom Kippur a day of awe and fasting—at their root they express an identical theme. What may seem haphazard, ruthless—a mere lottery—can be transformed through faith into something elevating, ennobling, and purposeful. . . . Esther's faith and fortitude transformed potential tragedy into salvation and celebration. Haman is ensnared by his own cruel *pur*, and in its place is the joy of redemption, Purim.

The Cycle of Seven

Menachem Genack, May 24, 1999

The cycle of seven is normally associated with the Sabbath, the Jewish day of rest concluding every week. This letter, instead, focuses on a lesser-known cycle of seven—the Jewish Jubilee year—which is celebrated at the conclusion of seven cycles of seven years.

THE CYCLE OF SEVEN is deeply embedded in the biblical calendar. In days (Sabbath), weeks (Shavuot, the Festival of Weeks), years (Sabbatical year), and seven cycles of seven years (Yovel, the Jubilee year), the number seven frames our time consciousness, directing our thoughts to the fundamental principle that God is the Creator of all reality and imposes order upon it.

In each of these holidays, man relinquishes, to a degree, his control and dominion over nature and the land, thereby proclaiming that the land and all Creation is God's, and only He grants man its use. Ultimately everything is God's possession, including man himself.

By refraining from work on the Sabbath, we acknowledge that creation is not ours but God's. Man thereby gives up part of the dominant role with which God endowed him in the mandate to conquer and subdue nature. Yet concomitantly he achieves a sense of freedom, for both himself and his household, as well as a sense of social justice—"that thy manservant and thy maidservant may rest as well as thou" (Deut. 5:14). In the cycle of seven weeks after Passover, which culminates in the holiday of Shavuot—the anniversary of the Great Theophany at Sinai—man subjugates his own will to that of God by accepting His revealed word. Our rabbis interpret the expression that the words of God were "graven [*charut*] upon the tables" (Exod. 32:16) as "do not read engraved [*charut*] but freedom [cheirut]" (Ethics of the Fathers, 6:2). By accepting the will of God, one achieves an existential freedom that cannot be crushed by the onerous forces of history and nature.

In the cycle of seven years, man again gives up certain of his powers, rights, and prerogatives. Man acknowledges that the land belongs to God, and that God alone bequeaths it to man. Here again the notions emerge of freedom and social justice. All that grows during the Sabbatical year is accessible to the poor, and outstanding loans are canceled.

The Yovel, or Jubilee year, has equivalent laws to the Sabbatical year. In addition, all lands sold in Israel in the preceding years return to their original owners at Yovel, emphasizing again that no one can acquire all the lands. This redistribution of wealth ensures that every Jew retains possession of the ultimate source of economic wealth and freedom—the land. Slaves are freed during the Yovel year. The statement quoted on the Liberty Bell, "Proclaim liberty throughout all the land unto all the inhabitants thereof" (Lev. 25:10), is the declaration made in the Torah with reference to the Yovel year. Yovel is the year of freedom; it is not simply an expression eliminating the external pressures of subjugation, but rather it establishes a positive environment of freedom that makes life on earth worth living.

As the cycles of seven culminate in the Jubilee year, we return to our ultimate source. According to the medieval Jewish commentator Nachmanides, the etymology of the word *yovel* comes from the word *yuval*—to be brought back to the source. It is the confluence of these two seemingly diametrically opposed ideas—that man is God's subject and all Creation belongs to God, on the one hand, and the concept of freedom and social justice proclaimed during the Yovel year on the other—that uniquely marks the Jewish concept of freedom. The irony of Jewish freedom is that it is achieved only by the recognition of our total dependence on and servitude to God.

In Western thought, freedom is defined by man's ability to independently make choices. However, the Jewish concept of freedom, which emerges from this progression from Sabbath to Yovel, is that ultimate freedom is man's ability to fulfill his potential as a creation of God, by submitting to His will. Man thereby becomes a transcendent being, not chained to time or place. Freedom is an in-depth experience, not a superficial one dependent on circumstance. Therefore, by adhering to God's will, man, who is created in the image of God, acts as a free agent.

The Seventh of Adar/July Fourth

Menachem Genack, 1999

This letter—reflections on the anniversary of Moses's death—recalls the evolving relationship between John Adams and Thomas Jefferson and the moving circumstances of their final departure from this world.

MOSES WAS BORN and died on the seventh of the month of Adar. Jewish tradition maintains that the coincidence of the anniversary of birth and death indicates that he had fulfilled the Divine mission with which he had been charged. God placed him in the world and removed him on the same calendar day, for his unique calling was accomplished.

The tragedy of death is mitigated by the knowledge that each person has a special role to play in this earthly drama. It is for a purpose that one is placed in and ultimately retired from the world. We remember Moses, God's messenger, as the model of a man who, once he realized his mission, was taken from the earth with a Godly kiss (Deut. 34:5; Avot D'Rebbe Nasson 12:5).

Thomas Jefferson and John Adams had been close friends when they served their fledgling new country together as ambassadors to the European courts. They both collaborated on that most wondrous document in political history, the Declaration of Independence. However, they became bitter rivals in the presidential election of 1800, when after an acrimonious campaign, Jefferson defeated Adams. Through the efforts of Dr. Benjamin Rush, another signer of the Declaration, the two antagonists were reconciled. These two massive intellects—in Rush's phrase "fellow laborers in erecting the great fabric of American independence"—began a correspondence that lasted fourteen years. Remarkably, both Founding Fathers died on the same day: July 4, 1826, the fiftieth anniversary of the Declaration. John Adams's last words were "Jefferson still lives"; but unbeknownst to him, Jefferson had died only a few hours earlier.

What incredible serendipity that these two giants should both expire on the jubilee of the birth of American independence. It was as if God sent a message that He had endorsed the great enterprise that they began, the United States of America. These two Founders, having found grace in God's eyes, like Moses, had completed their majestic mission.

Singing the Blues

Erica Brown, April 12, 2000

"People do not sing when they are feeling sensible," W. H. Auden is said to have stated. This letter traces the evolution of the Jewish people into a singing people.

WITH THE APPROACH OF PASSOVER, we turn our minds to the first fifteen chapters of Exodus. Although, surprisingly, Moses is not mentioned in the Passover Haggadah, he is the major protagonist of the Exodus narratives. It is he who is chosen to lead the Jews out of slavery and oppression, present them with the Decalogue, and bring them to the cusp of the Promised Land. Initially, however, Moses rejects the mission because he sees himself as inadequate to the task. His refusal is quite specific, "I am not eloquent" (Exod. 4:10). As readers, however, we can't help but question the veracity of Moses's claim. How can it be that several chapters later it is Moses, the one who cannot speak, who composes and leads the people in the "Song of the Sea," otherwise known as the "Song of Moses" (Exod. 15:1–18)? It is Moses who is picked by the Israelites to continue the recitation of the Ten Commandments, in preference to God Himself. The critical moments in Moses's leadership involve speech of the most eloquent order.

W. H. Auden once said that sensible people don't sing. His statement can be understood as more of a comment about music than about rational people. Music emanates from a special part of humanity's consciousness, a sacred and subtle place that touches the most profound longings within us. One might argue that the desire for freedom originates in that very same place. In times of oppression, our personal and communal intuitive sense of injustice, and our heightened immunity to suffering, intercept the music within us. Rabbi Joseph B. Soloveitchik drew our attention to the fact that before Moses arrived on the scene of oppression, we do not once hear the Israelites cry out in their anguished state. Immediately after Moses is introduced in chapter 2 of Exodus, we read that "the children of Israel sighed by reason of the bondage, and they cried, and their cry came up unto God by reason of the bondage" (Exod. 2:23). Pain is numbing and unspeakable when its expression cannot help change the circumstances. Once a savior is introduced, people can begin to feel, and to express their suffering. Acknowledging oppression is part of the process of redemption. What starts as silence becomes a sigh, and then a cry, and then a prayer, and then, eventually, intolerance for injustice. When we look at revolutionary moments in history, they often follow this pattern.

But there are two more steps in our text; there is the cry of victory, and then there is song. The Children of Israel experience this transformation communally. Moses experiences it personally. The "Song of the Sea" is a transformative moment in Moses's leadership; the song expresses not only the victory against the enemy outside of Moses, but also the triumph over the inadequacy within him. Before he could not speak; now he can sing. This triumph over injustice brings out the music within us all.

Rabbi Akiva and the Thirty-Third of the Omer

Menachem Genack, June 8, 2000

When we find ourselves amid destruction, it takes uncommon optimism to remain hopeful. The Talmudic sage Rabbi Akiva, and a curious holiday celebrating his legacy, provide an enduring message of optimism even in the most difficult of circumstances.

EACH YEAR, late in spring, is a holiday unlike any other on the Jewish calendar. It is called Lag BaOmer, which translates as the "thirty-third of the omer." Omer refers to the measure of barley that is offered in the temple on the second day of Passover. The holiday is called the Thirty-third of the Omer in reference to the biblical injunction to count the days between the barley offering on Passover and the Festival of Weeks ("Shavuot" in Hebrew) fifty days later (Lev. 23:15). This process is known as the "Counting of the Omer."

Rabbinic tradition records in the Talmud (Tractate Yevamot 62b) that as the result of a plague, Rabbi Akiva, the great second-century sage, lost all twenty-four thousand of his students during this same fifty-day period. Some have interpreted this "plague" as a metaphor for the unsuccessful Bar Kokhba Revolt against Rome (132–36 CE), in which Rabbi Akiva himself was ultimately martyred. Since the time of this devastating loss, the Counting of the Omer has been a time dedicated to remembering the terrible tragedy that occurred so many centuries ago. Joy is curtailed and, in particular, several of the laws of mourning are observed.

On Lag BaOmer, however—the thirty-third day of the omer—mourning gives way to celebration. While the common explanation for this holiday is that it was on this day that the plague abated, some have suggested a different explanation, one that provides a special insight into the indomitable faith of Rabbi Akiva. The Talmud says further (Tractate Yevamot 62b) that after the death of Rabbi Akiva's students, Rabbi Akiva, unbent, traveled to the south of Israel. There he found five new students and taught them the Torah. These five students became scholars and ultimately teachers, and from them Torah scholarship was rejuvenated.

It is Rabbi Akiva's capacity to persevere in the worst of times, and to do so with supreme optimism, that distinguishes him as the "greatest of the rabbis." The Thirty-third of the Omer thus celebrates Rabbi Akiva's resoluteness, despite an extraordinary setback, to forge a new beginning for the Jewish people.

Another Talmudic story is told about Rabbi Akiva that underscores his particular greatness. The Talmud (Tractate Makkot 24b) relates that a few of Rabbi Akiva's colleagues traveled one year with Rabbi Akiva to Jerusalem. They reached Mount Scopus, and there they tore their garments in grief, for they saw a fox scurrying from under the ruins of what had been the Holy of Holies, the Temple's inner sanctuary. All of the rabbis began to weep—save for Rabbi Akiva, who laughed.

"Why are you laughing?" the rabbis asked him. Rabbi Akiva replied, "Why are you weeping?" The rabbis, in response, quoted a verse that refers to the superior sanctity of the Holy of Holies: "'The stranger that cometh nigh shall be put to death' (Num. 1:51). And now we see foxes living here! Shouldn't we weep?"

In response, Rabbi Akiva justified his optimistic laughter by quoting verses that contain two opposing predictions, each offered by a prophet of God. It had been said of the First Temple that "Zion for your sake [will] be plowed as a field" (Mic. 3:12). In contrast, a later prophet, living in the time of the Second Temple, had predicted that "old men and old women [will] dwell in the streets of Jerusalem" (Zech. 8:4). Rabbi Akiva explained, "Until one of these prophecies was fulfilled, I had doubts that the other one would be fulfilled." Now that Zion had been "plowed as a field," however—to the point that foxes were living on the site of the Holy of Holies!—Rabbi Akiva felt certain that the promised revival and reconstruction of Jerusalem would also come to pass. Therefore upon seeing the foxes making use of the "field" that had once been the Temple, Rabbi Akiva remembered the dual prophecies and felt joy and optimism, rather than sadness and defeat. Upon hearing his words, Rabbi Akiva's colleagues said to him, "Akiva, you have comforted us, Akiva, you have comforted us."

Lag BaOmer is an occasion for us also to be comforted by Rabbi Akiva's great and inspiring optimism. In a time of desolation he created a new beginning, and amid destruction he was able to see the seeds of redemption. It is his example that inspires us to shape from what at times appears to be so little, the possibility for so much.

THE WHITE HOUSE

6/22/00

Dear Rabbi Genack,

I loved your missive on "Rabbi Akiva and the 33rd of the Omer," about which I was completely ignorant.

It's as you said a story both inspiring and instructive and it came on a day when I was in need of both.

Sincerely,

Bill Clinton

6/22/00

Dear Rabbi Genack,

I loved your missive on the "Rabbi Akiva and the 33rd of the Omer," about which I was completely ignorant.

It's as you said a story both inspiring and instructive and it came on a day when I was in need of both.

Sincerely,
Bill Clinton

ACKNOWLEDGMENTS

THIS BOOK could not have come to fruition without the invaluable assistance of a wide circle of friends and colleagues. First and foremost, I am deeply grateful to President Bill Clinton and Secretary Hillary Rodham Clinton for their support of this project; for their friendship; and for their extraordinary capacity to lead, to learn, and to laugh—especially at themselves. Barbara Berger of Sterling Publishing, my friend and editor, worked tirelessly to shepherd the book through the editing and publishing process, and improved and refined the manuscript in countless ways. Joelle Delbourgo, my literary agent, was a constant source of advice and encouragement. I wish to thank my colleagues at the OU, David Bashevkin, Cary Friedman, Simon Posner, and Gavriel Price, for their review of the manuscript and many helpful suggestions. I express appreciation as well to my secretaries, Sally Goldberg and the late Ethel Morrow, for their assistance. My good friends David Raab, Gil Student, and Joel Wolowelsky were patient sounding boards for me and could always be counted on for wise counsel. President Clinton's staff members have been a pleasure to work with. Ann Lewis, the former White House Communication Director, with whom I interacted often, was unfailingly helpful and gave freely of her time, experience, and sage advice. Thanks also to the president's current staff: Tina Flournoy, Chief of Staff; Doug Band, President Clinton's Counselor during his post-presidency; Hannah Richert, Advisor; and Steve Rinehart, Correspondence Director. Sara Ehrman, who served at the time as Deputy Political Director of the Democratic National Committee—and who is currently Senior Advisor to the S. Daniel Abraham Center for Middle East Peace—was a surrogate mother to so many of us, including the First Lady. I am especially grateful to Toras HoRav Foundation for so graciously allowing us to reprint excerpts from the writings of Rabbi Joseph B. Soloveitchik.

The staff of Sterling Publishing and OU Press are to be commended for their help and professionalism. At Sterling, I am grateful to cover designer Elizabeth Mihaltse, interior designer Christine Heun for the design concept, and publicist Lauren Cirigliano. Special thanks to book packager gonzalez-defino.com for production and layout. I am indebted to Rabbi Lord Jonathan Sacks for his eloquent preface, and, last but certainly not least, I am profoundly grateful to all the contributors whose essays grace this book.

WILLIAM JEFFERSON CLINTON

September 20, 2012

Rabbi Menachem Genack
Rabbinic Administrator and
    Chief Executive Officer
Union of Orthodox Jewish
    Congregations of America
11 Broadway
New York, New York 10004

Dear Rabbi Genack:

Thank you for the great birthday card—it
made me laugh. You were so nice to remember
me, and thanks for providing me with both
wisdom and humor over the years.

All the best to you.

Sincerely,

*Thanks for being
a true friend +*

*President Clinton with Rabbi Genack and his family, Englewood,
New Jersey, 2007. Photograph by Beatrice Moritz Photography.*

EDITOR AND CONTRIBUTORS

Menachem Genack, editor of the volume, is rabbi of Congregation Shomrei Enunah in Englewood, New Jersey, and CEO of OU Kosher.

Julius Berman, special counsel to the New York City law firm Kaye Scholer, has served as president of the Orthodox Union and chairman of the Conference of Presidents of Major American Jewish Organizations.

Benjamin Blech is an author, lecturer, and professor of Talmud at Yeshiva University.

Judith Bleich is professor of Judaic studies at Touro College.

Erica Brown is scholar-in-residence for the Jewish Federation of Greater Washington and its managing director for Education and Leadership.

Gail (Giti) Butler Bendheim is a practicing psychologist in New York.

Shalom Carmy is assistant professor of Jewish philosophy and Bible at Yeshiva University and editor of the journal *Tradition*.

Judah Copperman is founder and dean emeritus of the Michlalah-Jerusalem College for Women in Jerusalem.

Samuel J. Danishefsky, a member of the National Academy of Sciences, is Eugene W. Kettering Chair and Director of the Laboratory for Bioorganic Chemistry, Memorial Sloan-Kettering Cancer Center, and professor of chemistry at Columbia University.

Jeremy Dauber is Atran Associate Professor of Yiddish Language, Literature and Culture at Columbia University and director of the Institute for Israel and Jewish Studies.

Mark Dratch is executive vice president of the Rabbinical Council of America.

Yaakov Elman is Herbert S. and Naomi Denenberg Chair in Talmudic Studies and professor of Jewish history at Yeshiva University.

Emanuel Feldman is rabbi emeritus of Congregation Beth Jacob in Atlanta and editor emeritus of the journal *Tradition*.

Barry Freundel serves as rabbi of Congregation Kesher Israel in Washington, D.C.

Joseph Grunblatt is rabbi emeritus of Queens Jewish Center.

Roald Hoffmann, a Nobel Laureate in Chemistry, is Frank H. T. Rhodes Professor of Humane Letters Emeritus at Cornell University, School of Chemistry and Chemical Biology.

The late Lord Rabbi Immanuel Jakobovits served as Chief Rabbi of the United Hebrew Congregation of the Commonwealth.

Judith S. Kaye is of counsel at the Skadden law firm in New York City and served as chief judge of the State of New York.

David Kazhdan is professor of mathematics at the Hebrew University of Jerusalem and professor emeritus of mathematics at Harvard University. He held a MacArthur Fellowship from 1990–95.

Daniel C. Kurtzer, former U.S. ambassador to Egypt and later to Israel, is S. Daniel Abraham Professor in Middle Eastern Policy Studies at Princeton University's Woodrow Wilson School of Public and International Affairs.

Maurice Lamm is president of the National Institute for Jewish Hospice, and professor at Yeshiva University's affiliate rabbinical seminary in New York, where he held the chair in professional rabbinics.

Norman Lamm is former chancellor of Yeshiva University and Rosh Yeshiva of its affiliated Rabbi Isaac Elchanan Theological Seminary.

The late Bernard Lander was founding president of Touro College.

Suzanne Last Stone is professor of law at Benjamin N. Cardozo School of Law and director of its Center for Jewish Law and Contemporary Civilization.

Israel Meir Lau served as the Ashkenazi Chief Rabbi of Israel from 1993–2003. Currently, he is Chief Rabbi of Tel Aviv and chairman of the Yad Vashem council.

Joseph Lieberman, former senior U.S. senator from Connecticut, was Democratic nominee for vice president in 2000.

Martin E. Marty is Fairfax M. Cone Distinguished Service Professor Emeritus of the History of Modern Christianity at the University of Chicago Divinity School.

David McCullough is a best-selling author and historian, and a two-time winner of the Pulitzer Prize and the National Book Award.

Cynthia Ozick is an award-winning short-story writer, novelist, and essayist.

Simon Posner is executive editor of OU Press.

Michael Rosensweig occupies the Nathan and Perel Schupf Chair of Talmud at Yeshiva University.

Noa Rothman, a television producer and attorney, is the granddaughter of the late Yitzhak Rabin, prime minister of Israel.

Elyakim Rubinstein is a justice on the Supreme Court of Israel.

Lord Jonathan Sacks is Chief Rabbi of the United Hebrew Congregation of the Commonwealth.

The late Nahum M. Sarna served as chair of the Department of Near Eastern and Judaic Studies at Brandeis University.

Lawrence H. Schiffman, former chair of New York University's Skirball Department of Hebrew and Judaic Studies, is vice-provost of Undergraduate Education at Yeshiva University and Ethel and Irvin A. Edelman Professor of Hebrew and Judaic Studies.

David Shatz, is professor of philosophy at Yeshiva University and editor of the *Torah u-Madda Journal* and the MeOtzar HoRav series.

Uriel Simon is professor emeritus of Bible at Bar-Ilan University.

The late Ahron Soloveichik was Rosh Yeshiva of Yeshivas Brisk in Chicago.

Adin Steinsaltz is founder and head of the Israel Institute for Talmudic Publications.

Marc D. Stern is general counsel of the American Jewish Committee.

Shlomo Sternberg is George Putnam Professor of Pure and Applied Mathematics at Harvard University.

Joseph Telushkin, a noted author and lecturer, is rabbi of the Synagogue for the Performing Arts in Los Angeles.

Esther Wachsman is a volunteer involved with the SHALVA Center in Jerusalem, SHALVA Beit Nachshon, which is named after her martyred son.

Joel B. Wolowelsky, dean of faculty at the Yeshivah of Flatbush, is associate editor of the journal *Tradition* and the MeOtzar HoRav series.

The late Walter Wurzburger, Adjunct Professor of Philosophy at Yeshiva University and a synagogue rabbi in Toronto and then Lawrence, New York. He was a past president of the Rabbinical Council of America and the founding editor of the journal *Tradition*.

TEXTUAL CITATIONS

Source: King James Version

EPIGRAPH
What is man, that thou art mindful of him? (Ps. 8:4–5)
He crowns kings, yet kingship is His alone (Rosh Hashanah liturgy)

PREFACE
Keep therefore and do them (Deut. 4:6)
Seek the peace of the city (Jer. 29:7)

INTRODUCTION
Where there is no vision, the people perish (Prov. 29:18)
But they that wait upon the Lord (Isa. 40:31)
If my people, which are called by my name (2 Chron. 7:14)

I LEADERSHIP

Judah and Joseph
Then Judah came near unto him, and said, Oh my lord, let thy servant (Gen. 44:18)
The scepter shall not depart from Judah (Gen. 49:10)
And Judah acknowledged them, and said, She hath been more righteous than I (Gen. 38:26)
[I] have brought Agag the king of Amalek, and have utterly destroyed the Amalekites. But the people took of the spoil, sheep and oxen (1 Sam. 15:20–21)

Planning and Patience
Now when Jacob saw that there was corn in Egypt, Jacob said unto his sons. . . . Then Joseph could not refrain himself before all them that stood by him (Gen. 42–45)

The Trials of Leadership
With him I will speak mouth to mouth (Num. 12:8)
My servant Moses is not so, who is faithful in all mine house (Num. 12:7)
And I spake unto you at that time (Deut. 1:9)
How can I myself alone bear your cumbrance (Deut. 1:12)
We remember the fish, which we did eat in Egypt freely (Num. 11:5)
Wherefore hast thou afflicted thy servant? . . . the Lord spake unto Moses (Num. 11:11–15)
And I will come down and talk with thee there (Num. 11:17)

Abandoned by His Flock
And I besought the Lord. . . . But the Lord was wroth with me for your sakes (Deut. 3:23–26)
Yet now, if thou wilt forgive their sin (Exod. 32:32)

Moses
And she called his name Moses: and she said, Because I drew him out of the water (Exod. 2:10)
And they said, An Egyptian delivered us (Exod. 2:19)
That which is altogether just shalt thou follow (Deut. 16:20)

The Journey in the Desert
These are the journeys of the Children of Israel. . . . And these are their journeys according to their goings out (Num. 33:1–2)

Preparation for Leadership
And the thoughts of God are profound, and who can stand in His counsel (Ibn Ezra, extended commentary, Exod. 2:3)
And when she could not longer hide him, she took for him an ark of bulrushes (Exod. 2:3)
Oppressed from his oppressor (Maimonides, Laws of Sanhedrin 2:7)
And it came to pass in those days, when Moses was grown . . . and he spied an Egyptian smiting an Hebrew (Exod. 2:11)
And he looked this way and that way . . . slew the Egyptian, and hid him in the sand (Exod. 2:12)
Now when Pharaoh heard this thing, he sought to slay Moses. . . . Moses stood up and helped them, and watered their flock (Exod. 2:15–17)

Influence or Power?
Ye take too much upon you (Num. 16:3)
But there remained two of the men in the camp, [Eldad and Medad]. . . . [Moses said] Enviest thou for my sake? Would God that all the Lord's people were prophets! (Num. 11:26–29)
Lay thine hand upon him (Num. 27:18)
Put some of thine honour upon him (Num. 27:20)
"Lay thine hand upon him"—this was like one who takes a flame to light another flame. "Put some of thine honour upon him"—this was like one who pours liquid from one vessel to another (Midrash Rabbah, Num. 21:15)

The Greater Challenge
There shall not any man be able to stand before thee (Josh. 1:5)
Be strong and of a good courage. . . . Only be thou strong and very courageous (Josh. 1:6–7)
Have not I commanded thee? Be strong and of a good courage (Josh. 1:9)

The Hands of Moses
And . . . when Moses held up his hand. . . . But Moses' hands were heavy (Exod. 17:11–12)
Did the hands of Moses make or break the war? (Mishnah, Rosh Hashanah 3:8)

Jethro
And . . . Moses sat to judge the people. . . . [He] hearkened to the voice of his father in law (Exod. 18:13–24)

Envoys Extraordinaire
And he commanded them, saying, Thus shall ye speak unto my lord Esau (Gen. 32:4)
And Moses sent messengers. . . . Thus Edom refused to give Israel passage (Num. 20:14–21)
And Israel sent messengers. . . . And Sihon would not suffer Israel to pass (Num. 21:21–23)
And Israel smote him with the edge of the sword (Num. 21:24)
And Jephthah sent messengers unto the king of the children of Ammon (Judg. 11:12)
So Jephthah passed over unto the children of Ammon. . . . And he smote them from Aroer (Judg. 11:32–33)
And the children of Israel set forward. . . . [Balak] sent messengers therefore unto Balaam (Num. 22)
And Abram said, Lord God, what wilt thou give me (Gen. 15:2)
And Abraham [said] . . . go unto my country . . . take a wife unto my son Isaac (Gen. 24)

Here Am I
And Israel said unto Joseph, Do not thy brethren feed the flock in Shechem? (Gen. 37:13)
And it came to pass after these things, that God did tempt Abraham (Gen. 22:1)
And when they saw him afar off . . . they conspired against him to slay him (Gen. 37:18)
Abraham lifted up his eyes, and saw the place afar off (Gen. 22:4)
We shall see what will become of his dreams (Gen. 37:20)
And Abraham called the name of that place Jehovahjireh (Gen. 22:14)
So now it was not you that sent me hither, but God (Gen. 45:8)
For God did send me before you (Gen. 45:5)
And God sent me before you (Gen. 45:7)
I heard the voice of the Lord, saying, Whom shall I send . . . ? I said, Here am I; send me (Isa. 6:8)

Isaac's Enigmatic and Heroic Legacy
And Rebekah lifted up her eyes, and when she saw Isaac, she lighted off the camel (Gen. 24:64)
These are the generations of Isaac, Abraham's son: Abraham begat Isaac (Gen. 25:19)
And Abraham took the wood of the burnt offering, and laid it upon Isaac . . . and they went both of them together (Gen. 22:6)
And Abraham said, My son, God will provide himself a lamb for a burnt offering: so they went both of them together (Gen. 22:8)
And Isaac came from the way of the well Lahairoi. . . . [Rebekah] said unto the servant, What man is this that walketh in the field to meet us? (Gen. 24:62–65)

Human Anonymity and the Divine Plan
And there went a man from the House of Levi. . . . took to wife a daughter of Levi. And the woman conceived, and bare a son (Exod. 2:1–2)
Amram took him Jochebed . . . to wife; and she bare him Aaron and Moses (Exod. 6:20)
And the child grew . . . and he became her son. And she called his name Moses (Exod. 2:10)

Sarah and Esther
And Sarah was an hundred and seven and twenty years old (Gen. 23:1)
Now it came to pass in the days of Ahasuerus (Est. 1:1)
The princes also of Pharaoh saw her . . . [she] was taken into Pharaoh's house (Gen. 12:15)
And . . . Abimelech king of Gerar sent, and took Sarah (Gen. 20:2)
And Esther obtained favour in the sight of all them that looked upon her (Est. 2:15)

Breaking the Tablets
And it came to pass, as soon as he came nigh unto the camp (Exod. 32:19)
And the Lord said unto Moses, Go, get thee down. . . . They have turned aside quickly out of the way which I commanded them: they have made them a molten calf (Exod. 32:7–8)
And Moses . . . said, Lord, why doth thy wrath wax hot against thy people (Exod. 32:11)
Now therefore let me alone, that my wrath may wax hot against them (Exod. 32:10)
Yet now, if thou wilt forgive their sin (Exod. 32:32)
When Moses saw that there was no future hope for Israel, he united his life with theirs (Midrash Rabbah, Exod. 46:1)
You have entered the [gladiatorial] arena. . . . Either you conquer, or I conquer you (Midrash Rabbah, Exod. 28:1)
Three things did Moses do of his own understanding (Babylonian Talmud Shabbat 87a)
The first tables which thou brakest (Deut. 10:2)
Your courage is commended for having broken them (Babylonian Talmud Shabbat 87a)

Between a Grumbling People and a Jealous God
Ye take too much upon you . . . wherefore then lift ye up yourselves above the congregation of the Lord? (Num. 16:3)
Be holy unto your God (Num. 15:40)
Is it a small thing that thou hast brought us up out of a land that floweth with milk and honey, to kill us (Num. 16:13)
If these men die the common death . . . then the Lord hath not sent me. . . . then ye shall understand that these men have provoked the Lord (Num. 16:29–30)
Separate yourselves from among this congregation (Num. 16:21)
Shall one man sin, and wilt thou be wroth with all the congregation? (Num. 16:22)
And he spake . . . saying, Depart, I pray you, from the tents of these wicked men (Num. 16:26)
This do; Take you censers. . . . And put fire therein (Num. 16:6–7)
And Nadab and Abihu, the sons of Aaron, took either of them his censer. . . . And there went out fire from the Lord (Lev. 10:1–2)
And there came out a fire from the Lord (Num. 16:35)
But on the morrow all the congregation of the children of Israel (Num. 16:41)
Get you up from among this congregation (Num. 16:45)
Take a censer, and put fire therein from off the altar (Num. 16:46)
And Aaron . . . ran into the midst of the congregation. . . . the plague was stayed (Num. 16:47–50)

Jacob and Israel
Then Jacob was greatly afraid and distressed (Gen. 32:7)
And he passed over before them, and bowed himself to the ground seven times (Gen. 33:3)
Thy name shall be called no more Jacob, but Israel (Gen. 32:28)

The Royal Reach
One thing have I desired of the Lord, that will I seek after; that I may dwell in the house of the Lord all the days of my life (Ps. 27:4)

How Things End
And die in the mount whither thou goest up. . . . Because ye trespassed against me among the children of Israel (Deut. 32:50–51)
And wherefore have ye made us to come up out of Egypt . . . And the Lord spake unto Moses and Aaron, Because ye believed me not (Num. 20:5–12)

Swearing on Lincoln's Bible
The judgments of the Lord are true and righteous altogether (Ps. 19:9)

A Father's Sacrifice
Lay not thine hand upon the lad (Gen. 22:12)
Now I know that thou fearest God, seeing thou hast not withheld thy son (Gen. 22:12)

Attributes of a Leader
Moreover thou shalt provide out of all the people able men (Exod. 18:21)
Take you wise men, and understanding . . . and I will make them rulers over you (Deut. 1:13)
To teach us that if men with all the seven attributes are not found, then we select from those with four [attributes] (Midrash Rabbah, Deut. 1:10)
Where no counsel is, the people fall (Prov. 11:14)

II SIN AND REPENTANCE
For there is not a just man upon earth, that doeth good, and sinneth not (Eccles. 7:20)
And God called the light Day (Gen. 1:5)
And the Lord [proclaimed] . . . Keeping mercy for thousands, forgiving iniquity (Exod. 34:6–7)

When a Ruler Sins
If a soul shall sin through ignorance (Lev. 4:2)
And if the whole congregation of Israel sin through ignorance (Lev. 4:13)
And if any one of the common people sin through ignorance (Lev. 4:27)
When a ruler hath sinned (Lev. 4:22)
And the priest shall make an atonement for him (Lev. 4:26)
Fortunate is the nation whose ruler brings a sin-offering (Horayot 10b)

The Weeping Shofar
Thus saith the Lord; A voice was heard in Ramah. . . . Refrain thy voice from weeping (Jer. 31:14–16)
The Lord, his God, is with him, and the shout of a king is among them (Num. 23:21)
And shalt return unto the Lord thy God. . . . That then the Lord thy God will turn thy captivity, and have compassion upon thee (Deut. 30:2–3)

A Good Name
A good name is better than precious ointment (Eccles. 7:1)

Forging Mettle
Wait on the Lord: be of good courage (Ps. 27:14)

The Sins of Saul and David
Saul reigned one year (1 Sam. 13)
For, as the Lord liveth, which saveth Israel, though it be in Jonathan my son, he shall surely die. . . . And the people said unto Saul, Do what seemeth good unto thee (1 Sam. 14:39–40)
Samuel also said unto Saul, The Lord sent me to anoint thee (1 Sam. 15)
And the Lord said unto Samuel, How long wilt thou mourn for Saul? . . . And Saul spake to Jonathan his son, and to all his servants, that they should kill David (1 Sam. 16–19)
Then they told David, saying, Behold the Philistines fight. . . . And the Ziphites came unto Saul to Gibeah, saying, Doth not David hide himself in the hill of Hachilah (1 Sam. 23–26)
And it was told Joab, Behold, the king weepeth. . . . And all the people were at strife throughout all the tribes of Israel (2 Sam. 19:1–9)
Against thee, thee only, have I sinned (Ps. 51:4)
And it came to pass after this, that the king of the children of Ammon died (2 Sam. 10)
For David's sake did the Lord his God give him a lamp in Jerusalem (1 Kings 15:4)

Respecting the Office
Thou shalt in any wise set him king over thee (Deut. 17:15)
Honour thy father and thy mother (Exod. 20:12)
Thou shalt rise up before the hoary head (Lev. 19:32)
[A nation's ruler is the] heart of the nation (Maimonides, Laws of Kings, 3:6)

Noah
And he drank of the wine. . . . And he said, Cursed be Canaan (Gen. 9:21–25)

The Naked Prophet
And he went thither to Naioth in Ramah. . . . And he stripped off his clothes also, and prophesied before Samuel in like manner (1 Sam. 19:23–24)
Because thou hast rejected the word of the Lord, he hath also rejected thee from being king (1 Sam. 15:23)

Righteous Indignation
Now therefore be not grieved, nor angry with yourselves, that ye sold me hither (Gen. 45:5)
And the sons of Jacob came out of the field when they heard it (Gen. 34:7)
O my soul, come not thou into their secret (Gen. 49:6)

Night and Day
And God called the light Day, and the darkness he called Night (Gen. 1:5)
Behold his bed, which is Solomon's; threescore valiant men are about it . . . because of fear in the night (Song of Sol. 3:7–8)
To shew forth thy lovingkindness in the morning, and thy faithfulness at night (Ps. 92:2–3)

The Ascent of Judah
And Judah acknowledged them, and said, She hath been more righteous than I (Gen. 38:26)
For a just man falleth seven times, and riseth up again (Prov. 24:16)
Judah is a lion's whelp: from the prey, my son, thou art gone up (Gen. 49:9)

Second Chances
And the Lord spake unto Moses. . . . Let the children of Israel also keep the passover (Num. 9:1–14)
And there were certain men . . . that they could not keep passover. . . And those men said unto him, We are defiled by the dead body of a man (Num. 9:6–7)
And Moses said unto them, Stand still, and I will hear what the Lord will command (Num. 9:8)
And the Lord spake unto Moses, saying . . . The fourteenth day of the second month at even they shall keep it. . . . according to all the ordinances of the passover they shall keep it (Num. 9:9–12)
And Joseph wept when they spake unto him. . . . And he comforted them (Gen. 50:17–21)
And Joseph took an oath . . . ye shall carry up my bones from hence (Gen. 50:25)
Speak ye unto all the congregation of Israel, saying, In the tenth day of this month they shall take to them every man a lamb (Exod. 12:3)

III CREATION

In His Own Image
So God created man in His own image (Gen. 1:27)

Playing God: The Limits of Man's Creative Genius
In sorrow thou shalt bring forth children (Gen. 3:16)
And shall cause him to be thoroughly healed (Exod. 21:19)
For in six days the Lord made heaven and earth, the sea, and all that in them is (Exod. 20:11)

A Faulty Foundation: The Tower of Babel
Go to, let us build us a city and a tower, whose top may reach unto heaven (Gen. 11:4)
And they had brick for stone and slime had they for mortar (Gen. 11:3)
Be fruitful, and multiply, and replenish the earth (Gen. 9:1)
The whole earth was of one language (Gen. 11:1)
Nothing will be restrained from them, which they have imagined to do (Gen. 11:6)

The Message of the Rainbow
And I will remember my covenant, which is between me and you and every living creature of all flesh (Gen. 9:15)
Like the appearance of the rainbow in the midst of the clouds, so was the appearance of the Priest (liturgy for Yom Kippur)
And the whole earth was of one language, and of one speech (Gen. 11)
And God blessed them, and God said . . . Replenish the earth, and subdue it (Gen. 1:28)

Personal Privacy and Balaam's Donkey
And the Lord opened the mouth of the ass . . . And the ass saw me, and turned from me these three times (Num. 22:28–33)

Man's Image Transcends Death
Each and every individual is commanded by Jewish tradition to believe that the world was created for him alone, and that the world's continued existence depends on him (Babylonian Talmud, Sanhedrin 37a)
He will swallow up death in victory; and the Lord God will wipe away tears (Isa. 25:8)

Man's Dual Personality
It is not good that the man should be alone; I will make him an help meet for him (Gen. 2:18)
And Adam gave names to all cattle, and to the fowl of the air, and to every beast . . . but for Adam there was not found an help meet for him (Gen. 2:20)
And God said, Let us make man in our image. . . . Be fruitful, and multiply (Gen. 1:26–28)
And the Lord God formed man of the dust of the ground (Gen. 2:7)
And the Lord God . . . put him into the garden of Eden to dress it and to keep it (Gen. 2:15)
And the Lord God commanded the man, saying, Of every tree of the garden thou mayest freely

eat: But of the tree of the knowledge of good and evil, thou shalt not eat (Gen. 2:16–17)
And the Lord God caused a deep sleep to fall upon Adam . . . he took one of his ribs . . . and the rib, which the Lord God had taken from man, made he a woman (Gen. 2:21–22)

The Creation of Man
Man was created singly to teach that whoever destroys a single life is considered by Scripture as if he had destroyed an entire world (Babylonian Talmud, Sanhedrin 37a)

The Blessings of Adam and Noah
And God blessed them; and God said unto them, Be fruitful, and multiply. . . . wherein there is life, I have given every green herb for meat (Gen. 1:28–30)
And God blessed Noah and his sons, and said unto them, Be fruitful, and multiply. . . . even as the green herb have I given you all things (Gen. 9:1–3)
And the wolf also shall dwell with the lamb (Isa. 11:6)

One God—Two Sexes
So God created man in His own image (Gen. 1:27)
In the beginning God created the heaven and the earth (Gen. 1:1)
And God spake unto Moses and said unto him, I am the Lord (Exod. 6:2)
And the Lord God said, It is not good that the man should be alone (Gen. 2:18)

IV COMMUNITY

Freedom's Defense
And it shall come to pass, when your children shall say unto you, What mean ye by this service? . . . It is the sacrifice of the Lord's Passover (Exod. 12:26–27)
And thou shalt shew thy son in that day, saying, This is done because of that which the Lord did unto me (Exod. 13:8)
When thy son asketh thee in time to come . . . that thou shalt say unto him (Exod. 13:14)

Shabbat Behar and Justice Benjamin Nathan Cardozo
Ye shall proclaim liberty throughout all the land (Lev. 25:10)
The rabbis have power to expropriate property should it be for the general public good (Talmud, Tractate Gittin 36b)

Justice, Justice You Shall Pursue
That which is altogether just shalt thou follow . . . [Justice, justice you shall pursue] (Deut. 16:20)
And they shall answer and say, Our hands have not shed this blood (Deut. 21:7)
Is it even conceivable that the elders of the city are murderers? (Talmud, Tractate Sotah 45b)
Judges and officers . . . they shall judge the people with just judgment (Deut. 16:18)

Holiness
Ye shall be holy for I, the Lord your God, am holy (Lev. 19:2)
And one cried unto another, and said, Holy, Holy, Holy is the Lord of Hosts (Isa. 6:3)
Imitate His attributes: to clothe the naked, to visit the sick, to comfort mourners, to bury the dead (Talmud, Tractate Sotah 14a)
Ye shall walk after the Lord your God (Deut. 13:4)
And God blessed the seventh day, and sanctified it (Gen. 2:3)

You Shall Be Holy
And the Lord spake unto Moses . . say unto [the congregation], Ye shall be holy (Lev. 19:1–2)
And the Lord delivered unto me two tables of stone . . . on them was written according to all the words, which the Lord spake with you . . . in the day of the assembly (Deut. 9:10)
And God spake all of these words, saying I am the Lord thy God. . . . Thou shalt have no other gods before me. . . . Thou shall not covet (Exod. 20:1–17)
Honour thy father and thy mother (Exod. 20:12)
Ye shall fear every man his mother, and his father (Lev. 19:3)
Thou shalt not kill (Exod. 20:13)
Neither shalt thou stand against the blood of thy neighbour (Lev. 19:16)
Thou shalt not covet . . . any thing that is thy neighbour's (Exod. 20:17)
Thou shalt love thy neighbour as thyself (Lev. 19:18)

God of the Earth
And Abram said, Lord God, what wilt thou give me, seeing I go childless, and the steward of my house is this Eliezer of Damascus? (Gen. 15:2)

And I will make thee swear by the Lord, the God of heaven, and the God of the earth, that thou shalt not take a wife unto my son of the daughters of the Canaanites (Gen. 24:3)

The Lord God of heaven, which took me from my father's house. . . shall send His angel before thee (Gen. 24:7)

Before Abraham embarked on his life's work, God was not as yet recognized as the God of the earth (Midrash Rabbah, Gen. 59:11)

Transcending Limits

So all the cities which ye shall give to the Levites shall be forty and eight cities (Num. 35:7)

And ye shall measure from without the city on the east side two thousand cubits (Num. 35:5)

Education and the Family

Hear, O Israel: The Lord our God is one Lord: And thou shalt love the Lord thy God with all thine heart. . . . And these words . . . thou shalt teach them diligently unto thy children (Deut. 6:4–7)

My son, hear the instruction of thy father, and forsake not the law of thy mother (Prov. 1:8)

The Nazirite

All the days of his separation he is holy unto the Lord (Num. 6:8)

And he shall offer his offering unto the Lord (Num. 6:14)

All the days that he separateth himself unto the Lord he shall come at no dead body. He shall not make himself unclean for his father, or for his mother . . . when they die (Num. 6:6–7)

And the Lord said unto Moses, Speak unto the priests. . . . There shall none be defiled for the dead among his people: But for his kin, that is near unto him (Lev. 21:1–3)

And I raised up of your sons for prophets, and of your young men for Nazirites (Amos 2:11)

Jacob's God

Hear O Israel: The Lord our God is one Lord [added in liturgy: Blessed be the Name of His glorious Kingdom forever] (Deut. 6:4)

And Jacob called unto his sons, and said, Gather yourselves together, that I may tell you that which shall befall you. . . . our father Jacob opened [his mouth] and exclaimed, "Blessed be the name of His glorious kingdom forever and ever" (Gen. 49:1; Talmud, Tractate Pesachim 56a)

And they told him all the words of Joseph . . . when he saw the wagons which Joseph had sent to carry him, the spirit of Jacob their father revived (Gen. 45:27)

And the Lord said unto Jacob, Return . . . to thy kindred; and I will be with thee (Gen. 31:3)

The Two Midwives and the World's First Recorded Act of Civil Disobedience

The more they afflicted them, the more they multiplied and grew. And they were grieved because of the children of Israel (Exod. 1:12)

The midwives feared God, and did not as the king of Egypt commanded them, but saved the men children alive (Exod. 1:17)

Why have ye done this thing, and have saved the men children alive? (Exod. 1:18)

The Hebrew women . . . are delivered ere the midwives come in unto them (Exod. 1:19)

Therefore God dealt well with the midwives, and the people multiplied. . . . because the midwives feared God, that he made them houses (Exod. 1:20–21)

Adam and Cain

They heard the voice of the Lord God, walking in the garden (Gen. 3:8)

And He said, What hast thou done? The voice of thy brother's blood crieth unto me from the ground (Gen. 4:10)

And the Lord God called unto Adam, and said unto him, Where are thou? (Gen. 3:9)

And the Lord said unto Cain, Where is Abel thy brother? (Gen. 4:9)

Thy desire shall be to thy husband (Gen. 3:16)

If thou doest well, shalt thou not be accepted? . . . And unto thee shall be his desire (Gen. 4:7)

Unto Adam He said, Because thou hast harkened unto the voice of thy wife . . . cursed is the ground for thy sake (Gen. 3:17)

And now art thou cursed from the earth (Gen. 4:11)

Thorns also and thistles shall it bring forth to thee (Gen. 3:18)

When thou tillest the ground, it shall not henceforth yield unto thee her strength (Gen. 4:12)

And He drove out the man (Gen. 3:24)

Behold thou hast driven me out this day from the face of the earth (Gen. 4:14)

The Splitting of the Sea

There he made for them a statute and an ordinance, and there he proved them (Exod. 15:25)

Cities
And Cain . . . builded a city, and called [it] the name of his son, Enoch (Gen. 4:16–17)
And he called it Shebah: therefore the name of the city is Beersheba unto this day (Gen. 26:33)
Then Abram removed his tent, and came and dwelt in the plain of Mamre, which is in Hebron, and built there an altar unto the Lord (Gen. 13:18)
And Isaac said unto them . . . Let there be now an oath betwixt us (Gen. 26:27–33)
And Abraham called the name of that place Jehovahjireh (Gen. 22:14; Midrash Rabbah, Gen. 56:11)
And the Lord spake unto Moses in the plains of Moab . . . These six cities shall be a refuge, both for the children of Israel, and for the stranger (Num. 35)
Thou shalt truly tithe all the increase of thy seed. . . . and thou shalt eat there before the Lord thy God, and thou shalt rejoice (Deut. 14:22–26)

Tree of the Field
When thou shalt besiege a city a long time . . . thou shalt not destroy the trees . . . for thou mayest eat of them, and thou shalt not cut them down (for the tree of the field is man's life) (Deut. 20:19)
Only the trees which thou knowest that they be not trees for meat, thou shalt destroy and cut them down (Deut. 20:20)
And God blessed them, and God said unto them, Be fruitful, and multiply, and replenish the earth, and subdue it (Gen. 1:28)
See my world, how beautiful and praiseworthy it is. I made it for you. Be mindful that you do not destroy it (Midrash Rabbah, Eccles. 7:13)

V Faith

Exodus
And there went a man of the house of Levi, and took to wife a daughter of Levi (Exod. 2:1)
Why bring children into the oppressive bondage in Egypt? (Talmud, Tractate Sotah 12a)

The Almighty Has His Own Purposes
And when that year was ended [they] said unto him . . . buy us and our land for bread. . . . And Joseph bought all the land of Egypt for Pharaoh . . . [and] removed [the people] to cities from one end of the borders of Egypt even to the other end (Gen. 47:18–21)
Now there arose up a new king over Egypt, which knew not Joseph. And he said . . . the children of Israel are more and mightier than we: Come on, let us deal wisely with them (Exod. 1:8–10)
Thy seed shall be a stranger in a land that is not theirs, and shall serve them (Gen. 15:13)

God Unfair to Cain?
And . . . Cain was a tiller of the ground. . . . Cain brought of the fruit of the ground an offering. . . . But unto Cain and to his offering he had not respect. . . . [And the Lord said] If thou doest well, shalt thou not be accepted? and if thou doest not well, sin lieth at the door (Gen. 4:2–7)
And . . . Cain rose up against Abel his brother, and slew him (Gen. 4:8)
When thou tillest the ground, it shall not henceforth yield unto thee her strength; a fugitive and a vagabond shalt thou be. . . . and Cain builded a city (Gen. 4:12–17)

The Ram in the Thicket
And Abraham lifted up his eyes and looked, and behold behind him a ram caught in a thicket by his horns (Gen. 22:13)

The Royal Conflict: King David and Michal
And it was told king David, saying, The Lord hath blessed the house of Obededom and all that pertaineth unto him, because of the ark of God (2 Sam. 6:12)
And David danced before the Lord with all his might . . . [and] brought up the ark of the Lord with shouting, and with the sound of the trumpet (2 Sam. 6:14–15)
Michal Saul's daughter looked through a window, and saw king David leaping and dancing before the Lord; and she despised him in her heart (2 Sam. 6:16)
And [David] dealt . . . to every one a cake of bread (2 Sam. 6:19)
How glorious was the king of Israel to day who uncovered himself to day in the eyes of the handmaidens of his servants (2 Sam. 6:20)
It was before the Lord which chose me before thy father . . . to appoint me ruler . . . therefore will I play before the Lord. . . . [and] be base in mine own sight (2 Sam. 6:21–22)
Therefore they enquired of the Lord further, if the man should yet come thither. And the Lord answered, Behold he hath hidden himself among the stuff (1 Sam. 10:22)

And Michal, the daughter of Saul, tracing her lineage to Joseph and Rachel, approaches God with reserve, thought, inwardness, quiet . . . just as Rachel whispered her secrets to her sister Leah on the wedding day (Talmud, Tractate Megillah 13b)

Leaving the Wilderness: The Sin of the Spies

But the men that went up with [Caleb] said, We be not able to go up against the people, for they are stronger than we (Num. 13:31)

And Caleb stilled the people before Moses, and said, Let us go up at once (Num. 13:30)

Except the Lord build the house, they labour in vain that build it: except the Lord keep the city, the watchman waketh but in vain (Ps. 127:1)

Hannah's Prayer

And it came to pass, as [Hannah] . . . spake in her heart; only her lips moved, but her voice was not heard: therefore Eli thought she had been drunken (1 Sam. 1:12–13)

And Hannah answered and said, No, my lord, I am a woman of a sorrowful spirit: I have drunk neither wine nor strong drink, but have poured out my soul before the Lord (1 Sam. 1:15)

Then said Elkanah her husband to her, Hannah, why weepest thou? . . . am not I better to thee than ten sons? (1 Sam. 1:8)

And she was in bitterness of soul, and prayed unto the Lord, and wept sore (1 Sam. 1:10)

Out of the depths have I cried unto thee, O Lord (Ps. 130:1)

Elkanah knew Hannah his wife; and the Lord remembered her. . . . [Hannah] bare a son, and called his name Samuel, saying, Because I have asked him of the Lord (1 Sam. 1:19–20)

Abraham

And there came one that had escaped, and told Abram the Hebrew (Gen. 14:13)

Mercy and truth are met together; righteousness and peace have kissed each other (Ps. 85:10)

Shall not the Judge of all the earth do right? (Gen. 18:25)

The Expulsion of Ishmael and the Binding of Isaac

Let it not be grievous in thy sight because of the lad, and because of thy bondwoman (Gen. 21:12)

Take now thy son, thine only son Isaac, whom thou lovest (Gen. 22:2)

And Abraham rose up early in the morning, and took bread, and a bottle of water, and gave it unto Hagar . . . and she departed, and wandered in the wilderness (Gen. 21:14)

And Abraham rose up early in the morning . . . and took two of his young men with him, and Isaac his son . . . and rose up, and went unto the place (Gen. 22:3)

[And on the third day] Abraham took the wood of the burnt offering, and laid it upon Isaac his son (Gen. 22:6)

She cast the child under one of the shrubs . . . . . . [and] said, Let me not see the death of the child. And she sat over against him, and lift up her voice, and wept (Gen. 21:15–16)

And Abraham stretched forth his hand, and took the knife to slay his son (Gen. 22:10)

And the angel of God called to Hagar out of heaven, and said unto her, What aileth thee, Hagar? fear not (Gen. 21:17)

And the angel of the Lord called unto him [Abraham] out of heaven, and said . . . Lay not thine hand upon the lad (Gen. 22:11–12)

And God opened her eyes, and she saw a well of water . . . [she] gave the lad drink (Gen. 21:19)

And Abraham lifted up his eyes, and looked, and behold behind him a ram caught in a thicket by his horns . . . [He] offered him up for a burnt offering in the stead of his son (Gen. 22:13)

I will make [Ishmael] a great nation (Gen. 21:18)

That in blessing I will bless thee, and in multiplying I will multiply thy seed as the stars of the heaven. . . . And in thy seed shall all the nations of the earth be blessed (Gen. 22:17–18)

Get thee out of thy country . . . unto a land that I will shew thee (Gen. 12:1)

And I will make of thee a great nation (Gen. 12:2)

For in Isaac shall thy seed be called (Gen. 21:12)

Cast out this bondwoman and her son: for the son of this bondwoman shall not be heir with my son, even with Isaac (Gen. 21:10)

Many wonder at Abraham—how could he banish his own son, also evicting son and mother with nothing? (Ibn Ezra, Gen. 21:14)

Let it not be grievous in thy sight because of the lad, and because of thy bondwoman. . . . for in Isaac shall thy seed be called. And also of the son of the bondwoman will I make a nation, because he is thy seed (Gen. 21:12–13)

Then Abraham fell upon his face and laughed, and said in his heart, Shall a child be born unto him that is an hundred years old? (Gen. 17:17)

Sarah laughed within herself, saying, After I am waxed old shall I have pleasure (Gen. 18:2)
God hath made me to laugh, so that all that hear will laugh with me (Gen. 21:6)
Behold, thou art with child and shalt bear a son, and shalt call his name Ishmael (Gen. 16:11)
Fear not, for God hath heard the voice of the lad where he is (Gen. 2:17)

Pharaoh's Irony
And Pharaoh charged all his people, saying, Every son that is born ye shall cast into the river, and every daughter ye shall save alive (Exod. 1:22)
And the woman conceived, and bare a son. . . . And the child grew, and she brought him unto Pharaoh's daughter, and he became her son (Exod. 2:2–10)
There are many devices in a man's heart; nevertheless the counsel of the Lord, that shall stand (Prov. 19:21)

Looking Over Serah's Shoulder
And there arose not a prophet since in Israel like unto Moses (Deut. 34:10)
And the sons of Asher; Jimnah, and Ishuah . . . and Serah their sister (Gen. 46:17)
And the name of the daughter of Asher was Sarah (Num. 26:46)
And because he loved thy fathers, therefore he chose their seed after them (Deut. 4:37)

Go Forth
Now the Lord had said unto Abram, Get thee [go forth] out of thy country . . . unto a land that I will shew thee (Gen. 12:1)
And he said, Take now thy son, thine only son Isaac, whom thou lovest, and get thee [go forth] into the land of Moriah; and offer him there for a burnt offering (Gen. 22:2)
In Isaac shall thy seed be called (Gen. 21:12)
Behold now I have taken upon me to speak unto the Lord, which am but dust and ashes (Gen. 18:27)

A Book Unto Itself
[And] when the ark set forward, that Moses said, Rise up, Lord, and let thine enemies be scattered. . . . when it rested, he said, Return, O Lord, unto the many thousands of Israel (Num. 10:35–36)

The Two Camps
I am not worthy of the least of all the mercies . . . thou hast shewed unto thy servant; for with my staff I passed over this Jordan; and now I am become two bands (Gen. 32:10)
And said, If Esau come to the one company, and smite it, then the other company which is left shall escape (Gen. 32:8)
And Jacob went on his way, and the angels of God met him. And when Jacob saw them, he said, This is God's host: and he called the name of that place Mahanaim [two camps] (Gen. 32:1–2)
For He shall give His angels charge over thee, to keep thee in all thy ways (Ps. 91:11)

And Jacob Was Left Alone
And Jacob was left alone; and there wrestled a man with him until the breaking of the day (Gen. 32:24)
And Jacob called the name of the place Peniel: for I have seen God face to face, and my life is preserved (Gen. 32:30)
And it came to pass. . . Jacob . . . rolled the stone from the well's mouth (Gen. 29:10)
And Jacob . . . took the stone . . . and set it up for a pillar (Gen. 28:18)
And he said, Let me go, for the day breaketh. And he said, I will not let thee go, except thou bless me (Gen. 32:26)
And Jacob asked him, and said, Tell me, I pray thee, thy name. And he said, Wherefore is it that thou dost ask after my name? And he blessed him there (Gen. 32:29)

For I Shall Be With You
And Moses said unto the Lord, O my Lord, I am not eloquent. . . . And the Lord said unto him, Who hath made man's mouth? . . . have not I the Lord? (Exod. 4:10–11)
Who made Pharaoh mute, that he did not immediately order your execution, and his agents deaf, that they did not hear Pharaoh's order to have you killed? (Rashi, Exod. 4:11)
And he said, Certainly I will be with thee (Exod. 3:12)
Go in unto [come to] Pharaoh (Exod. 10:1)

Remembering History, Remembering Amalek
Write this for a remembrance in a book and rehearse it in the ears of Joshua: for I will utterly put out the memory of Amalek from under heaven (Exod. 17:14)
Remember what Amalek did unto thee by the way (Deut. 25:17)

VI DREAMS AND VISION

Joseph and His Brothers
And Jacob dwelt in the land wherein his father was a stranger (Gen. 37:1)
Thy seed shall be a stranger in a land that is not theirs (Gen. 15:13)
For, behold, we were binding sheaves in the field, and, lo, my sheaf arose. . . . and, behold, your sheaves stood round about, and made obeisance to my sheaf (Gen. 37:7)
And he dreamed yet another dream . . . behold, the sun and the moon and the eleven stars made obeisance to me (Gen. 37:9)
And his brethren envied him (Gen. 37:11)
And his brethren said to him, Shalt thou indeed reign over us? . . . And they hated him yet the more for his dreams, and for his words (Gen. 37:8)

Now and Tomorrow
Know of a surety that your seed shall be a stranger in a land that is not theirs . . . But in the fourth generation they shall come hither [into the Holy Land] again (Gen. 15:13, 16)
For I know him [Abraham] that he will command his children . . . and they shall keep the way of the Lord (Gen. 18:19)
And Sarah died in Kirjatharba. . . . [Abraham] spake unto the sons of Heth, saying, I am a stranger and a sojourner with you: give me a possession of a buryingplace with you (Gen. 23)

Of Dreams, Dreamers, and Nondreamers
Now Israel loved Joseph more than all his children, because he was the son of his old age: and he made him a coat of many colours (Gen. 37:3)
Joseph dreamed a dream, and he told it his brethren: and they hated him (Gen. 37:5)
Hear, I pray you, this dream which I have dreamed (Gen. 37:6)
And his brethren said to him, Shalt thou indeed reign over us? . . . And they hated him yet the more for his dreams, and for his words (Gen. 37:8)
And he told it to his father . . . and his father rebuked him, and said unto him, What is this dream that thou hast dreamed? (Gen. 37:10)
And when they saw him afar off . . . they conspired against him to slay him. . . . we will say, Some evil beast hath devoured him: and we shall see what will become of his dreams (Gen. 37:18–20)
And he dreamed, and behold a ladder set up on the earth (Gen. 28:12)
And it came to pass . . . . that I lifted up mine eyes, and saw in a dream. . . . And the angel of God spake unto me in a dream, saying, Jacob: And I said, Here am I (Gen. 31:10–11)

The Personalities of Noah and Abraham
And every living substance was destroyed which was upon the face of the ground . . . and Noah only remained alive, and they that were with him in the ark (Gen. 7:23)

The Strength to Dream
And when they saw him afar off . . . they conspired against him to slay him (Gen. 37:18–20)

The Seven Fat Years
And Joseph said unto Pharaoh, The dream of Pharaoh is one . . . the seven empty ears . . . shall be seven years of famine (Gen. 41:25–32)
Now therefore let Pharaoh . . . . store to the land against the seven years of famine (Gen. 41:33–36)

The First Blessing of the Day
Who gives the rooster [sechvi] *the understanding to distinguish between day and night* (Siddur, morning blessing)
The prophet Jeremiah was unable to declare God to be gibbor *[mighty]. Where is His might to be seen when gentiles raucously and blasphemously dance in His Temple?* (Talmud, Yoma 69b)
Who girds Israel with might (Siddur, morning blessing)

Where There Is No Vision, the People Perish
And it shall be unto you for a fringe, that ye may look upon it, and remember all the commandments of the Lord, and do them (Num. 15:39)
Nevertheless the people be strong that dwell in the land, and the cities (Num. 13:28)
But the men that went up with him said, We be not able to go up against the people; for they are stronger than we (Num. 13:31)
A land which the Lord thy God careth for: the eyes of the Lord thy God are always upon it, from the beginning of the year even unto the end of the year (Deut. 11:12)
And they brought up an evil report of the land . . . that eateth up the inhabitants (Num. 13:32)

Speak unto the children of Israel, and bid them that they make them fringes in the borders of their garments . . . [and] put upon the fringe of the borders a ribband of blue (Num. 15:38)
And there was under his feet as it were a paved work of sapphire stone, and as it were the body of heaven in his clearness (Exod. 24:10)
And see the land, what it is, and the people that dwelleth therein, whether they be strong or weak, few or many (Num. 13:18)
These are the names of the men which Moses sent to spy out the land (Num. 13:16)
Ye seek not after your own heart and your own eyes, after which ye use to go a whoring (Num. 15:39)

VII HOLIDAYS

The Fourth Commandment
Remember the sabbath day, to keep it holy. . . . For in six days the Lord made heaven and earth, the sea, and all that in them is, and rested the seventh day (Exod. 20:8–11)

Sound the Shofar
Blow up the trumpet in the new moon. . . . This he ordained in Joseph for a testimony, when he went out through the land of Egypt. . . . I removed his shoulder from the burden (Ps. 81: 3–6)
And ye shall hallow the fiftieth year, and proclaim liberty throughout all the land unto all the inhabitants thereof: it shall be a jubile unto you; and ye shall return every man unto his possession, and ye shall return every man unto his family (Lev. 25:10)

Qualitative Time
This month shall be . . . the first month of the year to you (Exod. 12:2)

Purim
And Aaron shall cast lots upon the two goats. . . . the [scapegoat] shall be presented alive before the Lord, to make an atonement with him (Lev. 16:8–10)

The Cycle of Seven
But the seventh day is the sabbath of the Lord thy God: in it thou shalt not do any work. . . . thy manservant and thy maidservant may rest as well as thou (Deut. 5:14)
And the tables were the work of God, and the writing was the writing of God, graven upon the tables (Exod. 32:16)
[Exod. 32:16 does] not read engraved [charut] but freedom [cheirut] (Ethics of the Fathers, 6:2)
Proclaim liberty throughout all the land unto all the inhabitants thereof (Lev. 25:10)

The Seventh of Adar/July Fourth
So Moses the servant of the Lord died (Deut. 34:5)
We remember Moses, God's messenger, as the model of a man who, once he realized his mission, was taken from the earth with a Godly kiss (Deut. 34:5; Avot D'Rebbe Nasson 12:5)

Singing the Blues
And Moses said unto the Lord, O my Lord, I am not eloquent (Exod. 4:10)
Then sang Moses and the children of Israel this song unto the Lord . . . The Lord shall reign for ever and ever (Exod. 15:1–18)
And it came to pass in process of time, that the king of Egypt died: and the children of Israel sighed by reason of the bondage, and they cried, and their cry came up unto God (Exod. 2:23)

Rabbi Akiva and the Thirty-Third of the Omer
And ye shall count unto you from the morrow after the sabbath, from the day that ye brought the sheaf of the wave offering; seven sabbaths shall be complete (Lev. 23:15)
As the result of a plague, Rabbi Akiva, the great second-century sage, lost all twenty-four thousand of his students during this same fifty-day period (Talmud, Tractate Yevamot 62b)
Rabbi Akiva's colleagues . . . saw a fox scurrying from under the ruins of what had been the Holy of Holies. . . . All of the rabbis began to weep—save for Rabbi Akiva, who laughed (Talmud, Tractate Makkot 24b)
The stranger that cometh nigh shall be put to death (Num. 1:51)
Zion for your sake [shall] be plowed as a field (Mic. 3:12)
Old men and old women [will] dwell in the streets of Jerusalem (Zech. 8:4)

INDEX